Road Biking™ Series

Road Biking™
Illinois

A Guide to the State's Best Bike Rides

Ted Villaire

FALCONGUIDES

GUILFORD, CONNECTICUT
HELENA, MONTANA

AN IMPRINT OF GLOBE PEQUOT PRESS

To buy books in quantity for corporate use
or incentives, call **(800) 962–0973**
or e-mail **premiums@GlobePequot.com.**

FALCONGUIDES®

FalconGuides is an imprint of Globe Pequot Press.
Falcon, FalconGuides, and Outfit Your Mind are registered trademarks and Road Biking is a trademark of Morris Book Publishing, LLC.

Maps by Ryan Mitchell © Morris Book Publishing, LLC
Photos by Ted Villaire unless otherwise indicated.
Layout: Sue Murray
Project editor: John Burbidge

Library of Congress Cataloging-in-Publication Data
Villaire, Ted, 1969-
  Road biking Illinois : a guide to the state's best bike rides / Ted Villaire.
      p. cm.—(FalconGuides)
  Includes index.
  ISBN 978-0-7627-4688-0
  1. Bicycle touring—Illinois—Guidebooks. 2. Cycling—Illinois—Guidebooks. 3. Illinois—Guidebooks. I. Title.
  GV1045.5.I3V55 2010
  796.6'409773—dc22

                        2010002386

Printed in the United States of America
10 9 8 7 6 5 4 3 2 1

Contents

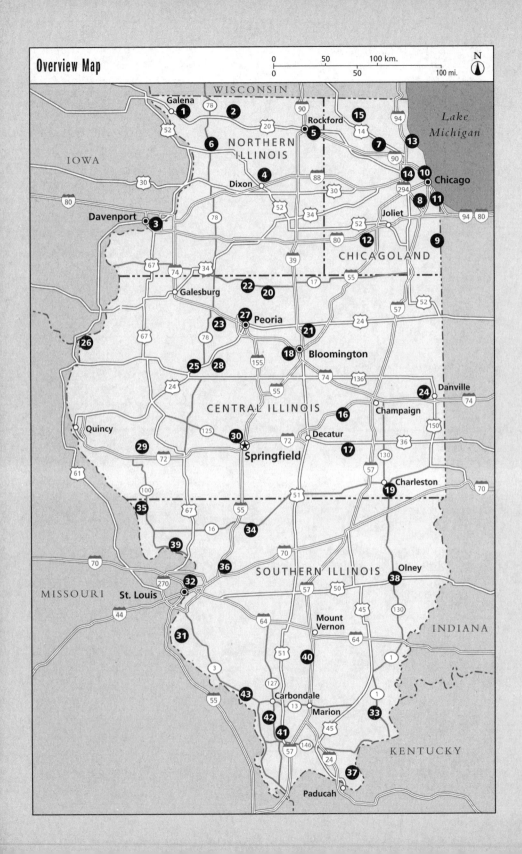

Overview Map

0   50   100 km.
0   50   100 mi.

N

WISCONSIN

Galena ● 1   78   ● 2   90   ● 15   94   *Lake Michigan*

52   Rockford ● 5   14   ● 7   ● 13

● 6   **NORTHERN ILLINOIS**   90

IOWA   ● 4   Dixon   88   294   ● 14 ● 10   Chicago

30   52   34   ● 8 ● 11

Davenport ● 3   78   ● 12   Joliet   94   80

67   74   34   52   52   39   17   55   **CHICAGOLAND**   ● 9

Galesburg ● 22   ● 20   57   52

● 27 Peoria   24

● 26   ● 23   67   78   ● 21

155   ● 18 Bloomington   74   136   Danville

● 25 ● 28   24   55   ● 24   74

Quincy   125   **CENTRAL ILLINOIS**   Champaign   150

● 29   72   ● 30   72   Decatur   36   130

Springfield   ● 16   ● 17   57

61   100   51   ● 19 Charleston   70

● 35   67   55

16   ● 34

● 39   70

● 36   **SOUTHERN ILLINOIS**   Olney

70   270   ● 32   57   50   ● 38   130

MISSOURI   St. Louis   INDIANA

44   ● 31   64   Mount Vernon   64   1

51   ● 40   45

3   127   1

● 43 Carbondale   ● 33

55   ● 42   13   Marion   45

● 41   146   **KENTUCKY**

57   24

● 37

Paducah

Foreword

As a bicyclist for most of my life and as executive director of the state's only statewide bicycle advocacy group, the League of Illinois Bicyclists, I have traveled Illinois from north to south and east to west. From my car and my bicycle, I have experienced the state's diverse topography, its people, its historical sites, its cultures, its food, and much more.

Over the years, I've learned that to travel on a bicycle rolling along by myself is enjoyable, but being with my family or my friends makes a trip even more special. Because the pace is slower on a bicycle and you're in the outdoors, the sights, the sounds, the smells of Illinois come closer to you than many people can ever imagine. The experience is magical when you're riding a bike.

Often the sight of a traveling bicyclist can be a discussion starter for the people you meet along the way. "Where'd you start?" "Where you headed?" The questions come easy from awed roadside observers during those chance meetings that are part of any enjoyable pedal.

Answering those questions comes easy, too, when you're familiar with Ted Villaire's *Road Biking Illinois*. Ted helps take the guesswork out of where to start and where to ride on those epic bicycling experiences that you'll be remembering and recounting for years to come.

Road Biking Illinois provides the necessary details for forty-three memorable Illinois rides. You can actually triple that number by doing each one in spring, summer, and fall, when the conditions vary enough to make them special rides in their own right. If you're hardy enough, some rides can even be done in winter.

Do all of Ted's rides, and you can boast experiencing the Land of Lincoln like few others. His *Road Biking Illinois* makes it happen easily enough for anyone looking for bicycling adventures of varying distances and challenges. Use this book first to dream, then to plan, then to ride. You'll be glad you did.

As a seasoned old-timer once told me, "I ride so that I can ride another day." Take those words to heart whether you ride one of Ted's short rambles or one of his long-distance classics. To ride another day means riding safely at all times. Wear a helmet, obey traffic laws, share the road, and be a defensive rider always on the lookout for potential hazards around you. If you plan to ride at twilight or night, be sure you have lights on the front and back of your bicycle so you can be seen by motorists.

Before starting on a bicycle trip, be prepared. Take a spare tube, tire levers, a hand pump or CO_2 cartridges, a patch kit, and a multipurpose bike tool. Remember to drink before you're thirsty to stay hydrated and to eat before you're hungry to maintain your energy. Wear sunscreen for protection from the sun's harmful rays and glasses to protect your eyes from road grit and insects. Also, consider carrying a cell phone just in case your bicycle can't be repaired on the roadside.

Some riders don't always take this into account: You not only represent yourself, but all riders. When motorists see a bicyclist do something he or she shouldn't on the road, they're likely to think all bicyclists behave like that. Whether we like it or not, we are bicycle ambassadors when we ride. How you ride may affect other bicyclists down the road.

Be a good bicycle citizen, and keep the rubber side down.

—Ed Barsotti
Executive Director, League of Illinois Bicyclists

Preface

I hope this book succeeds in making a strong case for the idea that Illinois is best explored on a bicycle. I also hope you'll see that the state is chock-full of interesting nooks and crannies accessible on bicycle—whether it's the beguiling natural beauty of its rivers, wetlands, and lakes or its rich offerings of historic sites, museums, and vibrant urban neighborhoods. In order to make this book useful to cyclists who have a variety of skill levels and interests, I chose the rides carefully, offering a fair mix of geography, terrain, length, and level of difficulty. While the rides are fairly well spread out within the state, you'll find a greater concentration around the population centers of Chicago, Saint Louis, and the cities of central Illinois. Of course, you'll also find a higher concentration of rides in the most scenic parts of the state.

While selecting the routes for this book, in many cases I relied on my own experience as a cyclist who loves exploring Midwestern back roads. In parts of the state where my knowledge was lacking, I reached out to cycling organizations and individuals in the local cycling communities and asked them to share a few of their favorite rides. I was immediately overwhelmed by their eagerness to help with my project. They sent route directions, they sent maps, and they sent elaborate ride descriptions. In some cases, I had the pleasure of joining local cycling clubs for group rides. On these rides I learned there's no better way to get to know a cycling route than tagging along with people who have been riding it over a period of years, and in some cases, decades. Some of these routes have been included in the book.

This book would have been much less interesting if it wasn't for the generosity of passionate cyclists throughout the state. First, thanks to Ed Barsotti, director of the League of Illinois Bicyclists, for contributing the foreword to the book and helping me contact leaders of bike clubs around the state. A hearty thank you also goes to Dean Schott, the league's outreach director. For sharing their knowledge of cycling routes in northern Illinois, I need to thank Dick Bowers and the Blackhawk Bicycle and Ski Club, B. J. Fenwick at Green River Adventure Sports, John H. McConnel Jr., Geoff Mumford and the McHenry County Bicycle Club, Roman Myszczak of the Chicago Area Tandem Society, Perry Perez, and Sandra Stengel.

Before researching this book, I never knew central Illinois possessed such a vibrant assortment of cycling clubs and organizations. The Decatur Bicycle Club, Champaign County Bikes, the Illinois Valley Wheelm'n, the Prairie Cycle Club, and the Springfield Bicycling Club all provided me with invaluable information. Individuals who offered guidance and suggestions in central Illinois included Dave Balfour, Dave Carpenter, Peter Cole, Steve Daggs, Bill Gillespie, Kent Harris, Pamela Henderson, Deborah Hutti, Sue Jones, Richard McClary, David McDivitt, John Stierman, Mark and Claudia Washburn, and Laurie Wilbur. Thanks to Sheldon Schafer for sharing the route information for his Peoria rides, and for providing me with a friendly place to stay.

In southern Illinois, my thanks goes to Annette and Jerry Bausman, Dan Becque, Loren Easter, Roger Kramer and the Belleville Area Bicycling and Eating Society, and Don Lawrence and the Carbonale Bicycle Club.

I would like to acknowledge the excellent work done by Todd Hill and others at the Illinois Department of Transportation in creating the eminently useful series of cycling maps that cover the entire state. These maps do a tremendous job of showing nearly every road in the state and rating them for bicycling. The urban cycling maps produced by the League of Illinois Bicyclists and the Active Transportation Alliance also proved to be extremely useful. And finally, thanks to the anonymous posters, List-serv users, and forum contributors who provided assistance via the Internet.

I'm grateful to friends who accompanied me on rides: Doug Burk, Kari Lyder-sen, and Tim Merello. Thanks to Cari Noga for her helpful suggestions on conducting research and to Rachel Schripsema for her valuable input on the photography. As always, thanks to my family for their support and encouragement. In particular, I'm grateful to my sister, Isabelle, who got the ball rolling by taking me on my first long rides.

Throughout the Galena Classic, the views of the Galena-area landscape are outstanding.

Introduction

People unfamiliar with Illinois may think that outside of Chicago, the state offers little to see and experience. They may think it's all flat cropland and assume the parks, the historic sites, and the small towns and cities are unimpressive or uninteresting. These misconceptions are immediately called into question once they start to see more of the state. Head to toe, Illinois offers a bounty of places to explore, whether it's small towns, urban historic areas, or scenic parkland containing lakes and hills.

Illinois greets cyclists with a warm embrace. The gentle terrain, the wealth of quiet rural roads, and small town friendliness conspire to make Illinois a perfect place for bicycle exploration. Additionally, cities throughout the state are quickly becoming more conducive to cycling as local municipalities establish more bike lanes, bike paths, and bike-friendly laws.

One part of Illinois often overlooked is the southern tip of the state, occupied largely by the 270,000-acre Shawnee National Forest. The forest, bordered by the Ohio River and Mississippi River, is one of the few parts of Illinois to escape the flattening effects of the last glacier. As a result, you'll find deep canyons, fantastic rock formations, rugged woodland, and many waterfalls. Its sandstone cliffs, quiet rocky streams, and high bluffs dotted with wildflowers give it a scenic beauty unparalleled in the state. The west side of the forest hosts a panoply of wineries and fruit farms. Fall is a particularly rewarding season to explore the Shawnee: oak, hickory, poplar, sumac, and ash trees guarantee an abundance of color. Rides in the vicinity of Shawnee National Forest start at classic destinations like Garden of the Gods, Giant City State Park, and the Little Grand Canyon.

Historically, the prairies of central and northern Illinois have occupied a special place in the minds of Americans. The promise of the most fertile farmland in the nation lured many a settler from the eastern United States and from abroad. After the settlers arrived en masse and farming became king, the prairie, unfortunately, vanished from the Prairie State. While it's true that this part of Illinois is best known for its corn and soy plants and a generally level topography, it's also true that there are numerous pockets of parkland, lakes, and recreation areas within striking distance of places like Bloomington, Champaign, Danville, Decatur, Springfield, Peoria, and Rockford.

The former prairies of central Illinois are lodged firmly in the public consciousness partly because they served as home to Abraham Lincoln. Indeed, the legacy of the sixteenth U.S. president is everywhere. Given that he traveled widely in the state as an itinerant lawyer, museums and historic sites in his honor crop up with regularity.

Along with the former prairie, the Illinois landscape is often defined by its network of great rivers. These major waterways—the Illinois, the Mississippi, and the Ohio—contain river barge traffic and pleasure boaters for much of the year. They have locks and dams and impressive latticed bridges. While cycling along these waterways, you'll encounter places where these rivers swell several miles in width. You'll see

Marquette Park occupies a pleasant stretch of the Mississippi River in Savanna.

wooded bluffs and vast swaths of bottomland and many thousands of acres of wetland. Cycling along the rivers also offers an opportunity to explore the many towns that grew up during a time when the rivers served as interstate superhighways. Smaller but no less beautiful Illinois rivers that you'll encounter include the Rock, the Sangamon, and the Fox.

Apart from having Lake Michigan in its front yard, the terrain of the Chicago area is not dissimilar from other parts of the state. The city tends toward flatness, while several outlying areas contain rolling wooded terrain. For good reason, Chicago has been identified as one of the best large cities for cycling. The many miles of attractive shoreline, the fascinating neighborhoods, and the ever-expanding cycling infrastructure allow for great riding.

Since Illinois covers nearly 400 miles between its north and south borders, the climate can vary considerably. As one would expect, the cycling season is extended in the south (as are the hot and sticky days of midsummer) and is a bit shorter in the north. In most of the state, many people don their windbreakers and cycling pants for recreational rides in late March. In the fall, some people keep riding into early November. Many consider spring and fall the best times of the year for riding. No extreme heat, the bugs are dormant, and you have the opportunity to enjoy the color displays that come with flowers blooming and leaves turning.

Road and Traffic Conditions

When putting together these cycling routes, the top priority was choosing quiet and safe roads. Given the predominantly rural landscape of Illinois, roads conducive to cycling are not hard to find. Occasionally, though, it becomes tricky to create a loop using only quiet roads. That's why, now and then, busy roads are unavoidable. Rest assured, these sections are brief, and the text will point out heavy traffic conditions. Also, please bear in mind that traffic patterns may change due to new construction, rerouting of roads, etc.

In most of Illinois, heavy traffic rarely presents a problem. It's a different story in Chicagoland. Interestingly enough, the worst traffic scenarios for cyclists often occur not in the city, but in the outlying areas where bicycling infrastructure is minimal. These are the places where a cornfield may become a housing development, a shopping mall, or a school practically overnight. When this happens, quiet rural roads suddenly become major thoroughfares—oftentimes without the needed infrastructure improvements. The good news is that drivers in Chicago and most suburbs are accustomed to having cyclists in their midst, and therefore tend to treat us with a good bit of respect.

A handful of the rides in this book use short stretches of gravel roads for the purpose of creating full loops. Cyclists with wider road-biking tires will have no trouble. Those who ride on the skinniest of tires, however, may want to consider going with a wider model. (Wider road-biking tires—say 25c or wider—also tend to get fewer flats and last longer than skinny racing tires.)

A number of the rides make use of the state's extensive collection of rail trails. Many cyclists, myself included, enjoy taking a break from cycling on roads in order to cruise along a scenic bike path. With more than 600 miles of existing rail trails and nearly 150 miles of trails currently in development, Illinois has one of the best networks of rail trails in the Midwest. It would be a darn shame not to enjoy these trails when the opportunity presents itself. In most cases, the trails are paved. In the absence of pavement, the trail surface will be crushed gravel—which tends to be surprisingly smooth and will accommodate road bikes with no trouble. The maps within this book indicate sections of the routes that follow trails.

Equipment

Particularly for the longer rides featured in this guide, you might consider using a road bike with at least ten speeds. Road bikes tend to have lighter frames, narrower tires, and drop handlebars—all qualities that enhance comfort for longer rides. Hybrids and mountain bikes will work, too, but expect to get tired more quickly because you're using more bike than you need.

The equipment and supplies needed for a bike ride will vary depending on the climate and the length of the ride. If the sun is hot, for example, you'll want to bring lip balm, sunscreen, and more water than you think you'll need. If there's a slight

Illinois is full of historic barns, such as this one on the Evergreen Lake–Lake Bloomington cruise.

chance of rain, you might consider bringing a rain jacket, rain pants, and a waterproof helmet cover.

While some pieces of equipment are variable, there are certain items you should always have on a ride: Think helmet. Think water and snacks. Think patch kit and pump. Patch kits, of course, are worthless unless you know how to use them. Many people bring spare tubes in case their tube gets damaged beyond repair. Don't forget a map—not just the ones in this book, but also other local maps in case you want to stray from the route. And how about bringing at least a few bucks for a phone call or some fruit from a roadside stand?

As far as apparel, padded shorts significantly reduce chafing. Riding gloves protect your hands from blisters, numbness, and—if you happen to take a spill—the road surface. In hot weather, quick-drying clothing will add to your comfort considerably.

The list of nonessentials can be long and complicated: Many people like to bring gadgets like cell phones, GPS devices, and cameras. If you're taking a long ride, consider bringing front and rear lights. Rides sometimes get extended as a result of repairs or undue lingering.

Safe Riding

In Illinois, like other places around the country, bicycles are legal vehicles on the road and cyclists have all the rights and responsibilities of motorists. For the most part, cyclists must abide by the laws that regulate automobile traffic: This means observing traffic signs, signaling turns, and riding with the traffic. Typical traffic no-no's for bicyclists are riding against traffic, failing to observe red lights and stop signs, not using proper lights or reflectors when riding at night, and riding with earphones. Under Illinois law, cyclists should ride as close to the right side of the road as practical, except when passing another cyclist, making a left turn, or when it becomes necessary to avoid objects in the road.

One of the great joys of cycling is riding with others. Cyclists tend to be social people who are quick to embrace the companionship of other riders. Attentive riding companions will point out details that you may miss, such as scenery and wildlife, as well as hazards along the way. Group riders routinely call out "car back" or "car up" to alert other cyclists of approaching traffic. Also, cyclists often call out hazards as they see them, such as potholes, loose gravel, pedestrians, or dogs. When riding in a group, be sure not to clog the roadway if cars are trying to pass.

When riding in rural Illinois, there's no getting around this fact of life: Dogs sometimes give chase. Most of the time, the dog's intentions seem harmless enough—all bark and no bite. Harmless or not, it's still an alarming experience. Since dogs decide to chase cyclists for a variety of reasons, it's best to have a variety of responses up your sleeve. Here are a few that may work: (1) pedal fast and outrun it, (2) yell at the dog authoritatively and order it to go home, (3) squirt it in the face with your water bottle, and (4) hop off the bike and keep the bike between you and the dog. The most extreme measure involves giving it a dose of pepper spray. Different situations call for different responses or a combination of responses. However you react, be sure to keep calm. I've seen riders get in accidents because they were so rattled by a dog on the chase.

Another imposing sight on the rural roads of Illinois are huge tractors used for planting and harvesting. If a tractor the size of a small house is heading toward you, slow down. Be mindful that the driver may not be looking for cyclists as he or she lumbers from one field to another. If the load is big and the road is narrow, pull off and let the tractor pass. As the tractor passes, be sure to give the driver a friendly wave.

How to Use This Book

The rides in this book are broken into one of four categories representing different levels of difficulty. Keep in mind that mileage is one factor that contributes to the difficulty of a ride. Hills, the likelihood of wind, and lack of roadside amenities can all play roles a ride's difficulty.

Rambles are the easiest and shortest rides in the book, accessible to almost all riders, and should be easily completed in one day. They are less than 35 miles long and are generally on flat to slightly rolling terrain.

Cruises are intermediate in difficulty and distance. They are generally 25 to 50 miles long and may include some moderate climbs. Cruises will generally be completed easily by an experienced rider in one day, but inexperienced or out-of-shape riders may want to take two days with an overnight stop.

Challenges are difficult, designed especially for experienced riders in good condition. They are usually 40 to 60 miles long and may include some steep climbs. They should be a challenge even for fairly fit riders attempting to complete them in one day. Less experienced or fit riders should expect to take two days.

Classics are long and hard. They are anywhere from around 60 miles and up. They can include steep climbs and high-speed downhills. Even fit and experienced riders may want to take two days. These rides are not recommended for less fit and less experienced riders unless they are done in shorter stages.

UTM Coordinates

Readers who use either a handheld or car-mounted GPS (global positioning system) unit can punch in the UTM (Universal Transverse Mercator) for each starting point and have the GPS lead the way. The UTM coordinates are to be used with NAD 27 datum (rather than WGS83 or WGS84). Along with the UTM coordinates, the zone is also given. All coordinates were generated using mapping software, rather than taking readings "in the field."

Maps

Each ride in the book lists pertinent pages in the *DeLorme: Illinois Atlas & Gazetteer*. This atlas offers a fair amount of topographical information, identifying lakes, cities, rivers, hills, all roads, and many parks. For cyclists who want a map that depicts nearly every pond and creek, every roll in the landscape, and an abundance of local landmarks, the 7.5-minute topographical maps from the United States Geological Survey (USGS) will do the trick. These maps are also listed for each of the rides. One useful set of maps that seemed redundant to list with each ride is the Illinois Department of Transportation's series of nine Illinois Official Bicycle Maps. While these maps lose much detail in populated areas, they provide the invaluable service of showing traffic volume for the majority of the roads in the state. Visit www.dot.state.il.us/bikemap/state.html for more information.

Mileage Markers on the Maps

While charting the routes described in this book, I used a GPS device to continuously track my progress via satellite. Maps and mileage delineations for this book are based on the GPS routes I created. While I have found this procedure accurate in determining mileage covered, it unfortunately doesn't mean our numbers will match up precisely. If you're using a bike odometer, keep in mind that these have to be calibrated carefully; just changing to a larger tire can make a noticeable difference.

While GPS devices are generally more accurate, they too can lead you astray. If you backtrack or pursue a side trip and forget to subtract this distance from the total mileage covered, that, of course, will create a different mileage reading. The best policy is to use the mileage markers on the maps as a rough guide that provides you with a close—but not exact—determination of distance traveled.

Rides at a Glance

(Listed by category and distance)

Rambles

11 miles	Peoria Sculpture and Architecture Ramble, ride 27
16 miles	Crow Creek Ramble, ride 20
18 miles	Beverly–Oak Lawn Ramble, ride 8
18 miles	Olney Ramble, ride 38
22 miles	Lewistown Ramble, ride 25
22 miles	Shawnee–Pomona Ramble, ride 42
25 miles	Chain of Rocks Ramble, ride 32
25 miles	Nickelplate–Quercus Grove Ramble, ride 36
26 miles	Kickapoo State Park Ramble, ride 24
26 miles	Nauvoo Ramble, ride 26
28 miles	Chicago South Side Ramble, ride 11
29 miles	Shawnee Hills Wine Trail Ramble, ride 41
29 miles	Shawnee West Ramble, ride 43
30 miles	Chicago Lakefront and Boulevard Ramble, ride 10
30 miles	Rockford Ramble, ride 5
30 miles	Salt Creek Ramble, ride 14
30 miles	Sand Ridge State Forest Ramble, ride 28
32 miles	Amish Country Ramble, ride 17
34 miles	Hillsboro Ramble, ride 34
34 miles	Woodstock Ramble, ride 15
35 miles	Rend Lake Ramble, ride 40

Cruises

30 miles	Barrington Cruise, ride 7
35 miles	Evergreen Lake–Lake Bloomington Cruise, ride 21
35 miles	Kampsville River Bluff Cruise, ride 35
35 miles	Lena–Pecatonica River Cruise, ride 2
35 miles	North Shore Cruise, ride 13
35 miles	Rock River Cruise, ride 4
37 miles	Garden of the Gods Cruise, ride 33
38 miles	Charleston Cruise, ride 19
39 miles	Springfield Cruise, ride 30
41 miles	American Bottoms Cruise, ride 31
43 miles	Illinois River Cruise, ride 22
45 miles	Cedar Lake Cruise, ride 9
46 miles	Allerton Park–Monticello Cruise, ride 16

Challenges

44 miles	Ohio River Challenge, ride 37
45 miles	Jubilee College Challenge, ride 23
46 miles	Quad Cities Challenge, ride 3
48 miles	I&M Canal Challenge, ride 12
58 miles	Pere Marquette Challenge, ride 39

Classics

56 miles	Galena Classic, ride 1
60 miles	Savanna Classic, ride 6
64 miles	Bloomington Classic, ride 18
75 miles	Siloam Springs–Griggsville Classic, ride 29

Map Legend

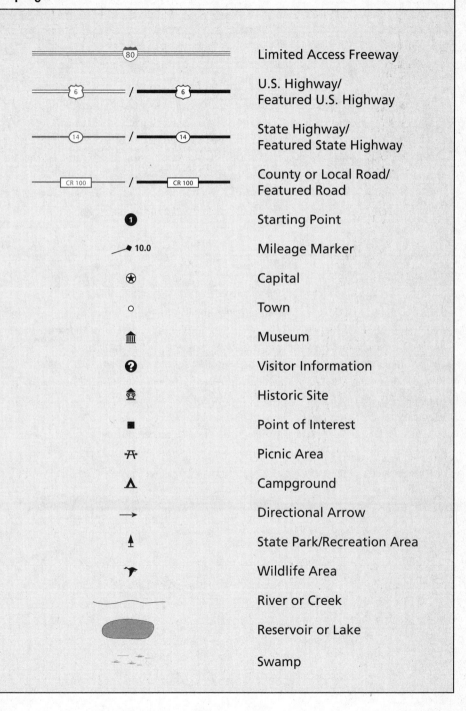

80	Limited Access Freeway
6 / **6**	U.S. Highway/ Featured U.S. Highway
14 / **14**	State Highway/ Featured State Highway
CR 100 / CR 100	County or Local Road/ Featured Road
1	Starting Point
10.0	Mileage Marker
⊛	Capital
○	Town
🏛	Museum
❓	Visitor Information
🏛	Historic Site
■	Point of Interest
⛱	Picnic Area
▲	Campground
→	Directional Arrow
🌲	State Park/Recreation Area
🦅	Wildlife Area
～	River or Creek
⬭	Reservoir or Lake
～	Swamp

Northern Illinois

Road biking in northwestern Illinois will infuse your life with joy. I guarantee it. This is especially true in the Galena region, where high hills, knobs, and steep ravines will pose repeated challenges as they instill a deep appreciation for the landscape. Unlike most of the rest of the state, which was scraped flat during past glaciations, the glaciers missed northwestern Illinois and adjacent portions of Iowa and Wisconsin. As a result, the northwestern corner of the state competes with southernmost Illinois for topographical diversity.

On the Galena Classic ride, you'll come within a couple miles of Charles Mound, the highest point in Illinois, just before seeing the small limestone canyon at Apple River State Park. In Galena, rows of historic buildings perched almost one on top of another progress up the steep hillside leading from the Galena River.

In north-central Illinois, the Rock River angles southwest toward the Quad Cities, where it meets up with the Mississippi. While exploring the narrow Rock River Valley on the Rockford Ramble and the Rock River Cruise, you'll enjoy scenic vistas and wooded bluffs carved from the surrounding prairie. Just north of Oregon stands the awe-inspiring 50-foot concrete sculpture of a Native American overlooking the Rock River. Near Dixon, you'll pass the John Deere Historic Site and the Nachusa Grasslands, one of the largest prairies in the state.

Though limestone bluffs abut much of the Mississippi River in Illinois, one of the most dramatic examples is at Mississippi Palisades State Park. At the beginning of the Savanna Classic, you'll take in the jaw-dropping views from the top of these stone cliffs.

1 Galena Classic

If you live in Illinois, you've likely heard of Galena—a small historic town situated on a bluff not far from the Mississippi River. It's one of the state's biggest tourist destinations, but what the throngs of visitors often fail to fully experience is the beautiful countryside surrounding the town. The outlying landscape hosts some of the hilliest, most scenic terrain in Illinois. If you've cycled in this far northwest corner of the state, the thought of pedaling this area again will likely bring a smile to your face. It's a pleasant mix of hills—some quite big by Illinois standards—small dairy farms, lush woodland, winding streams, and mostly quiet roadways. Through much of the second half of the ride, the roadway twists and curves like a wriggling snake.

Start: In Galena at the trailhead parking lot for the Galena River Trail, located immediately south of the US 20 bridge over the Galena River.
Length: 57.5 miles.
Terrain: Delightfully hilly and rolling along most of the route. The hills around Galena are some of the steepest and most scenic in the Prairie State.

Traffic and hazards: Most of this ride follows quiet roads. The sections that use Stagecoach Trail are busier and traffic can move fast, but motorists seem accustomed to cyclists and provide a wide berth while passing. In certain places—particularly near Galena—roads seem to change names randomly. Navigation can be tricky; the Miles and Directions below will guide you through the tough spots.

Getting there: From Chicago and points east, take I-90 (Northwest Tollway) northwest. Just before Rockford, exit I-90 and head west on I-39, which soon merges with US 20. Stay on US 20 all the way to Galena. In Galena, turn right on Park Avenue just before crossing the Galena River on US 20. Turn left after 2 blocks on Bouthillier Street (the old train depot on the corner now serves as Galena's Visitor Information Center). Continue over the train tracks. The trailhead parking area is located at the far end of the lot after passing underneath US 20. Park at the Galena River Trail parking area. Coordinates for starting point: 15T 711486E 4698266N

The Ride

In the 1830s, as a result of a booming lead-mining industry, Galena's population of 1,000 far outnumbered the one hundred residents of Chicago. All the commerce established Galena as one of the busiest Mississippi River ports in the 1850s. Many of the buildings from the era still stand on Main Street and within the very compact downtown area. Indeed, 85 percent of the town's buildings are listed on the National Register of Historic Places.

While there's plenty to enjoy about the historic town of Galena, there are also some things to avoid. Main Street can be annoying, with its heavy traffic and stores hawking decorative stuffed animals and sweatshirts bearing cutesy sayings. Especially

on busy weekends, Main Street is easier to endure on a bike: You can enjoy looking at the historic buildings and get through the traffic and crowds more quickly.

The route out of Galena brings you down Main Street and through a residential stretch of houses perched on the side of a bluff above the Galena River's floodplain. A mile or so outside of town, prepare to leave the flatland behind: The next 2 miles provide a few short downhills, but mainly your pistons are pumping upward. Soon these efforts start to pay off—while continuing a gradual climb, don't forget to raise your head to see the expansive views of the countryside. Immense vistas of the farms and woodland to the south and north unfold before you. At 5 miles, the road descends and you'll fly across the Galena River. Start climbing again, and soon views in nearly every direction compete with the need to watch the road in front of you.

As Stagecoach Trail dips now and then into ravines—some containing small streams—the route offers pleasing views of a pastoral landscape with swaths of woodland and occasional gatherings of Holsteins in green fields. This road probably hasn't changed much since it was a 40-mile stagecoach route between Galena and the town of Lena to the east. The stagecoach route was likely in operation from the mid-1830s until the mid-1850s, when the railroad arrived in the area. On the left is a sign for the nearby village of Scales Mound. Just north of Scales Mounds is a hill called Charles Mound—the highest point in Illinois at 1,235 feet above sea level.

Heading south from Stagecoach Trail, the route zigzags along a few quiet farm roads on the way to a little gem in the state parks system called Apple River Canyon State Park. The park boasts some delightful picnicking spots with views of the small canyons carved out by the Apple River. If you've got the time, this is great place to enjoy a piece of fruit, admire the surroundings, and give your hardworking, hill-climbing legs a bath in the cool river.

South of the park, Townsend Road immediately takes you on a sometimes gradual and sometimes screaming descent that continues for a couple of miles. Pure joy. By now, you'll see a pattern emerge on this ride: The longer descents often lead to a river crossing—in this case, of the Apple River.

After crossing the Apple River, you'll follow a crooked road to higher ground. The intersection of Schapville Road and Scout Camp Road is followed by a 1.5-mile—mostly gradual—descent. Cross the Hells Branch of the Apple River, climb a bit, and then head back down to cross Mill Creek. In Schapville, look for the Zion Presbyterian Church, a classic country church built in 1886.

After Schapville, the route climbs a couple hundred feet and then gently undulates. The views along this stretch of roadway bring to mind idyllic pastoral paintings of the nineteenth century: a series of overlapping hills adorned with lush greenery, happy farm animals, and the occasional garnet-colored barn. Rawlins Road brings you off the ridge and gradually descends about 350 feet before crossing the invitingly

◀ *Exposed sandstone walls line the banks of the Apple River.*

Galena Classic

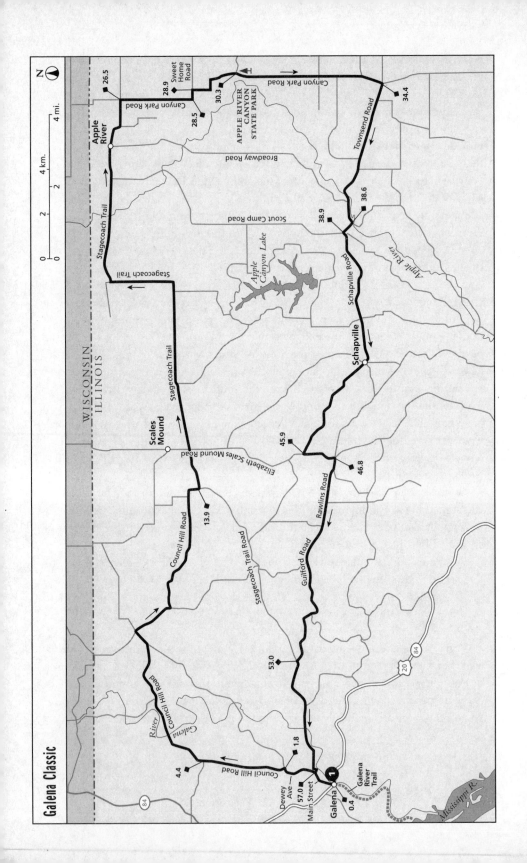

named Smallpox Creek. Two lesser climbs bring you back to Stagecoach Trail, and then over the Galena River again and back into town.

If you've still got energy to burn after arriving back in Galena, take a pleasant spin on the 3.4-mile Galena River Bike Trail, which starts at the parking area for this ride. The smooth, crushed gravel trail runs along the river and adjoining wetlands for much of the route. Unfortunately, the trail ends just shy of meeting up with the Mississippi.

Miles and Directions

0.0 Start riding back toward the visitor center parking area entrance.

0.25 Turn right on Park Avenue.

0.4 Turn right on US 20 and cross the bridge over the Galena River.

0.5 Turn right on Main Street and enter the green floodgates before passing all the cutesy shops. Continue straight out of town on Main Street. At Meeker Street, Main Street turns into Broadway Street, and soon Broadway Street turns into Dewey Avenue. Then, after the curve, Dewey Avenue turns into Council Hill Road.

1.8 Bear left on Council Hill Road.

4.4 Continue straight ahead on Council Hill Road. While enjoying this roller coaster ride, be sure to stay on Council Hill Road. The road takes a couple of sharp turns at junctions, first to the right and then to the left.

13.9 At Stagecoach Trail, turn left. Shortly after the junction with Stagecoach Trail is the turnoff for the small community of Scales Mound. The town is a half mile off West Stagecoach Trail and has gas stations as well as a public park with water and restrooms.

26.5 Turn right on Canyon Park Road.

28.5 Turn left on Sweet Home Road.

28.9 Turn right on Canyon Park Road.

30.3 Arrive at Apple River Canyon State Park.

34.4 Turn right on Townsend Road.

38.6 Turn right on Scout Camp Road.

38.9 Turn left on Schapville Road.

45.9 Turn left on Elizabeth Scales Mound Road (CR 4).

46.8 Turn right on Rawlins Road.

48.7 Continue straight ahead on Guilford Road as Rawlins Road turns to the right.

53.0 Turn left on Stagecoach Trail.

55.0 On the way into Galena, Stagecoach Trail becomes Field Street, Claude Street, and then Meeker Street.

56.3 Turn left on Bench Street.

57.0 Turn right on Main Street, then immediately turn left on US 20 to cross the bridge.

57.3 Turn left on Park Avenue.

57.4 Turn left on Bouthillier Street and enter the parking area.

57.5 Return to the start.

Local Information

Galena/Jo Daviess County Convention & Visitors Bureau: 101 Bouthillier St., Galena; (877) 464-2536; www.galena.org.

Local Events/Attractions

Galena/Jo Daviess County History Museum: The exhibit focusing on lead mining in the area is fascinating and includes mining tools, photos of miners, and a mine shaft; 211 South Bench St., Galena; (815) 777-9129; www.galena historymuseum.org.

Restaurants

Fried Green Tomatoes: Upscale Italian; 213 North Main St., Galena; (815) 777-3938; www .friedgreen.com.

Vinny Vanucchi's Little Italy: Classic Italian; good destination for a group; pleasant patio; 201 South Main St., Galena; (815) 777-8100; www.vinnysgalena.com.

Accommodations

Apple River Canyon State Park: Wooded campground offers fairly private campsites; 8736 East Canyon Rd., Apple River; (815) 745-3302; http://dnr.state.il.us/lands/landmgt/parks/ r1/apple.htm.

Blanding Landing Recreation Area: Pleasant campground operated by the U.S. Army Corps of Engineers on the banks of the Mississippi River,

about 10 miles south of Galena; 5720 South River Rd., Hanover; (800) 645-0248 or (815) 591-2326.

Grant Hills Motel: Clean, affordable motel located a mile east of Galena; outdoor pool; 9372 US 20, Galena; (877) 421-0924 or (815) 777-2116; www.granthills.com.

Bike Shops

Fever River Outfitters: Rents and sells outdoor equipment, including bicycles; 525 Main St., Galena; (815) 776-9425; www.feverriver outfitters.com.

Restrooms

Start/finish: The Galena River Trail parking area has a portable toilet. Water is available at the visitor center.

Mile 13.9: Turn left on North Elizabeth Scales Mound Road for a one-half mile trip to the village of Scales Mound. There are gas stations in town, as well as a public park offering restrooms and water.

Mile 30.3: Apple River Canyon State Park has restrooms and water.

Maps

USGS: Elizabeth NE quad, Galena quad, Scales Mound East quad, Scales Mound West quad.

DeLorme: Illinois Atlas & Gazetteer: Pages 15 and 16.

2 Lena-Pecatonica River Cruise

This ride takes you through the Pecatonica River Valley and the rolling farmland north of Lena. On the way to one of the highest points in Illinois, you'll pass through the village of Winslow, where you can fill your water bottles from a gushing artesian well. After passing through the historic town of Lena, you'll head back to the starting point at Lake Le-Aqua-Na State Park.

Start: Near the guardhouse at Lake Le-Aqua-Na State Park, located just north of the Lena.
Length: 34.9 miles.
Terrain: Rolling terrain with some hills.

Traffic and hazards: While traffic is minimal on the entire route, expect to see a few more cars on Lake and Galena Roads. Use caution on the long downhill on Galena Road.

Getting there: From Chicago and points east, take I-90 (Northwest Tollway) northwest. Just before Rockford, exit I-90 and head west on I-39, which soon merges with US 20. Stay on US 20 to Galena Road (CR 6). Turn right on Galena Road and head into Lena. In Lena, turn right on Freedom Street (CR 7). The entrance to the park is on the left. Stay to the right and park in the lot next to the guardhouse. Coordinates for starting point: 16T 267249E 4700400N

The Ride

Before heading out, take a quick lap around the small but picturesque 40-acre Lake Le-Aqua-Na. (The name of this lake and state park sounds like it's a taken from a Native American language, but it's not—it's a commingling of the words *Lena* and *aqua*. As one might guess, a naming contest was behind that choice.) Exiting the park, the hilly terrain allows long views of the surrounding fields and woods.

At about 3 miles into the ride, the road begins descending gradually toward the Pecatonica River, a sinuous 120-mile-long tributary of the Rock River. Just after crossing the Pecatonica, look in the floodplain on the right for the small oxbow lake formed when the river abandoned its original meandering course and cut a new channel.

A mile before entering the community of Winslow, the Pecatonica appears again, twisting through the floodplain on the left. After crossing the river and entering Winslow, follow the sign for Paradise Cove, a nifty little community park containing the town's treasure, a gushing artesian well that is the source of Winslow's water supply. Water from the artesian well (flowing at 444 gallons a minute, they say) passes over a small waterwheel on its way to Indian Creek; the town also created a little waterfall by piping the water to the top of a small rocky ledge. A picnic table and a few mowed trails are located at the back of the park. Take a cue from the locals filling up their jugs and have a drink.

Following Warren Road out of town brings you past the town's water tower (one presumes the town has no trouble keeping it filled) and up to a ridge with more fine

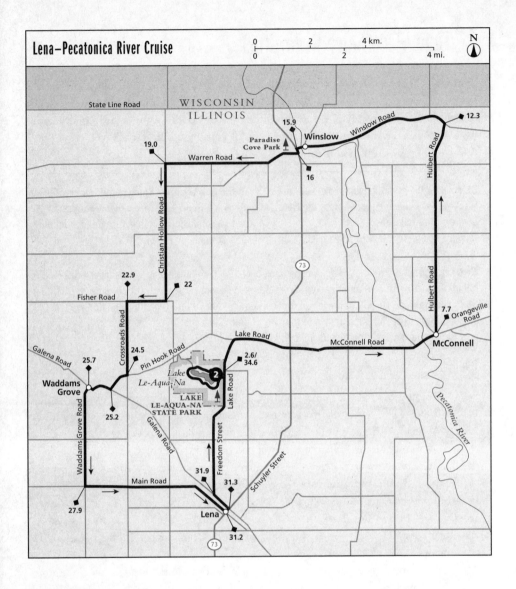

Lena–Pecatonica River Cruise

0   2   4 km.

0   2   4 mi.

N

State Line Road

WISCONSIN
ILLINOIS

Paradise
Cove Park

15.9

Winslow

Winslow Road

12.3

19.0

Warren Road ←

16

Christian Hollow Road

73

Hulbert Road

Hulbert Road

22.9

22

7.7

Orangeville Road

Fisher Road

Crossroads Road

Lake Road

McConnell Road

McConnell

Galena Road

25.7

24.5

Pin Hook Road

2.6/
34.6

Waddams
Grove

Lake
Le-Aqua-Na

2

25.2

LAKE
LE-AQUA-NA
STATE PARK

Lake Road

Galena Road

Freedom Street

Schuyler Street

Pecatonica River

Waddams Grove Road

27.9

Main Road

31.9

31.3

Lena

31.2

73

views of the surrounding countryside. While cruising over this rolling terrain, keep an eye to the left for a quarry—the exposed patterns of rock and dirt provide a snapshot of the local geological strata.

The rolling farmland along Crossroads Road was one of the many places in the region that saw a clash during the Black Hawk War of 1832. The war was a short-lived conflict that showcased the horrific treatment of Native Americans during European settlement of the continent. The conflict arose when the Sauk leader Black Hawk and his followers resisted pressure to move away from their traditional land and relocate across the Mississippi River. Black Hawk and his group eventually were violently removed, and in at least a couple of instances, his followers were massacred by the U.S. military as they were retreating from the disputed territory.

As you climb for a half-mile up to Galena Road on Pin Hook Road, look at the hill to the left and you'll see the second-highest natural point in Illinois at 1,150 feet. (Charles Mound, located about 15 miles northwest, is the highest point in the state at more than 1,200 feet.) The air feels thinner, doesn't it? Enjoy the screaming descent into the small community of Waddams Grove, and then pedal through gently rolling farmland toward the town of Lena.

On the way into Lena, you'll pass the town's brick water tower, built in 1896. A couple other historic structures are near the corner of Schuyler Street and Galena Road. At the northwest corner of this intersection stands a mill that has been in continuous operation since it opened in 1855. A few doors southeast on Galena Road (Lena Street) stands a stately yellow limestone building (the only house angled on a diagonal from the road) that was once a popular stopover on the stagecoach route between Chicago and Galena. Called Dodds Inn, it reportedly had many famous guests, including Abe Lincoln, Jefferson Davis, and Horace Greeley. Currently, it's a private residence.

From downtown Lena, it's about 3.5 miles of rolling terrain back to the parking area at Lake Le-Aqua-Na State Park.

Miles and Directions

0.0 Start by making a counterclockwise loop around Lake Le-Aqua-Na.

2.6 Leaving the park, turn left on Lake Road. Lake Road becomes McConnell Road after crossing SR 73.

7.7 After crossing the Pecatonica River, turn left on Hulbert Road.

12.3 Turn left on Winslow Road.

15.9 Turn left on SR 73 in the town of Winslow. Stop at Paradise Cove Park on the right.

16.0 Turn right on Warren Road.

19.0 Turn left on Christian Hollow Road.

22.0 Turn right on Fisher Road.

22.9 Turn left on Crossroads Road.

24.5 Turn right on Pin Hook Road.

25.2 Turn right on Galena Road. Watch for traffic on this downhill.

25.7 Turn left on Waddams Grove Road.

27.9 Turn left on Main Road.

31.2 Turn left on Schuyler Street.

31.3 Turn left on Galena Road.

31.9 Turn right on Freedom Street. Freedom Street soon becomes Lake Road.

34.6 Turn left into Lake Le-Aqua-Na State Park.

34.9 Arrive back at parking area.

Local Information

Freeport/Stephenson County Convention and Visitors Bureau: 4596 US 20 East, Freeport; (815) 233-1357 or (800) 369-2955; www .stephenson-county-il.org.

Local Events/Attractions

Lena Area Historical Museum: Open weekends May to September; 427 West Grove St., Lena; (800) 369-2955.

Restaurants

Lena Drive Inn: A '60s-era carhop drive-in with all the food you'd expect; 304 North Freedom St., Lena; (815) 369-4317.
Uncle Bob's: Decent diner fare, good pies; 126 West Main St., Lena; (815) 369-5177.

Accommodations

Lake Le-Aqua-Na State Park: Two camping areas; 8542 North Lake Rd., Lena; (815) 369-

4282; http://dnr.state.il.us/lands/landmgt/ parks/r1/leaquana.htm.

Bike Shops

Freeport Bicycle Company: 120 South Chicago Ave., Freeport; (815) 235-2014; www.freeport bikes.com.

Restrooms

Start/finish: Pit toilets and a drinking fountain are located across the park road from the guardhouse.
Mile 16.0: Paradise Cove Park has a portable toilet and drinking water. There's also a gas station/ convenience store in Winslow.
Mile 31.9: Gas station in Lena.

Maps

USGS: Lena quad, Warren quad, Monroe quad, Orangeville quad.
DeLorme: Illinois Atlas & Gazetteer: Page 16.

3 Quad Cities Challenge

This ride is crammed with appealing places to explore. The first section traces the Mississippi River south through a few parks and Moline's newly rejuvenated downtown. After crossing the Mississippi via Rock Island, you'll embark on a 24-mile loop through the Iowa cities of Bettendorf and Davenport. In Bettendorf, the Duck Creek Trail guides you along a dozen miles of scenic greenway punctuated by a series of open, grassy parks.

Start: Illiniwek Forest Preserve in Hampton, located a few miles north of the Quad Cities.
Length: 45.9 miles.
Terrain: Climb and descend major hills at mile 15.3 and mile 28, respectively. The rest of the ride is flat.
Traffic and hazards: This route has less than 10 miles of on-street riding; the rest follows

several paved bike trails—all in good condition. While crossing the Mississippi River twice on the Governors Bridge, pay heed to the signs asking you to walk your bike. The grated metal surface on the bridge is uneven in places and could catch a wheel. Waverly Street in Davenport has no shoulder and gets busy with traffic at times; fortunately, the traffic is slow moving.

Getting there: From I-80 northeast of the Quad Cities, exit heading south on SR 84. After passing Fishermen's Corner Campground, enter the Illiniwek Forest Preserve on the right. Coordinates for starting point: 15T 716291E 4604148N

A handful of impressive bridges span the Mississippi River near the Quad Cities.

The Ride

Illiniwek Forest Preserve, the starting point for this ride, overlooks a dam that stretches for half a mile across the width of the Mississippi River. The park serves as a perfect place to watch the progression of river barges lumbering up and down the waterway and passing through the locks. Starting south on the Mississippi River Trail from Illiniwek Park, you'll breeze by a small local-history museum and an old-fashioned ice cream shop in the sleepy riverside village of Hampton. South of Hampton, the lightly wooded grounds of Empire Park contain a trailside visitor center with displays focusing on the ecosystem of the Mississippi River.

Getting closer to Moline, the trail traces the top of a levee through a series of industrial areas and then threads its way through Riverside Park, which is pressed between the Mississippi River and River Drive. Like Rock Island to the south, Moline has its roots in farm machinery manufacturing. John Deere's headquarters still reside in Moline, and Rock Island once was home to International Harvester.

In downtown Moline, the trail brushes against the backside of the I Wireless Center, a 12,000-seat entertainment venue and home to the local American Hockey League team, the Quad City Flames. Tucked among a strip of industrial buildings in

Moline is a pedestrian bridge that leads out to Sylvan Island, a 36-acre wooded park that once hosted a steel mill and a rock-crushing operation.

Just before mounting the Governors Bridge and heading toward Rock Island (the island as opposed to the city), the 70-foot-tall glass structure that houses the Quad City Botanical Center appears on the left. Inside is a tropical garden with a 15-foot waterfall that splashes down amid palm trees, orchids, and bromeliads. On Rock Island, you'll pass a replica of Fort Armstrong, built in the early 1700s as the first European settlement on the island. After this original settlement, various military installations came and went. During the Civil War, the island hosted a Confederate prison camp (a cemetery on the island contains the graves of 2,000 prisoners who died at the camp). Not long after the Civil War, the military established an armory that now has a museum attached to it.

While on Rock Island, many travelers stop at the Mississippi River Visitor Center, which offers a bird's-eye view of boats passing through Mississippi River Lock 15. To reach the visitor center, you have to enter the gates to the island. Guards require photo identification, and they are notorious for being very strict about who gets access. Don't be surprised if you are turned away for some reason.

As the river path whisks you upstream along the Mississippi's Iowa shoreline, you'll soon pass a collection of restaurants, small shops, and historic buildings in the village of East Davenport. Even though the city of Davenport long ago annexed East Davenport, the village retains a distinctive identity. Part of that identity is preserved in the handsome Victorian mansions perched on a bluff overlooking the river.

After a bit of on-street riding, the Duck Creek Trail—the longest stretch of green space in the Quad Cities area—guides you along a winding creek bordered by open, grassy banks. While crossing the creek nearly a dozen times on steel bridges, you'll encounter patches of bottomland woods and occasional rocky outcroppings peeking from the sides of wooded bluffs. Given the creek's residential surroundings, the number of tree stumps gnawed by beavers comes as a surprise. The east half of the trail often conveniently bypasses busy cross streets by going underneath. The west half of the trail, however, often meets up with local traffic at crosswalks.

After completing the Duck Creek Trail and putting in a few more miles of on-street riding, you'll arrive back at the shore of the Mississippi for a lap around Credit Island Park. The 2-mile-long island contains swaths of open, grassy parkland as well as bottomland woods, marshland, and lagoons.

Passing under the latticed arches of the Centennial Bridge signals your arrival in downtown Davenport. After passing the outside wall of the baseball stadium where the minor-league Quad Cities River Bandits play, you'll arrive at the elegant LeClaire Park band shell, built in the 1920s on the riverbank. On your way back to the Governors Bridge, the trail runs next to another riverboat casino and under the suspended space-age walkway that leads to it.

After retracing your path on the Mississippi River Trail and returning to the starting point at Illiniwek Forest Preserve, you'll have the opportunity to nearly double

Quad Cities Challenge

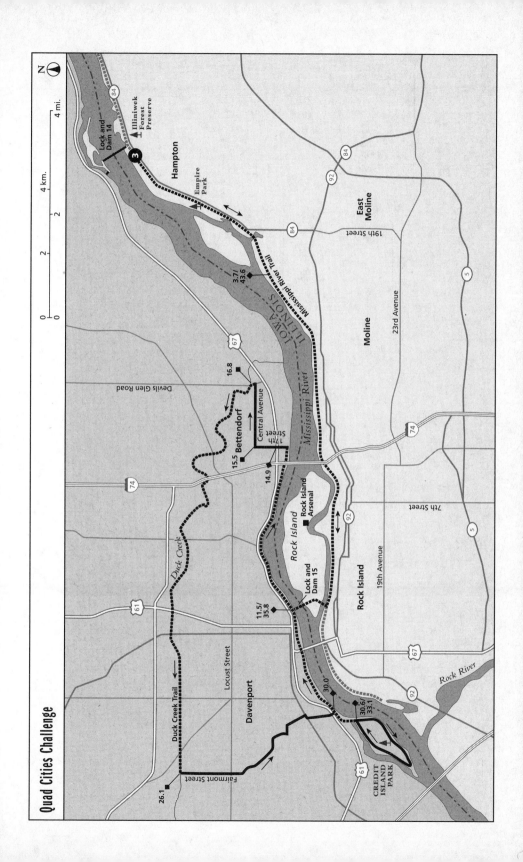

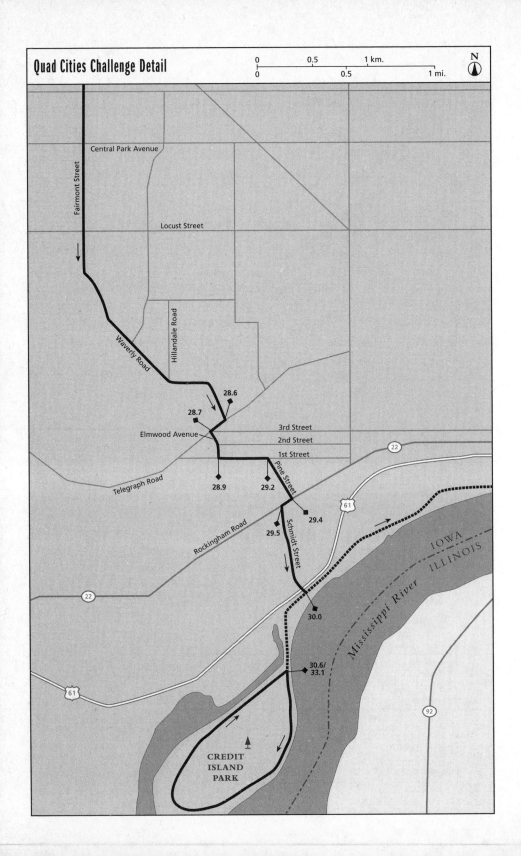

Quad Cities Challenge Detail

0   0.5   1 km.
0   0.5   1 mi.

N

Central Park Avenue

Fairmont Street

Locust Street

Hillandale Road

Waverly Road

28.6

28.7

Elmwood Avenue

3rd Street

2nd Street

1st Street

Telegraph Road

28.9

29.2

Pine Street

29.4

Rockingham Road

29.5

Schmidt Street

22

61

30.0

30.6/
33.1

22

61

92

IOWA

ILLINOIS

Mississippi River

CREDIT
ISLAND
PARK

the mileage by continuing north on the trail. Most of this 20-mile northern section of trail runs alongside the well-trafficked route of SR 84. Fortunately, the trail strays from the highway for interludes of varying length, most notably in the towns of Rapids City, Port Byron, and Cordova. North of Cordova, the trail and SR 84 head inland away from the river, and the final few miles of the trail take you by a sprawling Mississippi backwater and thick bottomland woods that are a part of the Upper Mississippi River National Fish and Wildlife Refuge. The trail ends at Albany Mounds State Historic Site, containing nearly a hundred Native American mounds—one of the largest collections of American Indian mounds in the nation (see my book, *Best Rail Trails Illinois*, for a complete description of the route).

Miles and Directions

0.0   Head south toward the Quad Cities on the Mississippi River Trail.

10.7   Take the Governors Bridge to Rock Island and then continue on to Davenport, Iowa.

15.0   Before the trail ends at the Isle of Capri Casino, take the paved path down to street level. Turn left on 17th Street and follow it over the railroad tracks.

15.3   Jog to the left and then continue ahead on 17th Street.

15.5   Turn right on Central Avenue.

16.8   Turn left on Devils Glen Road.

16.9   Take the path to the right and pass under the bridge to start the Duck Creek Trail.

26.1   Instead of following the path all the way to the end, you'll turn off just a quarter mile before the end on Fairmont Street. Look for the spur trail on the left about 0.2 mile after passing under a set of railroad tracks. Turn right on Heatherton Drive and then immediately left on Fairmount Street. Continue ahead on Fairmount Street as it turns into Waverly Road.

28.6   Turn right on Telegraph Road.

28.7   Turn left on Elmwood Avenue.

28.9   Turn left on 1st Street.

29.2   Turn right on Pine Street.

29.4   Turn right on Rockingham Road.

29.5   Turn left on Schmidt Road.

30.0   Cross US 61 to catch the Mississippi River Trail. Turn right and head out to Credit Island Park.

30.6   Bear left where the park road splits on Credit Island.

35.8   Cross the Governors Bridge and return to Illinois.

36.6   Head upstream to your starting point at Illiniwek Forest Preserve.

45.9   Return to Illiniwek Forest Preserve.

Local Information

Great River Trail Guide: (309) 277-0937, ext. 113; www.greatrivertrail.com.

Quad Cities Convention and Visitors Bureau: 1601 River Dr., Suite 110, Moline; (800) 747-7800; www.visitquadcities.com.

Local Events/Attractions

Celebration River Cruises: The 800-passenger *Celebration Belle* is one of the largest functioning riverboats on the Upper Mississippi; the trail passes the boarding area; 2501 River Dr., Moline; (309) 764-1952; www.celebration belle.com.

Mississippi River Visitor Center: Overlooking Lock and Dam 15, the center is operated by the U.S. Army Corps of Engineers; west end of Rock Island; (309) 794-5338.

Rock Island Arsenal Museum: Focuses on firearms and the history of the arsenal; Rock Island Arsenal, Rock Island; (309) 782-5021; http ://riamwr.com/museum.htm.

Restaurants

Bent River Brewery: Nice selection of beers brewed on-site, including a jalapeño beer; 1413 5th Ave., Moline; (309) 797-2722; www .bentriverbrewery.com.

Bier Stube: German food served in a comfortable atmosphere; 415 15th St., Moline; (309) 797-3049; www.bier-stube.com.

Remember When Ice Cream and Candies: Old-fashioned ice cream parlor right on the route; back deck overlooks the Mississippi River; 625 1st Ave., Hampton; (309) 752-0362.

Accommodations

Illiniwek Forest Preserve: Starting point for this ride; pitch a tent on the river's edge; located on SR 84 north of Hampton; (309) 496-2620.

Stoney Creek Inn: New, outdoorsy-themed hotel in downtown Moline, right alongside the path; 101 18th St., Moline; (309) 743-0101; www.stoneycreekinn.com.

Bike Shops

Bike and Hike Shop: 3913 14th Ave., Rock Island; (309) 788-2092.

Restrooms

Start/finish: Restrooms and water are available at Illiniwek Forest Preserve.

Mile 3.7: Water and restrooms are available at the River Harbor parking area.

Mile 11.2: The Mississippi River Visitor Center on Rock Island has restrooms and water. (Turn right on Rodman and stop at the guardhouse. The visitor center is immediately on the left.)

Mile 14.6: Restrooms are available at the trail parking area just west of I-74.

Mile 30.7: Credit Island has restrooms and water.

Mile 35.4: Restrooms and water are available at the boat launch.

Maps

Quad Cities Metro Bicycling Map, the League of Illinois Bicyclists, 2550 Cheshire Dr., Aurora; www.bikelib.org.

USGS: Davenport East quad, Milan quad, Silvis quad.

DeLorme: Illinois Atlas & Gazetteer: Pages 22, 23, and 30.

4 Rock River Cruise

Among the many attractions on this ride are the charming town of Oregon, the John Deere Historic Site, and a handful of picturesque parks where you'll be enveloped in the local scenery. For those with an urge to explore a genuine Illinois prairie, this ride takes you past one of the largest pieces of preserved prairie in the state.

Start: Mill Springs Day Use Area at Franklin Creek Natural Area, located west of Dixon.
Length: 34.7 miles.
Terrain: Consistently rolling with a few small climbs.

Traffic and hazards: The first and last mile of the route is dirt road. Use caution on the brief segments of the route along SR 2 and SR 64. Both of these roads are fairly busy.

Getting there: From Chicago and points east, take I-88 (East-West Tollway) west to Rochelle. Exit north on SR 251 and turn left (west) on SR 38. Follow the highway to Franklin Grove and turn right on State Street (CR 25). Quickly turn left on Old Mill Road, which takes you into the Franklin Creek State Natural Area. Look for the Mill Springs Day Use Area on the left. Coordinates for starting point: 16T 305090E 4636022N

The Ride

The ride starts at Franklin Creek State Natural Area, a lovely park little known outside of the immediate area. Either at the end or the beginning of the ride, be sure to explore the path in back of the parking area. This paved trail follows picturesque Franklin Creek to springs where water emerges from under a rock outcropping on the side of a hill.

As you're heading out of the park, you'll pass a newly rebuilt gristmill modeled after the original cornmeal- and flour-producing mill built at the site in 1847. Unlike many gristmills that have been rebuilt, this one uses the same technology as the original mill: Water turns the four-ton wheel located outside the mill, and the turning of the wheel powers the gears, belts, and a vertical shaft that turn the grinder on the first floor. As you're leaving the mill, look to the left for some rocky outcroppings above Franklin Creek.

The next several miles of riding take you across a series of creeks and through rolling terrain that is part of the Nachusa Grasslands, one of the largest prairie remnants in Illinois (toward the ride's end you'll have the opportunity to explore more of this prairie).

After crossing the Rock River, consider dropping in at the John Deere museum, which includes the former residence and blacksmith workshop of this agricultural icon. There's also a series of exhibits focusing on Deere's main innovation in 1837: changing plow blades from iron to steel. Steel worked better because the rich Midwest soil didn't cling to the steel blade as it did to the iron blade. While it seems

like a modest contribution to farming technology, by all accounts Deere's plow did work better, and thereby hastened the settlement of the Midwest and the prairie in particular.

Continuing over the gently rolling landscape north toward Oregon, occasional views open up as you pass small farms, pastures, old barns, and patches of thick woodland. More long views appear on Oregon Trail Road. In particular, you'll see a couple of landmarks in the town of Oregon: the Ogle County Courthouse and the bluffs above the Rock River.

Before crossing the Rock River again in Oregon, you may want to take a closer look at the handsome courthouse, built in 1891. The courthouse lawn contains a monument by the Illinois artist Laredo Taft. Oregon claims several works by Taft, the best one located just 1.5 miles north of town in Lowden State Park. The 50-foot concrete statue of a Native American—often identified as Black Hawk—is perched dramatically on a bluff overlooking the Rock River (see Miles and Directions for this worthwhile side trip).

Turning onto Lowden Road, the traffic quiets down considerably as you ride under a canopy of oak and hickory toward Lowden-Miller State Forest. This forest once belonged to Frank Lowden, a former U.S. congressman and Illinois governor. Lowden lived for a time on the property with his family (Lowden's wife, Florence, was the daughter of George Pullman, the owner of the Chicago train car manufacturer).

The Nachusa Grasslands—a 2,500-acre natural area that is owned and operated by The Nature Conservancy—appears on the right during the last several miles of the ride. An information kiosk is located at the visitor entrance on Lowden Road, just past the entrance to the preserve's office. Occasional sandstone outcrops as well as rocky soil and streams made this grassland difficult to farm and saved large pieces of it from the plow. From the parking area, take a short walk on the mowed path up to the high point to take in the subtle drama of the landscape's rolling green waves. You'll see birds chirping madly and dashing among the compass plants, spiderworts, and coneflowers. From the grassland, it's a short trip back to Franklin Creek.

Miles and Directions

0.0 Turn left on Old Mill Road from the Mill Springs Day Use Area at Franklin Creek State Natural Area.

0.2 Turn right on Twist Road.

1.3 Turn left on Naylor Road.

4.3 Turn right on Maples Road, then make a quick right on Lost Nation Road.

4.5 Turn left on Grand Detour Road.

6.2 Turn right on SR 2.

◀ *Rocky outcroppings adorn the banks of Franklin Creek.*

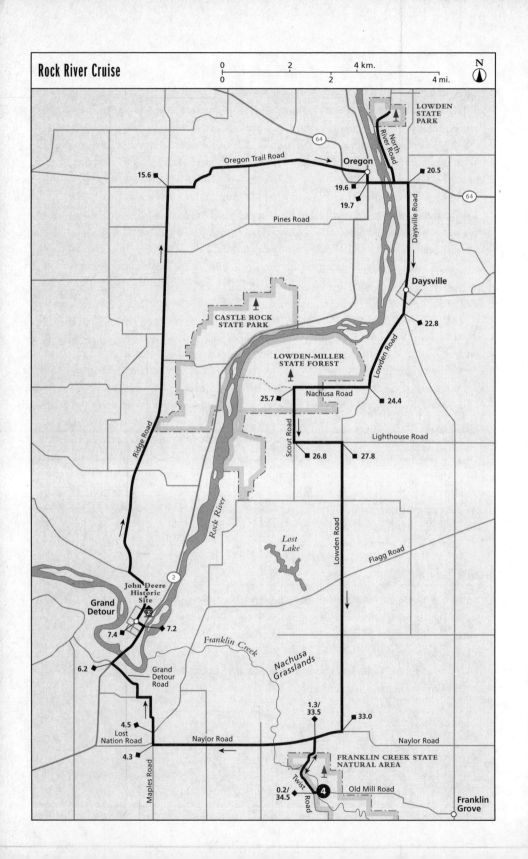

Rock River Cruise

0   2   4 km.

0   2   4 mi.

N

LOWDEN STATE PARK

North River Road

64

Oregon Trail Road

Oregon

15.6

20.5

64

19.6

19.7

Pines Road

Daysville Road

Daysville

22.8

CASTLE ROCK STATE PARK

LOWDEN-MILLER STATE FOREST

Lowden Road

25.7   Nachusa Road   24.4

Scout Road

Lighthouse Road

26.8   27.8

Ridge Road

Rock River

Lost Lake

Lowden Road

Flagg Road

2

John Deere Historic Site

Grand Detour

7.4   7.2

6.2

Franklin Creek

Nachusa Grasslands

Grand Detour Road

1.3/ 33.5

33.0

4.5

Lost Nation Road

Naylor Road

Naylor Road

4.3

Maples Road

Twist Road

0.2/ 34.5

4

Old Mill Road

FRANKLIN CREEK STATE NATURAL AREA

Franklin Grove

7.2	Turn left on Broad Street.
7.4	Turn right on Ridge Road. Several miles ahead, pass a parking area for hiking trails that are part of Castle Rock State Park.
15.6	Turn right on Oregon Trail Road. In Oregon, Oregon Trail Road becomes Monroe Street.
19.6	Turn right on 3rd Street.
19.7	Turn left on SR 64. Crossing the Rock River, take the pedestrian/bike path on the left.
20.2	**Side trip:** Go 1.5 miles north on River Road to Lowden State Park to see the towering statue of a Native American. Ride carefully on River Road—it can be busy.
20.5	Turn right on Daysville Road.
22.8	Turn right on Lowden Road.
24.4	Turn right on Nachusa Road.
25.7	Turn left on Scout Road. Side trip: For a fairly quick trip to the Rock River, keep straight ahead on Nachusa Road past Scout Road. You'll have to walk your bike for a half mile to the river; the park does not allow bicycling on the trails.
26.8	Turn left on Lighthouse Road.
27.8	Turn right on Lowden Road.
31.3	Nachusa Grasslands kiosk and trailhead.
33.0	Turn right on Naylor Road.
33.5	Turn left on Twist Road.
34.5	Turn left on Old Mill Road.
34.7	Return to Mill Springs Day Use Area.

Local Information

Blackhawk Waterways Convention and Visitors Bureau: 201 North Franklin Ave., Polo; (800) 678-2108 or (815) 946-2108; www.bwcvb.com.

Lee County Tourism: 113 South Peoria Ave., Dixon; (815) 288-1840; www.encounterleecounty.com.

Local Events/Attractions

Franklin Creek Natural Area Grist Mill: Milling demonstrations; open on weekends; 1872 Twist Rd., Franklin Grove; (815) 456-2878; http://dnr.state.il.us/lands/landmgt/parks/r1/franklin.htm.

John Deere Historic Site: The gift shop has that pair of John Deere oven mitts you've always wanted; South Main, Grand Detour; (815) 652-4551; www.deere.com/en_US/attractions/historicsite.

Nachusa Grasslands Preserve: Volunteers and staff conduct periodic tours, bird walks, and other special events; 8772 South Lowden Rd., Franklin Grove; (815) 456-2340.

Restaurants

La Vigna: Italian food; located on the route; 2190 South Daysville Rd., Oregon; (815) 732-4413.

White Pines Lodge Restaurant: Home-style fare; occasional dinner theater; 6712 West Pines Rd., Mount Morris; (815) 946-3817; www.whitepinesinn.com.

Accommodations

Chateau Lodge: 1326 SR 2, Oregon; (815) 732-6195; www.chateaulodge.com.

The Patchwork Inn: 122 North 3rd St., Oregon; (815) 732-4113; www.patchworkinn.com.

White Pines Inn/White Pines Forest State Park: One of the oldest Illinois state parks offers camping, cabins, and a restaurant (see above); 6712 West Pines Rd., Mount Morris; (815) 946-3817.

Bike Shops

Green River Adventure Sports: 148 South Peoria Ave., Dixon; (815) 288-1079; http://green riveradventuresports.com.

Restrooms

Start/finish: The Mill Springs Day Use Area has restrooms and a water fountain.
Mile 6.7: John Deere Historic Site has restrooms and water.

Mile 18.6: Oregon Park West has restrooms and water.
Mile 25.5: Equestrian area at Lowden-Miller State Forest has a portable toilet.

Maps

USGS: Franklin Grove quad, Daysville quad, Dixon East quad, Grand Detour quad, Oregon quad.
DeLorme: Illinois Atlas & Gazetteer: Pages 25 and 17.

5 Rockford Ramble

Get a full taste of the Rockford area while touring newer suburbs, older residential neighborhoods, and many acres of parkland. The highlight of this ride is a 7-mile-long path that winds along the grassy banks of the Rock River. While passing through downtown Rockford, you'll have an opportunity to check out a few quality museums clustered together across the river.

Start: Rock Cut State Park, located at the northeast edge of Rockford.
Length: 30.1 miles.
Terrain: Mostly flat and gently rolling; a few small hills appear along the way as well.

Traffic and hazards: About 19 miles of this route follow paved paths; the rest of the route is on quiet side streets. While following the path on Charles Street, keep an eye peeled for cars pulling into the path at driveways and cross streets.

Getting there: From I-39/90 northeast of Rockford, exit west on Riverside Boulevard. Turn right on Perryville Road. Several miles ahead, turn right on Lane Road (SR 173). Enter the park on the left and turn right where the park road splits. Follow signs to the Lakeview Picnic Area. Park in the lot on the left, near the shore of Pierce Lake. Catch the beginning of the trail across the park road from the parking area. Coordinates for starting point: 16T 336329E 4690145N

The Ride

As the third-largest city in Illinois, Rockford claims a rich history as a Midwestern manufacturing center. While much of the manufacturing is gone, Rockford remains vibrant, with a handful of historic neighborhoods built during a time when the city's economic engine was purring. The city also has a collection of burgeoning suburbs and an active downtown area. The main focus of the city is the big, wide Rock River, which winds through the center of the city and a variety of neighborhoods.

The ride begins on the shore of Pierce Lake within Rock Cut State Park. The park is packed with trails, fishing spots, and picnic areas as well as hills, creeks, and

Sinnissippi Park features a formal rose garden alongside a pleasant lagoon.

large swaths of rehabilitated prairie. The initial stretch of trail takes you through lush woods alongside Willow Creek and over a couple of pedestrian bridges spanning the gravel-bottomed creek.

Leaving the park behind, the route follows the Perryville Road Trail as it snakes alongside Perryville Road on a big S-curve. The open, rolling landscape along Perryville Road seems to dissipate the somewhat hectic atmosphere created by the patches of strip malls and shopping complexes.

Just south of Riverside Boulevard, the path runs through the Keeling-Puri Peace Plaza, a wayside park dedicated to world peace. Within the plaza are quotes from famous people, flower gardens, and a collection of forty flags representing all the nationalities that have populations within the Rockford area. At Guilford Road, you might consider a side trip several blocks to the right for a visit to a local history museum featuring a Victorian village with twenty-four historical buildings filled with artifacts of the era.

After gliding through quiet suburban neighborhoods along Trainer Road, you'll soon arrive at Charles Street and resume riding on a paved trail. Leaving Charles Street, the route tours older leafy neighborhoods where the terrain becomes rolling and, at times, hilly. Before reaching downtown, the route cuts through an industrial

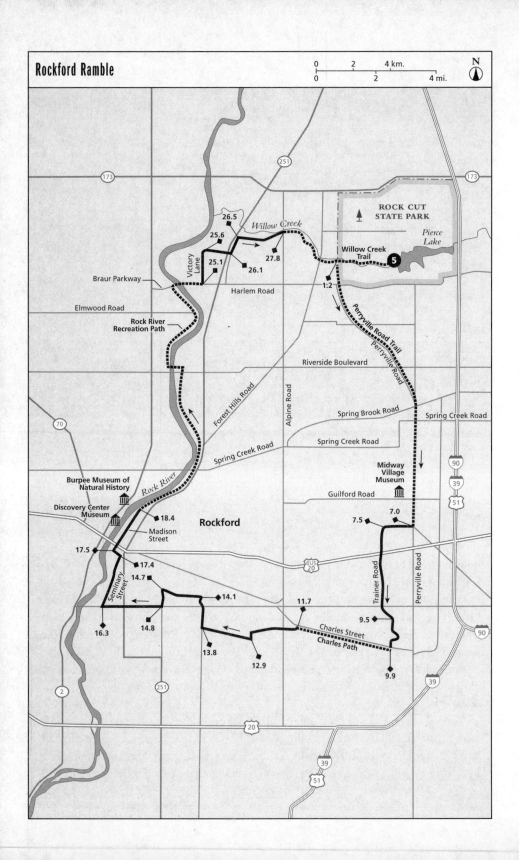

Rockford Ramble

0   2   4 km.
0   2   4 mi.

N

ROCK CUT
STATE PARK

Pierce
Lake

Willow Creek

Willow Creek
Trail

5

26.5

25.6

25.1

27.8

26.1

1:2

Victory
Lane

Braur Parkway

Harlem Road

Elmwood Road

Rock River
Recreation Path

Perryville Road Trail

Perryville Road

Riverside Boulevard

Forest Hills Road

Alpine Road

Spring Brook Road

Spring Creek Road

Spring Creek Road

Spring Creek Road

Midway
Village
Museum

Burpee Museum of
Natural History

Rock River

Guilford Road

Discovery Center
Museum

18.4

Rockford

Madison
Street

7.0

7.5

17.5

Trainer Road

17.4

14.7

14.1

11.7

9.5

Seminary
Street

16.3

14.8

13.8

12.9

Charles Street

Charles Path

9.9

Perryville Road

area on Seminary Street before sweeping past a collection of handsome Victorian homes at the crest of a hill.

In downtown Rockford, you might consider stopping at one of the city's museums located side-by-side on the opposite shore of the river. The Burpee Museum of Natural History contains the world's most complete skeleton cast of a juvenile *T. rex* as well as a two-story prehistoric coal forest. Other exhibits focus on topics such as regional geology and local Native American history. The Discovery Center Museum contains some 200 hands-on art and science exhibits aimed at kids and adults, and the Rockford Art Museum is noted for its collection of nineteenth- and twentieth-century American art as well as its changing exhibits.

After picking up the Rock River Recreation Path just north of downtown, one of the first stops along the way is Sinnissippi Park. The park's greenhouse alongside the trail contains a variety of plants, a few live animal displays, and a fish pond. In the fall, the greenhouse explodes with 4,000 colored mums. The park also contains formal rose gardens, lagoons, and a series of walking paths.

As the trail unfolds along the shore of the river, a series of outdoor sculptures crop up along the way. Most are abstract metal creations, but a few are not, such as the small gathering of large rock people standing in a grove of pine trees. Continuing north, you'll encounter a few brief on-street sections between the parks. Shorewood Park is covered with stately oaks and has grandstands overlooking the river. After another block or so of on-street riding, you'll reclaim the path as it crosses a bridge over a lagoon at Martin Park.

Once you've crossed a pedestrian bridge over the Rock River, the path drops down a steep bluff and then traces the foot of a blond sandstone wall. The combination of exposed rock and dense riparian woods makes this stretch of trail feel like a shady canyon. As you pass through Veterans Memorial Park, follow signs for the Braur Bridge (the path ends shortly after crossing the bridge). A couple more miles of on-street riding brings you to a path that curves beside Willow Creek and leads you back into the tangled woodland of Rock Cut State Park.

Miles and Directions

0.0   Catch the trail across the park road from the Lakeview Picnic Area and head west.

1.2   At the first junction with a paved path, turn right and then immediately turn left to follow the Perryville Road Trail along Perryville Road.

4.8   At Spring Brook Road, the trail switches sides of the street.

6.5   **Side trip:** At Guilford Road, consider a short side trip to the Midway Village Museum.

7.0   Follow Garret Lane right.

7.5   Turn left on Trainer Road.

9.5   Turn left on Rolling Hedge Lane.

9.6   Turn right on Valencia Drive.

9.7   Turn right on Hedgewood Road.

Rockford Ramble Detail

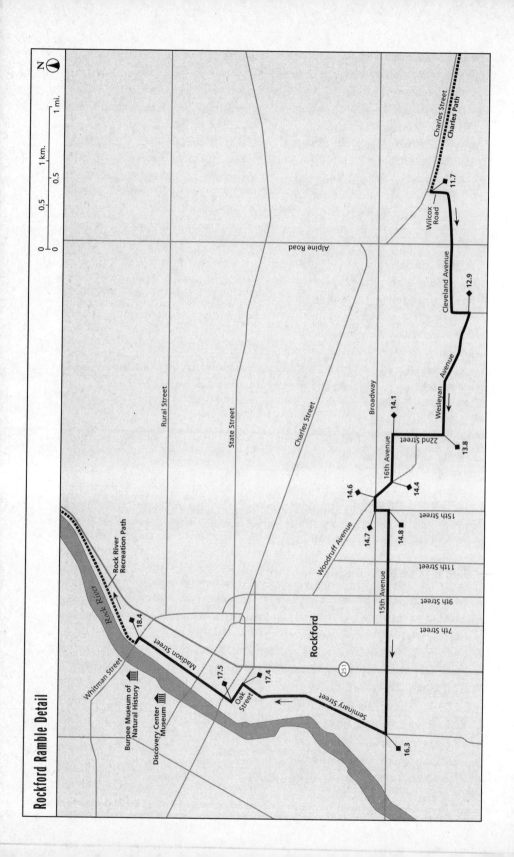

9.9	Turn right on Charles Street. Catch the paved path that runs on the south side of Charles Street.
11.7	Turn left on Wilcox Road. Bear right on Wilcox Road as it becomes Cleveland Avenue, then bear left as Cleveland Avenue becomes Montana Avenue.
12.9	Turn right on Wesleyan Avenue.
13.8	Turn right on 22nd Street.
14.1	Turn left on 16th Avenue.
14.4	Turn right on Woodruff Avenue.
14.6	Turn left on Broadway.
14.7	Turn left on 15th Street.
14.8	Turn right on 15th Avenue (that's right—you're turning from 15th Street onto 15th Avenue).
16.3	Turn right on Seminary Street; after the train tracks, Seminary Street becomes 2nd Avenue.
17.4	Turn left on Oak Street.
17.5	Turn right on Madison Street.
18.4	Just before the underpass, turn left and go through the parking lot. The trail starts at the opposite end of the parking lot.
22.1	Take the pedestrian path across the river. On the other side of the river, go up to the stoplight to cross Riverside Boulevard, then head back toward the river to catch the path heading north.
25.1	At the end of the Rock River Recreation Path, turn left on Victory Lane.
25.6	Turn right on Machesney Road.
26.1	Turn left on Frontage Road.
25.6	Turn right on Minns Drive.
27.8	Catch the Willow Creek Trail on the right.
30.1	Return to the Lakeview Picnic Area at Rock Cut State Park.

Local Information

Northern Illinois Tourism Development Office: 200 South State St., Belvidere; (815) 547-3740; www.visitnorthernillinois.com.

Rockford Area Convention and Visitors Bureau: 102 North Main St., Rockford; (800) 521-0849; www.gorockford.com.

Rockford Park District: 401 South Main St., Rockford; (815) 987-8800; www.rockfordpark district.org.

Local Events/Attractions

Burpee Museum of Natural History: 737 North Main St., Rockford; (815) 965-3433; www .burpee.org.

Discovery Center Museum: 711 North Main St., Rockford; (815) 963-6769; www.discovery centermuseum.org.

Midway Village Museum: 6799 Guilford Rd., Rockford; (815) 397-9112; www.midwayvillage .com.

Rock Cut State Park: 7318 Harlem Rd., Loves Park; (815) 885-3311; http://dnr.state.il.us/ lands/landmgt/parks/r1/rockcut.htm.

Rockford Art Museum: 711 North Main St., Rockford; (815) 968-2787; www.rockfordart museum.org.

Sinnissippi Greenhouse and Gardens: 1300 North 2nd St., Rockford; (815) 987-8858.

Restaurants

Carlyle Brewing Company: Serves bratwurst, hot pretzels, and sandwiches in addition to a variety of beers brewed on-site—homemade root beer, too; 215 East State St., Rockford; (815) 963-2739; www.carlylebrewing.com.

Thai Basil Fusion: Good Thai food served in a contemporary atmosphere; 1531 West Lane Rd., Machesney Park; (815) 633-9400; www .thaibasilonline.com.

Water Street Cafe: Breakfast and lunch with a Euro approach and outdoor seating; next to the river downtown; 115 North Water St.; Rockford, (815) 962-3310.

Accommodations

Rock Cut State Park: Large, well-shaded campground; see contact information above.

Sweden House Lodge: Indoor pool; 4605 East State St., Rockford; (815) 398-4130; www .swedenhouselodge.com.

Bike Shops

Rockford Bicycle Co.: Large, full-service shop; the route runs by the front door; 4169 North Perryville Rd., Loves Park; (815) 636-0664; www.rockfordbikes.com.

Restrooms

Start/finish: Restrooms and water are available at the concessionaire near Rock Cut State Park's boat launch (continue ahead on the park road for a half mile from the Lakeview Picnic Area).

Mile 7.7: A park with a portable toilet is on the corner of Garrett Lane and Trainer Road.

Mile 19.3: Restrooms and water are available in the Sinnissippi Greenhouse.

Mile 24.5: Vault toilets and water are available at the Headquarters Forest Preserve, which is located across Braur Parkway just before crossing the Braur Bridge.

Maps

USGS: Caledonia quad, Rockford South quad, Rockford North quad.

DeLorme: Illinois Atlas & Gazetteer: Page 18.

6 Savanna Classic

The first part of this ride takes you along a ridge and over the big rolling hills for which northwest Illinois is known. The second part leads you through several small picturesque towns, through the Mississippi's bottomlands, and alongside the river itself. At about the halfway point, you may want to consider budgeting time in Mount Carroll, where you'll find brick streets, Victorian homes, restaurants, a courthouse square, and a very weird funhouse.

Start: Lookout Point parking area in Mississippi Palisades State Park.

Length: 59.5 miles.

Terrain: There are ridges, bluffs, rolling hills, bottomland woods, wetlands, and Mississippi River bank. Much of the first half of the ride is rolling and hilly; the second half is flat to gently rolling. Prepare yourself for one very steep uphill in Savanna.

Traffic and hazards: A couple of short sections of this route follow SR 78 and SR 84. Both roads can be busy, but drivers seem accustomed to cyclists. Several miles of this route include gravel roads that are fairly smooth and in good condition. If riding on skinny road tires, be especially careful on the steep downhills.

Getting there: Savanna is located in the northwest corner of Illinois. From Chicago and points east, take I-90 (Northwest Tollway) northwest. Before Rockford, exit I-90 and head west on I-39, which soon merges with US 20. Stay on US 20 past Elizabeth and turn left on SR 84. Follow SR 84 to the Mississippi Palisades State Park's north entrance on the left. Entering the park, take the first right; continue past the camp store and head up the bluff. Follow signs for the Lookout Point parking area. Coordinates for starting point: 15T 734946E 4667858N

The Ride

This ride starts at one of the most striking natural locales in the entire state of Illinois. From the observation platform at the edge of the parking area in Mississippi Palisades State Park, you'll have immense views of the Mississippi River from a 250-foot-high dolomite cliff. From up here, Old Man River looks like an enormous wetland with large stretches of open water: The river is 2 miles across and includes dozens of islands, fingers of land, and grassy backwater wetlands.

After saddling up at Lookout Point, you'll exit the state park through a nifty backdoor route that is only accessible by foot and bike. Once out of the park, Scenic Ridge Route lives up to its name, offering splendid views as it snakes along the top of a ridge through a pastoral landscape with occasional homes and farms. Nearly a dozen miles into the ride, you'll come down off the ridge, cross Camp Creek, start climbing again, and then follow a similar pattern for the Plum River.

Arriving in the town of Mount Carroll, the redbrick county courthouse cuts an impressive figure as it sits high on a tree-shaded block bordered by brick streets. Across the street, one can imagine stagecoaches parked in front of the Hotel Glen View, built in 1866. One of the main attractions in Mount Carroll, though, is the Raven's Grin Inn, a bizarre playground/spook house located in an old mansion downtown. A series of hidden doorways, secret passageways, and winding hallways takes visitors to scenes and exhibits around the house that offer an equal measure of weird humor and ghoulishness. Heading out of Mount Carroll, you'll encounter rolling hills, patches of farmland, and quiet roads. While following Carroll Creek, look for the occasional rocky outcroppings on the walls above the creek.

Scenic Bluff Road curves south along the dividing line between the bluffs on the left and the flat former river bottom to the right. On one side, the landscape is heavily wooded and seems to rise straight up. The other side is covered with cropland—flat as a tortilla—continuing west for a couple of miles to the edge of the Mississippi. Along this road, you'll a pass a large quarry swarming with cliff swallows and pigeons.

On the way to the tiny town of Thomson, visitors learn that this village holds the distinction of being the Melon Capital of the World. Along with melons, Thomson is known for having a new, unopened prison. On Riverview Road, you can't miss the huge Thomson Correctional Center, one of Illinois' newest maximum-security prisons. State budget woes have kept this 1,600-cell prison mostly unoccupied several years after its construction. In early 2010 a plan was underway to move terrorism suspects from Guantanamo Bay, Cuba, to this prison

At nearly the half-century mark, Riverview Road bends to the right and the Mississippi River comes into view. Waterbirds flock to the river's accompanying wetlands, which are part of a huge complex managed by the U.S. Fish and Wildlife Service. Herons, egrets, pelicans, and various ducks may be visible from a wetlands viewing area located across the road from the Fish and Wildlife Service's Ingersoll Wetlands Learning Center.

After a short (and busy) stretch on SR 84, you'll enjoy a much quieter 3-mile ride into Savanna along the paved Great River Trail. Right away the trail passes the Spring Lake Unit of the Upper Mississippi River National Wildlife and Fish Refuge. If you want to see more of the river, this is the place. From here, you can walk (or ride a mountain or hybrid bike) on about 10 miles of rough gravel trails following levees out into the river.

The Great River Trail weaves between wetland and wooded areas and, just before reaching Savanna, crosses an impressive 1,100-foot-long pedestrian bridge arching over wetlands and railroad tracks. Coming off the bridge, keep straight ahead until you reach Marquette Park, a small riverside park beside the Savanna-Sabula Bridge. On the way out of Savanna, be prepared for a short but brutal climb: The road up this impossibly steep bluff curves back and forth menacingly. Returning to the Scenic Ridge Route, it's a short ride to the trail that brings you back to the Lookout Point parking area.

Miles and Directions

0.0 From the Lookout Point parking area, start riding toward the main park road.

0.2 Upon hitting the main park road, continue ahead on the narrow park service road that is marked authorized vehicles only. The park prohibits cars on this half-mile-long gravel road but allows bicycles and pedestrians.

0.9 Turn left on Scenic Ridge Route.

5.9 Scenic Ridge Route turns into South Derinda Road.

8.4 Turn right on CR 10.

8.7 Turn right on Massbach Road.

12.0 Stay right on Massbach Road as it turns into Breuning Road.

12.3 The road name changes from Breuning Road to Elizabeth Route (some road signs refer to this as Elizabeth Road).

13.2 Stay right as Elizabeth Route turns into Zion Road.

13.8 Turn left on Elizabeth Route.

20.7 Turn right on SR 78.

22.6 Turn right on Market Street.

22.8 Turn left on Mill Street.

23.2 Turn right on Scenic Palisades Road. Near Carroll Creek, you'll encounter brief stretches of dirt road.

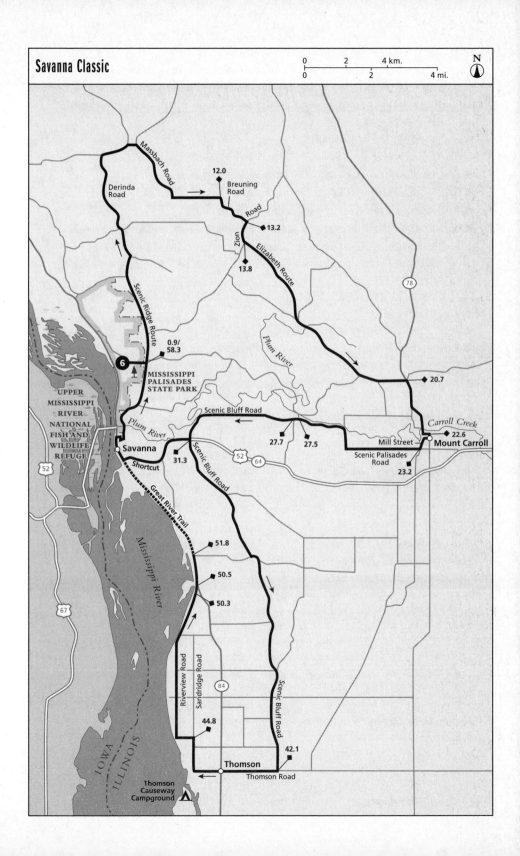

Savanna Classic

0   2   4 km.

0   2   4 mi.

N

Massbach Road

12.0

Breuning Road

Derinda Road

13.2

Zion Road

13.8

Elizabeth Route

78

Scenic Ridge Route

Plum River

0.9/58.3

6

MISSISSIPPI PALISADES STATE PARK

20.7

UPPER MISSISSIPPI RIVER NATIONAL FISH AND WILDLIFE REFUGE

Plum River

Scenic Bluff Road

Carroll Creek

27.7   27.5

Mill Street

22.6

Mount Carroll

52

Savanna

31.3

Scenic Bluff Road

52

64

Scenic Palisades Road

23.2

Shortcut

Great River Trail

51.8

50.5

50.3

Mississippi River

67

Riverview Road

Sandridge Road

84

Scenic Bluff Road

44.8

42.1

IOWA

ILLINOIS

Thomson

Thomson Causeway Campground

Thomson Road

27.5 Scenic Palisades Road turns into Scenic Bluff Road.

27.7 Just after crossing Carroll Creek, take the right fork at this unmarked junction.

31.3 A mile or so south of SR 64, keep a close eye on street signs as Scenic Bluff Road takes a couple of sharp turns. **Option:** Trim the route by 21.5 miles by turning right on SR 64, which can be busy at times. Pick up the route again at mile 55.6.

42.1 Turn right on Thomson Road.

43.8 After crossing SR 84, Thomson Road becomes Main Street.

44.8 After Main Street curves right, it becomes Sandridge Road.

45.5 Turn left on Sandpatch Road.

46.0 Sandpatch Road curves right and becomes Riverview Road.

50.5 Turn left on SR 84. Use caution and stay to the right: This is the busiest road of the ride.

51.8 After the airport, watch for the spot where the train tracks cross SR 84. On the left side of the road after the train tracks, look for the yellow posts that mark the entrance to the paved Great River Trail.

52.7 Arrive at the Spring Lake Unit of the Upper Mississippi River National Wildlife and Fish Refuge.

55.5 Turn right on Division Street.

55.6 Turn left on SR 84.

55.8 Turn right on Clay Street/Scenic Ridge Route. Get ready for a short but intense climb.

58.7 Turn left on the park service road (it's at parking area 6 and appears opposite Messmer Road).

59.5 Arrive back at the Lookout Point parking area.

Local Information

Blackhawk Waterways Convention and Visitors Bureau: 201 North Franklin Ave., Polo; (800) 678-2108 or (815) 946-2108; www .bwcvb.com.

Local Events/Attractions

Ingersoll Wetlands Learning Center: Operated by the U.S. Fish and Wildlife Service, Savanna District; visitor information and bookstore; 7071 Riverview Rd., Thomson; (815) 273-2732.

Raven's Grin Inn: Located just off Main Street in Mount Carroll, this historic house has been transformed into a sometimes spooky, often strange, funhouse; 411 North Carroll St., Mount Carroll; (815) 244-4746; www.hauntedravens grin.com.

Thomson Depot Museum: Limited hours of operation; 907 Main St., Thomson; (815) 259-2361.

Restaurants

Aunt Mannies Kitchen: Basic diner fare; breakfast and lunch only; homemade desserts; 417 Main St., Savanna; (815) 238-8123.

Accommodations

Mississippi Palisades State Park: 240 campsites, camp store, great hiking trails; 16327 A, SR 84, Savanna; (815) 273-2731; http://dnr .state.il.us/lands/landmgt/parks/r1/palisade .htm.

Super 8: Indoor pool; 101 Valley View Dr., Savanna; (815) 273-2288; www.the.super8 .com/savanna11339.

Thomson Causeway Recreation Area: Beautiful camping spot on the Mississippi River; mostly caters to RVs; Lewis Ave. and Main St., Thomson; (815) 259-2352.

Bike Shops

Arnold's Bike and Embroidery: Great selection for a small-town bike shop; provides rentals; get your bike shorts embroidered while you're there; 319 Main St., Thomson; (815) 259-8289.

Restrooms

Start/finish: The Lookout Point parking area has restrooms.

Mile 22.6: The gas station in Mount Carroll has restrooms and water.

Mile 43.8: The gas station in Thomson has restrooms and water.

Mile 50.3: Water and restrooms are available at the Ingersoll Wetlands Learning Center.

Mile 52.7: The Spring Lake Unit of the Upper Mississippi River National Wildlife and Fish Refuge has a portable toilet.

Mile 55.5: Marquette Park in Savanna has restrooms.

Maps

USGS: Savanna quad, Blackhawk quad, Pleasant Valley quad, Mount Carroll quad, Wacker quad, Thomson quad.

DeLorme: Illinois Atlas & Gazetteer: Pages 15, 16, and 24.

Chicagoland

L ike so much of Illinois, the landscape in the Chicago region is the legacy of the glaciers that covered the area. These glaciers created the local rivers— the Fox, the Des Plaines, the DuPage, the Kankakee, and the Illinois—and they steamrolled much of the region, making it as flat as the surface of Lake Michigan. While the surface is mostly level, topographical exceptions abound. Rides in this section focus on some areas with hilly woodland, such as the Woodstock Ramble near the Wisconsin border, the North Shore Cruise with its many ravines, and the Barrington Cruise featuring oak-covered hills. A couple of the rides—the Chicago Lakefront and Boulevard Ramble and the North Shore Cruise—take you along the Chicago area's star attraction, Lake Michigan.

Chicago, they say, is a city of neighborhoods. Several rides in this section offer opportunities to tour attention-grabbing urban neighborhoods, such as Beverly, Pilsen, Pullman, Hyde Park, and a host of areas on the north side of the city. By adding bike lanes, bike racks, and plenty of street signs directed at cyclists, Chicago, in recent years, has developed a reputation as a great place for cycling. The suburbs, unfortunately, have been slow to follow suit. Some have done much to enhance their cycling infrastructure, but others have done little.

While routes throughout this book typically follow quieter roads, this is not always possible in the city. Particularly during high traffic times, there is often no escaping thick traffic, sometimes backed up for blocks. The good news is traffic tends to travel slowly in the Chicago area and the drivers are accustomed to cyclists and behave accordingly.

If city riding is what you would like to get away from, consider the tours of nearby suburbs, such as Oak Park, Riverside, and Mount Greenwood. For those who want to get farther away from the city, the Woodstock Ramble, the Cedar Lake Cruise, and the I&M Canal Challenge take you beyond the outer edges of the metropolitan area to places where quiet country roads unfold for many miles.

7 Barrington Cruise

Given the bustle of the surrounding suburban landscape, the rural character of this ride seems unlikely. As you encounter the oak-covered hills, sprawling marshlands, and farms mixed in with a scattering of often-palatial houses, you'll find yourself congratulating the local residents who fought to preserve the area's rural charm.

Start: Lions Park, located on the shore of the Fox River in Fox River Grove.
Length: 28.9 miles.
Terrain: You'll encounter woodland, prairie, wetlands, and hills—some are steep, but none are very large.

Traffic and hazards: The two short stretches on Lake-Cook Road tend to be busy. Approach these sections of roadway with care.

Getting there: *Automobile:* Take I-90 northwest of Chicago to Barrington Road and head north. In Barrington, turn left on Northwest Highway (US 14). Turn left on Algonquin Road and then turn right on River Road. Park in Lions Park at the end of the road. *Public transportation:* The ride starts a half mile from the Fox River Grove Metra station on the Union Pacific District Northwest Metra Line. From the Metra station, take Lincoln Avenue left (southwest). Turn right on Beachway Drive, left on Millard Avenue, and right on River Road. Start from Lions Park on the right. Coordinates for starting point: 16T 398604E 4672193N

The Ride

When Chicago businessmen and their families began coming to Barrington after World War I, they were attracted to the rural setting and saw the potential to create a genteel atmosphere in the Chicago suburbs. They transformed old farms into estates and established numerous horse farms and riding facilities. Many houses were built to mimic English countryside manors or, in some bizarre cases, fortified castles from medieval England. Reinforcing this carefully cultivated air of English gentry, the area is sometimes referred to as "the Barringtons" because five local communities have "Barrington" in their names.

The first part of the ride takes you over the wooded bluffs that rise along the Fox River. Hills that line the opposite shore of the Fox occasionally peek through the trees while you're passing over the high point of the bluff. Descending to the river's edge, you'll follow a wavy ribbon of asphalt that parallels the 150-yard-wide waterway. River homes with big porches and inviting yards line the sides of the river.

Leaving the river behind, you'll make a short but steep climb back up the bluff. Spring Creek Road takes you through a landscape of cropland, wooded spots, various types of farms, and a small cemetery dating from 1842.

Lake-Cook Road marks the beginning of Spring Creek Valley Forest Preserve—4,000 acres of densely tangled woodland, tranquil prairie, and reedy marshes

Barrington's farmland is mostly gone, but some barns remain.

active with birds. Signs along the road indicate efforts to rid the area of invasive plants and restore the native landscape. Interrupting the savannas and wetlands are oak- and hickory-laden hills—some of which may prompt you to drop into the granny gear while climbing. Mixed in with the woods and open space are horse farms, scattered houses, and the occasional lavish estate.

Before turning on Otis Road, a vast marshland with acres of cattails and open water is cradled by the landscape on the left. More wetlands and a sprinkling of little lakes accompany the route into the village of Barrington.

Given the tony atmosphere of Barrington, one wouldn't guess it was the location of the final shootout between the FBI and the notorious gangster "Baby Face" Nelson. During the 1934 shootout, two FBI agents were killed; Nelson died a short time later from seventeen bullet wounds.

Soon after Barrington, the route cuts through the links at the Barrington Country Club and then passes the Grigsby Prairie, a swath of grassland managed by local citizens. Near the end of the ride, along the rolling wooded hills of Plum Tree Road, you'll pass an enormous mansion-castle (you may expect to see archers standing guard on its turrets). Returning to Lions Park, take some time to relax on the shore of the Fox River before heading home.

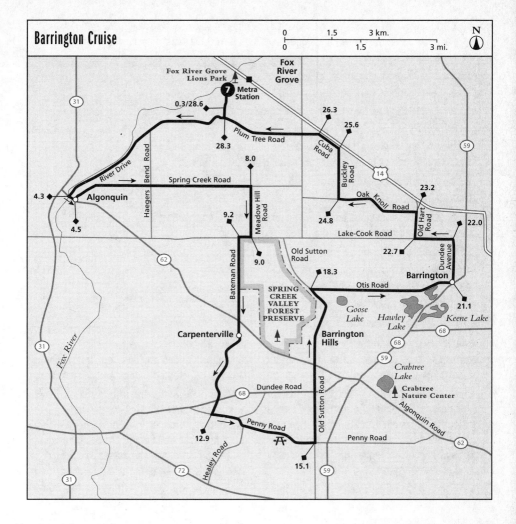

Barrington Cruise

Miles and Directions

0.0 From Lions Park, head south (away from the Fox River) on River Road.

0.3 Turn right on Algonquin Road, then follow it left through a sharp turn. Stay right on Algonquin Road at the junction with Old Hunt Road and Plum Tree Road. At Haegers Bend Road, Algonquin Road becomes River Road.

4.3 Turn left on SR 62/Algonquin Road. This road is typically very busy; use care riding along this stretch or consider walking your bike on the sidewalk for this 2-block stretch.

4.5 Turn left on Highland Avenue, which soon turns into Spring Creek Road.

8.0 Turn right on Meadow Hill Road (watch closely for a somewhat hidden street sign).

9.0 Turn right on Lake-Cook Road (stay close to the shoulder on this busy road).

9.2 Turn left on Bateman Road.

12.9 Turn left on Penny Road. Bear right at the slightly confusing intersection of Penny Road and Healy Road. The Penny Road Pond picnic area is the only forest preserve picnic area you'll encounter.

15.1 Turn left on Old Sutton Road.

18.3 Turn right on Otis Road.

21.1 Turn left on Dundee Avenue (access downtown Barrington by turning right on Station Avenue).

22.0 Turn left on Lake-Cook Road.

22.7 Turn right on Old Hart Road (the next street after Hart Road).

23.2 Turn left on Oak Knoll Road.

24.8 Turn right on Buckley Road.

25.6 Where Buckley Road ends, turn left on Cuba Road (no street sign). On Cuba Road immediately turn right on West Cuba Road (no street sign).

26.3 Bear left on Plum Tree Road.

28.3 Turn right on Algonquin Road.

28.6 Turn left on River Road.

28.9 Return to Lions Park.

Local Information

Barrington Area Chamber of Commerce: 325 North Hough St., Barrington; (847) 381-2525; www.barringtonchamber.com.

Chicagoland Regional Tourism Development Office: 2301 South Lake Shore Dr., Chicago; (312) 795-1700; www.chicagolandtravel.com.

McHenry County Convention and Visitors Bureau: 5435 Bull Valley Rd., Suite 324-B, McHenry; (815) 363-6177; www.visitmchenry county.com.

Local Events/Attractions

Crabtree Nature Center: Features some of the best hiking trails in the area; 3 Stover Rd. (enter on Palatine Rd., between Barrington Rd. and Algonquin Rd.), Barrington; (847) 381-6592.

Goebbert's Pumpkin and Farm Market: Large market with a cafe; 40 West Higgins Rd., South Barrington; (847) 428-6727; www.pumpkin farms.com/SBarrington.html.

Lake County Discovery Museum: Impressive local museum contains largest postcard collection in the world; 27277 Forest Preserve Dr., Wauconda; (847) 968-3400; www.lcfpd.org/discovery_museum.

Restaurants

Barrington Chocolate and Ice Cream Shop: Also sells homemade fudge and pie; close to the route; 140 South Cook St., Barrington; (847) 381-9973; www.barringtonchocolate.com.

Egg Harbor Cafe: Local chain serves up breakfast and lunch; 210 South Cook St., Barrington; (847) 304-4033; www.eggharborcafe.com.

Millrose Brewing Co.: Steak, seafood, and sandwiches; 45 South Barrington Rd., South Barrington; (847) 382-7673; www.millrose restaurant.com.

Port Edward Restaurant: Seafood and steak; dining areas overlook the Fox River; 20 West Algonquin Rd., Algonquin; (847) 658-5441; www.portedward.com.

Accommodations

Days Inn Barrington: 405 West Northwest Hwy., Barrington; (847) 381-2640.

Victorian Rose Garden Bed and Breakfast: 314 Washington St., Algonquin; (847) 854-9667; www.sleepandeat.com.

Bike Shops

Prairie Trail Bike Shop: Located on the Prairie Trail; 315 Railroad St., Algonquin; (847) 658-1154.

Village CycleSport: 203 West Northwest Hwy., Barrington; (847) 382-9200; http://village cyclesport.com.

Restrooms

Start/finish: Portable toilets in Lions Park.

Mile 5.4: Presidential Park has restrooms and water.

Mile 14.4: Penny Road Pond picnic area has a portable toilet.

Mile 22.0: The Starbucks in Barrington has restrooms.

Maps

USGS: Barrington quad, Crystal Lake quad, Streamwood quad.

DeLorme: Illinois Atlas & Gazetteer: Page 20.

8 Beverly-Oak Lawn Ramble

This ride opens with a short stint on a heavily wooded section of the Major Taylor Trail, one of the newest trails in Chicago. The route in Beverly takes you by a collection of historic mansions, including one that was modeled after an Irish castle. From Beverly, you'll head west through the quiet streets of Mount Greenwood and pass some of the local cemeteries for which the area is known. After tours of the suburban towns of Oak Lawn and Evergreen Park, you'll return to Beverly to gawk at more of the sprawling mansions.

Start: Dan Ryan Woods Forest Preserve, parking lots 15 and 16, near the intersection of Western Avenue and 83rd Street.

Length: 17.9 miles.

Terrain: Flat urban residential neighborhoods, with occasional small hills in the Beverly area.

Traffic and hazards: Most of these streets are quiet; a few short sections of the route follow busier roads.

Getting there: *Automobile:* Take I-94 south from downtown Chicago. Exit at 79th Street and head west to Damen Avenue. Turn left on Damen Avenue, then turn right on 83rd Street. Park in the Dan Ryan Woods Forest Preserve's parking lots 15 and 16, located on the right. *Public transportation:* Take the Rock Island Metra Line to the 91st Street station in Beverly. The Major Taylor Trail runs along the east side of the railroad tracks. Coordinates for starting point: 16T 443571E 4621316N

The Ride

Known for its historic homes, quiet streets, and racially integrated population, Beverly is one of the most likeable neighborhoods in Chicago. The large lawns, rolling topography, and close-knit community atmosphere give the area an unusual appeal. Along Longwood Drive you'll encounter a progression of mansions built in various styles, many with wooded surroundings and landscaped yards and gardens.

Before arriving in Beverly, though, you'll follow the first leg of the Major Taylor Trail as it gradually curves along an old railroad embankment on the eastern edge of the Dan Ryan Woods Forest Preserve. Dense stands of trees rise high above the trail and lean overhead, creating a tunnel of branches and shrubs. When the trail leaves the 20-foot-high embankment and returns to street level, the forest preserve continues to sprawl on the right, occasionally dotted with wetlands and marsh grasses.

On Longwood Drive in Beverly, take note of the small ridge that runs parallel to the street on the right. This several-mile-long glacially deposited moraine is called Blue Island. Some 14,000 years ago, at the tail end of the last ice age, this ridge was actually an island when Lake Michigan's water level stood 60 feet higher and the shoreline meandered farther inland.

The hilly topography provides a pleasing environment for the well-kept historic mansions along Longwood Drive. The first block heading south takes you past a couple of houses built in the Prairie style, one of which was designed by Frank Lloyd Wright (9914 South Longwood Drive). At 10200 South Longwood Drive sits a mansion built in 1890 in the Colonial Revival style by Horace E. Horton, founder of the Chicago Bridge and Iron Co. Probably the best-known community landmark, the Castle, at 103rd Street and Longwood Drive, is a replica of an Irish castle built in 1886 by real estate developer Robert C. Givins. As the story goes, Givins built the limestone castle in an effort to woo a bride from Ireland. Owned by the Beverly Unitarian Church since 1942, the structure has an assortment of ghost stories attached to it.

In the neighborhood of Mount Greenwood, you'll pass a couple of large cemeteries. The Mount Greenwood Cemetery at 111th Street and California Avenue happens to be where Major Taylor is buried. Major Taylor, whose name was given to the trail you encountered earlier, was an African-American track cyclist who dominated the sport at the turn of the century—at a time when it was the most popular spectator sport in the country—winning world championships in 1899, 1900, and 1901. Mount Greenwood has long been a popular spot for the dead: The community is sometimes called Seven Holy Tombs in honor of seven large cemeteries in the area. Local historians say that some commercial areas in Mount Greenwood developed because funeral-goers needed nearby places to eat and drink after burials.

Crossing the Chicago city limits takes you into Oak Lawn, one of the largest suburbs in Cook County. The town was fairly small until about 1960, when it started to swell with whites fleeing Chicago during the era of white flight. In recent years, the complexion of the town has become more varied. The route passes a few of Oak Lawn's many commercial areas, as well as its huge hospital complex, which employs some 3,500 people.

At 107th Street and Laramie Avenue, you can cross a pedestrian bridge to Wolfe Wildlife Refuge and then follow a half-mile-long bike path through 45 acres of wetlands surrounding Stony Creek.

As you return eastward, the route zigzags through Evergreen Park, known as the "Village of Churches" on account of the thirteen established congregations serving a community 4 square miles in size. Another detail to know about Evergreen Park is

Beverly-Oak Lawn Ramble

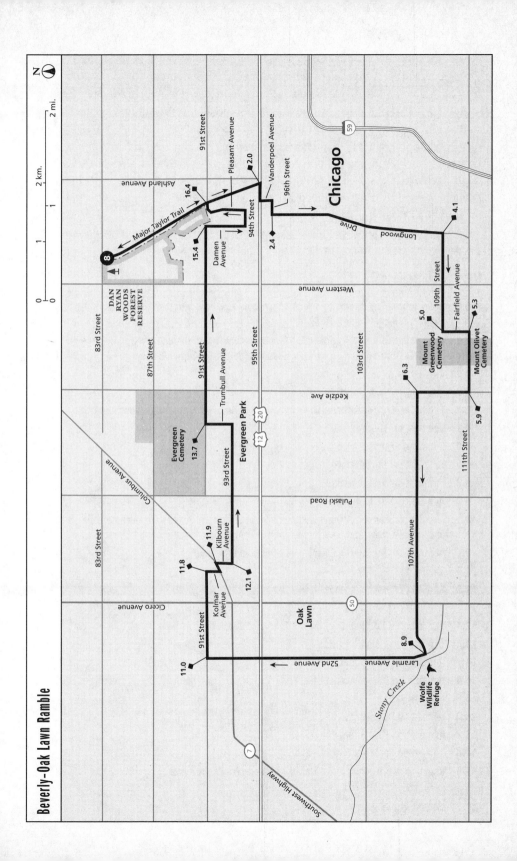

that it's the hometown of the Unabomber. Up until he left for Harvard University at age sixteen, Ted Kaczynski spent most of his youth in Evergreen Park.

The last leg of the ride takes you again to the tree-laden streets and stately homes of Beverly. A string of impressive mansions pop up along Pleasant Avenue, including another designed by Frank Lloyd Wright (9326 South Pleasant Avenue). The Queen Anne–style house at 9319 South Pleasant Avenue was the residence of Impressionist artist John H. Vanderpoel. (His works can be seen in the Vanderpoel Gallery at the Beverly Art Center.) The Colonial Revival–style house at 9203 South Pleasant Avenue was built by the first director of the Art Institute of Chicago and designed by the museum's lecturer in architecture.

A short trip through the forest preserve brings you back to the starting point at the north end of the Major Taylor Trail.

Miles and Directions

0.0 Head north on the Major Taylor Trail from the parking area and then follow it as it takes a sharp turn right, heading south.

2.0 Where the trail abruptly ends at the fence, continue south through the grocery store parking lot. At 95th Street, turn right. Proceed with care: 95th Street is busy.

2.2 Turn left on Vanderpoel Avenue.

2.3 Turn right on 96th Street.

2.4 Turn left on Longwood Drive, lined with many of Beverly's famous mansions.

4.1 Turn right on 109th Street.

5.0 Turn left on Fairfield Avenue.

5.3 Turn right on 111th Street.

5.9 Turn right on Kedzie Avenue.

6.3 Turn left on 107th Street.

8.9 Turn right on Laramie Avenue. Take the bike path over the bridge to follow a half mile or so of bike trails that run through Wolfe Wildlife Refuge.

9.4 At 103rd Street, Laramie Avenue becomes 52nd Avenue.

11.0 Turn right on 91st Street.

11.8 Turn right on Kolmar Avenue.

11.9 Turn left on Columbus Avenue and then immediately turn right on Kilbourn Avenue.

12.1 Turn left on 93rd Street.

13.4 Turn left on Turnbull Avenue.

13.7 Turn right on 91st Street.

15.4 Turn right on Damen Avenue.

15.8 Turn left on 94th Street.

16.0 Turn left on Pleasant Avenue.

16.3 Turn right on 91st Street.

16.4 Turn left on the Major Taylor Trail.

17.9 Return to the parking area at Dan Ryan Woods Forest Preserve.

Local Information

Chicago Convention and Tourism Bureau: 2301 South Lake Shore Dr., Chicago; (312) 567-8500; www.choosechicago.com.

Chicago Department of Transportation: 30 North LaSalle St., Suite 1100, Chicago; (312) 744-3600; www.cityofchicago.org/Transportation.

Chicago Southland Convention and Visitors Bureau: 2304 173rd St., Lansing; (708) 895-8200 or (888) 895-8233; www.visitchicago southland.com.

Local Events/Attractions

Beverly Arts Center: Features gallery exhibitions and a gift shop; hosts films and live music; 2407 West 111th St., Chicago; (773) 445-3838; www.beverlyartcenter.org.

Beverly Hills Cycling Classic: Held in July, this annual 100K criterium bike race through Beverly is paired with the annual Tour de Beverly Family Ride; organized by the Beverly Area Planning Association; (773) 233-3100; www.bapa.org.

Restaurants

Franconello's: Italian cuisine; located in an old storefront at 10222 South Western Ave., Chicago; (773) 881-4100.

Koda Bistro and Wine Bar: Well-regarded upscale eatery; 10352 South Western Ave., Chicago; (773) 445-5632; http://kodabistro.com.

Millie's Ice Cream Shoppe and Deli: Old-style place with a soda fountain; located right on the route; 5172 West 95th St., Oak Lawn; (708) 423-9293.

Southtown Health Foods: Offers groceries and a smoothie bar; 2100 West 95th St., Chicago; (773) 233-1856; www.southtownhealthfoods.com.

Accommodations

Benedictine Bed and Breakfast: Run by a Catholic monastery in the Bridgeport neighborhood on Chicago's south side; 3111 South Aberdeen St., Chicago; (773) 927-7424; www.chicagomonk.org.

J. Ira and Nicki Harris Family Hostel: Huge, clean, affordable hostel located downtown; dorm-style rooms and a limited number of private rooms; 24 East Congress Pkwy., Chicago; (312) 360-0300; www.hichicago.org.

Bike Shops

Beverly Bike and Ski: One of the few bike shops on the far south side; 9121 South Western Ave., Chicago; (773) 238-5704; www.beverly allseasons.com.

Restrooms

Start/finish: Dan Ryan Woods has restrooms and water.

Mile 8.9: A portable toilet is located at the Wolfe Wildlife Refuge (turn left on Laramie Avenue from 107th Street.)

Mile 10.5: The intersection of 52nd Street and 95th Street has a selection of chain restaurants.

Maps

USGS: Blue Island quad.

DeLorme: Illinois Atlas & Gazetteer: Page 29.

9 Cedar Lake Cruise

This ride takes you through a scenic setting that straddles the Illinois-Indiana state line just 40 miles south of downtown Chicago. The landscape features gently undulating farmland broken up regularly by swaths of woodland, occasional small hills and ravines, and streams that braid the landscape. At the ride's halfway point, you'll explore the Indiana community of Cedar Lake, a former resort town on the shore of a gleaming natural lake.

Start: Goodenow Grove Forest Preserve in eastern Will County south of Crete.
Length: 44.7 miles.
Terrain: Gently rolling farmland, wooded areas, and a small town on a lake.

Traffic and hazards: For riders sporting spaghetti-thin tires, approach with caution the occasional sections of pavement with potholes and patches of loose gravel.

Getting there: From Chicago, take I-94 south to I-80. At this junction, continue straight ahead on SR 394. Turn left on Goodenow Road and then left again on Dutton Road. Park at the Plum Creek Nature Center. Coordinates for starting point: 16T 449333E 4583282N

The Ride

It's easy to see why people once flocked to Cedar Lake for their vacations: Bluffs decorate the northern shore of the lake and sprawling wetlands—said to be among the largest in Indiana—border the south shore. The lake is large enough to instill a feeling of grandeur, but small enough to lend it intimacy. Known for its wooded shoreline, the 787-acre lake was originally named Lake of the Red Cedars.

Around the turn of the century, Cedar Lake claimed dozens of hotels, several steamboat tour lines, and numerous upscale lakeside cottages. Trains brought visitors in from Chicago and other population centers. Luminaries such as the retailer John G. Shedd (benefactor of the Shedd Aquarium), the Armour brothers (of meatpacking fame), and the famous foot doctor William Scholl owned vacation property on Cedar Lake, while nationally known bands played in ballrooms and pavilions on the lakefront. As automobiles allowed people to vacation in more out-of-the way destinations, Cedar Lake's status as a resort community dissolved. Except for some newer developments, the homes now tend to be modest, and there is little to indicate the community's former life as a popular vacation spot.

Before getting to Cedar Lake, you'll spend the first 10 miles of this ride exploring vast expanses of farmland, occasionally sprinkled with farmhouses and barns set back from the road. Watch the roadside for small streams twisting through the cornfields and under the road; look overhead for red-tailed hawks and American kestrels perched on the power lines and poles waiting for a rodent snack.

The scenic roads on the Cedar Lake Cruise host a few gradual downhills.

On State Line Road, cropland gives way to a series of small wooded ravines; little streams multiply, and wetlands flood the low spots. The approach to Cedar Lake reveals a landscape where the new world meets the old: New housing developments are surrounded by farmland, and the curving streets of subdivisions meet up with the straight old farm roads.

Along the shore of Cedar Lake, Lauerman Street squeezes between a marina on the left and the vast wetland on the right. This outsize marshland was part of the lake at one time, before its southern shore was drained and built up. After taking in the full lake views at the boat launch on Lake Shore Drive, the road follows a thin strip of land between the 60-foot-high bluff and the modest lake houses. When the road mounts the bluff on the lake's northern tip, whip out your camera for shots of the water from the roadside viewing platform.

After contending with the hustle-bustle along 133rd Avenue and crossing US 41, you'll return to farmland and encounter several scenic pieces of roadway. White Oak Road is particularly pleasing for its accompanying wooded ridge on the right. The gently rolling topography of Bemes Road is interrupted by an enormous horse care and training facility. Stony Island Avenue takes you through woodland that gradually slopes down before cutting left and dipping down to cross the sublime Plum Creek.

Many creeks on the route have been straightened to prevent flooding, but the wriggling form of Plum Creek certainly has not. The 41st mile of the ride introduces you to the dense, tangled bottomland woods that occupy the northern section of Goodenow Grove Forest Preserve. As you climb out the ravine created by Plum Creek, a wooded slope drops down steeply on the left.

Wrapping up the ride at Goodenow Grove Forest Preserve, you might consider exploring the park's hills, grasslands, ravines, and more of Plum Creek along several miles of trails. At the very least, take a walk up the sledding hill for a view of the surrounding area and then stroll the quarter-mile-long Trail of Thoughts, which starts adjacent to the nature center in the Nodding Oaks picnic area.

Miles and Directions

0.0 Leave Goodenow Grove Forest Preserve via Dutton Road, the same way you entered. At Goodenow Road, jog to the left and continue heading south on Park Avenue.

2.4 Turn left on Eagle Lake Road.

3.9 Turn right on Stony Island Avenue.

8.9 Turn left on CR 1200 North. No street sign is posted, but it is easy enough to navigate because it's where Stony Island Avenue ends.

11.2 Turn right on State Line Road/CR 1800 North.

12.3 Turn left on 185th Avenue.

13.6 Turn left on Hadders Road.

14.1 Turn right on 181st Avenue.

14.6 Turn left on White Oak Avenue.

17.6 Turn right on 157th Avenue. Be careful while crossing US 41.

19.6 Turn left on Parrish Avenue.

21.4 Turn right on 142nd Place.

21.9 Turn right on Lauerman Street, which turns into 147th Avenue as it curves.

22.8 Turn left on Cline Avenue, which becomes Lake Shore Drive.

23.0 Turn right on 145th Avenue.

23.4 Turn left on Morse Street.

25.9 Turn left on Lake Shore Drive. On the west side of Cedar Lake, Lake Shore Drive turns into 133rd Avenue and then farther out it becomes 135th Avenue. Use care on 133rd Avenue: Traffic can be busy, and there are many commercial driveways along the way.

28.9 Turn right on White Oak Avenue, which becomes 125th Court as the road turns left.

30.9 Turn right on Calumet Avenue.

31.4 Turn left on 121st Avenue.

32.3 Turn right on State Line Road.

32.9 Turn left on Bemes Road.

35.2 Turn right on Stony Island Avenue.

37.3 Stony Island Avenue becomes Burville Road as it curves left.

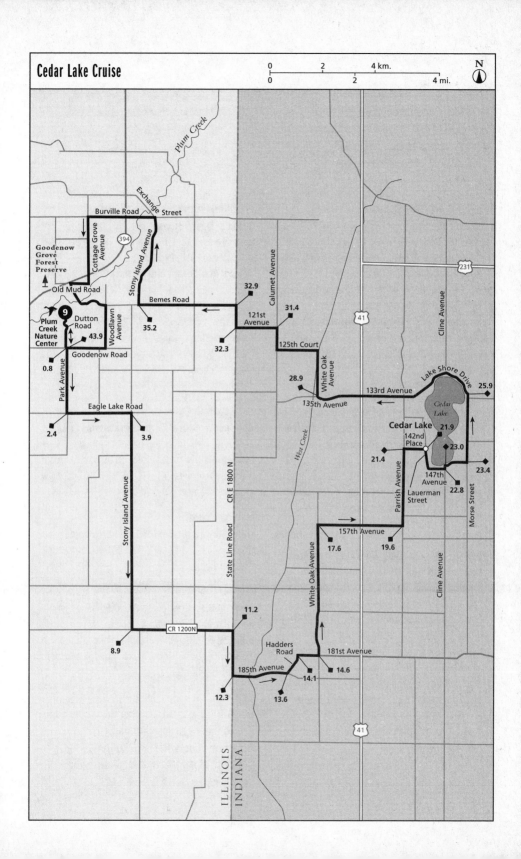

Cedar Lake Cruise

0   2   4 km.
0   2   4 mi.

N

Plum Creek

Exchange Street

Burville Road

Goodenow Grove Forest Preserve

Cottage Grove Avenue

394

Old Mud Road

Stony Island Avenue

Bemes Road

9

Plum Creek Nature Center

Dutton Road

43.9

Woodlawn Avenue

Goodenow Road

0.8

Park Avenue

35.2

32.9

32.3

121st Avenue

Calumet Avenue

31.4

125th Court

White Oak Avenue

28.9

135th Avenue

133rd Avenue

41

231

Cline Avenue

Lake Shore Drive

25.9

Cedar Lake

Cedar Lake

142nd Place

21.9

23.0

23.4

21.4

Parrish Avenue

147th Avenue

Lauerman Street

22.8

Morse Street

Cline Avenue

2.4

Eagle Lake Road

3.9

Stony Island Avenue

CR E 1800 N

State Line Road

West Creek

157th Avenue

17.6

19.6

White Oak Avenue

8.9

CR 1200N

11.2

12.3

185th Avenue

Hadders Road

13.6

14.1

181st Avenue

14.6

41

ILLINOIS
INDIANA

38.9 Turn left on Cottage Grove Avenue. As Cottage Grove Avenue curves right it becomes Old Mud Road.

40.8 Turn left on Bemes Road.

42.0 Turn right on Woodlawn Avenue.

43.0 Turn right on Goodenow Road.

43.9 Turn right on Dutton Road.

44.7 Return to Plum Creek Nature Center at Goodenow Grove Forest Preserve.

Local Information

Cedar Lake Chamber of Commerce: 7927 Lake Shore Dr., Cedar Lake, IN; (219) 374-6157.

Chicago Southland Convention and Visitors Bureau: 2304 173rd St., Lansing; (708) 895-8200 or (888) 895-8233; www.visitchicago southland.com.

Goodenow Grove Forest Preserve: Includes the Plum Creek Nature Center; 27064 South Dutton Rd., Beecher; (708) 946-2216; www.fpdwc .org/goodenow.cfm.

Local Events/Attractions

Barn and Field Flea Market: Antiques and collectibles, right on the route; open weekends; 9600 West 151st St., Cedar Lake, IN; (219) 696-7368.

Cedar Lake Summerfest: Four-day event over July 4 includes activities such as a cardboard boat race, checkers tournament, live music, boat and land parade, and talent show; Morse St. and Constitution Ave., Cedar Lake, IN; (219) 374-4444; www.cedarlakesummerfest.com.

Lake of the Red Cedars Museum: Housed in a former hotel; exhibits focus on the history of Cedar Lake; open early May to Labor Day, limited hours of operation; 7308 West 138th Pl., Cedar Lake, IN; (219) 374-7000.

Lemon Lake County Park: 400-acre park with 5 miles of hiking trails and an impressive 27-hole disc golf course; located less than 1 mile east of Cedar Lake; 6322 West 133rd Ave., Crown Point, IN; (219) 945-0543 or (219) 755-3685; www.lakecountyparks.com/lemonlake.html.

Restaurants

Bolda's Dawg House: Yes, Chicago-style hot dogs are available in Indiana; 9720 West 133rd Ave., Cedar Lake, IN; (219) 374-3466.

Carlo's Restaurant and Pizzeria: 13231 Wicker Ave. (US 41), Cedar Lake, IN; (219) 374-5500.

Cedar Lake Kitchen: Basic diner fare; 9525 West 133rd Ave., Cedar Lake, IN; (219) 374-8888.

Princess Cafe: Upscale dining with a menu focusing on steak and seafood; 502 South Dixie Hwy., Beecher; (708) 946-3141; www.theprincess cafe.com.

Accommodations

Goodenow Grove Forest Preserve: Primitive camping; see contact information above.

Hometown Inn and Suites: 1139 West Lincoln Hwy., Schererville, IN; (219) 322-7000; www .hometowninnschererville.com.

Bike Shops

Trek Bicycle Store: 651 East Lincoln Hwy., Schererville, IN; (219) 322-2453; http://trek bikestore.com.

Restrooms

Start/finish: Goodenow Grove Forest Preserve has restrooms and water.

Mile 27.5: A gas station/convenience store on 133rd Avenue in Cedar Lake offers a restroom and refreshments.

Maps

USGS: Dyer IL quad, Beecher East IL/IN quad, Lowell IN quad, S. John IN quad.

DeLorme: Illinois Atlas & Gazetteer: Page 37.

DeLorme: Indiana Atlas & Gazetteer: Page 18.

10 Chicago Lakefront and Boulevard Ramble

Enjoy a classic Chicago bike ride along the Lakefront Path as it winds past harbors, beaches, the dazzling skyline, and the big blue lake. After passing the museum campus and Soldier Field, you'll leave the well-beaten biking path and head into the vibrant neighborhoods of Pilsen and Little Village and then meet up with the Chicago boulevard system. The boulevards guide you through three large Chicago parks sprinkled with gardens, lagoons, and elegant park buildings. The final section of the route tours several of Chicago's north-side neighborhoods.

Start: Montrose Harbor, located where Montrose Avenue meets Lake Michigan in Chicago.
Length: 29.6 miles.
Terrain: Grassy parks, residential neighborhoods, and occasional light industrial areas. The terrain is flat.
Traffic and hazards: Most streets on this route do not have heavy traffic. During the summer, the north section of the Lakefront Path gets congested. For lighter crowds, go earlier in the day. The route follows a few one-way streets, which need to be avoided if following the route in reverse. You'll encounter speed bumps on a few streets. While riding in any urban area, keep aware of your surroundings.

Getting there: *Automobile:* From downtown Chicago, head north on Lake Shore Drive. Exit at Montrose Avenue and turn right toward the lake. Park in the large lot. Catch the trail as it heads south along Lake Shore Drive. *Public transportation:* To reach the starting point, catch bus 78 heading east from either the Montrose station on the Brown Line "L" Train or the Wilson station on the Red Line. The bus will bring you to the corner of Marine Drive and Montrose Avenue. From this intersection, head under Lake Shore Drive. Coordinates for starting point: 16T 446575E 4645599N

The Ride

It's no mystery why Chicago cyclists love the Lakefront Path: The views of the skyline, the grassy expanses, the boats lined up in the harbors, and the big beguiling lake make for unparalleled riding. While the lakeshore is indeed one of the best places in Chicago for riding, it's certainly not the only good place to ride in the city. This route follows the much-loved trail along the lakefront, but it also leads you to destinations such as the Prairie Avenue Historic District, the Pilsen neighborhood, and the city's boulevard system.

Heading south from Montrose Harbor, the path winds through many acres of grassy parkland scattered with trees. There's also a golf course, an attractive brick clock-tower park building, and dozens of boats moored in Belmont Harbor. The greenway goes on hiatus at the Fullerton Pavilion, a Prairie-style structure built in the early twentieth century as a "fresh air sanitarium" to promote good health among the infirm. (The building is now home to a cafe and a summer theater.)

South of the pavilion, the path squeezes between Lake Shore Drive on the right and North Avenue Beach on the left. At the south end of North Avenue Beach sits a beach house designed to look like an ocean liner that has been parked in the sand. Getting closer to the Loop, the path continues to be wedged—sometimes uncomfortably—between a traffic-choked six-lane thoroughfare and the lake.

In the warmer months, Oak Street Beach has plenty going on, whether it's jugglers, BMX trick riders, or in-line skaters whizzing through a slalom coarse. After passing Navy Pier (the largest tourist trap in the state) and making an awkward crossing of the Chicago River along the lower level of North Lake Shore Drive, you'll roll along acres of boats docked in Chicago Harbor. Across South Lake Shore Drive in Grant Park, you can't miss the 150-foot geyser shooting from Buckingham Fountain.

From the fountain, the route passes along the backside of the John G. Shedd Aquarium. The paneled glass wall facing the path contains the largest indoor saltwater pool in the world, home to a family of beluga whales and a handful of performing dolphins. To the right is the huge marble structure of the Field Museum. The building contains a vast collection of natural science exhibits, as well as the skeleton of the largest and most complete *T. rex* ever found.

South of the Field Museum is Soldier Field—the Chicago Bears' home turf—built in 1922 and the recipient of an unfortunate facelift in 2003 when a glass and steel addition was dropped on the top of the existing neoclassical structure. Soldier Field is where you'll head west away from the lake and over the new pedestrian bridge that crosses the train tracks.

The west end of the bridge drops you off at the Prairie Avenue Historic District, which became the city's most fashionable neighborhood following the Chicago Fire of 1871. Although many of the rambling Victorian mansions were demolished in the mid-twentieth century, the remaining buildings provide a sense of the neighborhood's former character. Two of these sumptuous multilevel brick homes are now museums: the Clarke House and the Glessner House.

Continuing along 18th Street takes you over the South Branch of the Chicago River, under the Dan Ryan Expressway, and into Pilsen. Once home to a large population of Eastern Europeans, many of whom were Czechs, it's now home to the largest concentration of Latinos in Chicago. Visitors will enjoy the lively shopping district along 18th Street, the delicious smells from local restaurants, the many murals, and the attractive nineteenth-century architecture.

In the Little Village neighborhood, you'll connect with Marshall Avenue, which is part of a system of boulevards that were designed to connect Chicago's major parks. Here on Chicago's west side, the boulevards connect three great parks—Douglas, Garfield, and Humboldt—each to be visited on this route. William Le Baron Jenney—a landscape designer, architect, and engineer now considered the father of the skyscraper—originally designed all three parks in the late nineteenth century. The renowned Prairie-style designer Jens Jensen oversaw a second phase of improvements for these parks during the early twentieth century.

The views of the Chicago skyline along the Lakefront Path are outstanding.

Douglas Park has gardens, lagoons, paths, and an eye-catching open-air structure designed by Jensen called the Flower Hall. As you head west from Douglas Park, you'll pass attractive gray stone houses overlooking the leafy boulevard. In Garfield Park you'll find more quiet lagoons with islands, as well as several notable park buildings, including an elegant bandstand and a gold-domed field house with a wildly ornate facade. Garfield Park's most impressive building, though, is its glass and steel conservatory, which houses one of the largest publicly owned botanical gardens in the world. Some 5,000 plant species grow within six enormous glassed-in rooms. Built in 1908, Jensen designed the structure to resemble a giant haystack.

At Division Avenue, in Humboldt Park, sculptures of bison stand inside a formal flower garden on the left side of Sacramento Boulevard. On the right, the graceful arches of the Prairie-style Humboldt Park Boat House create a pleasant spot to look over the lagoon fringed with cattails and walking paths.

At one time, many of the city's boulevards were bordered by stately brick mansions like those along Logan Boulevard. Built by wealthy people attracted to the boulevards' greenways, most of the mansions on the other boulevards fell into disrepair and were demolished to make way for newer homes.

After crossing the Chicago River again, the route cuts through the Julia Lathrop Homes, built in 1938 as the first Chicago housing project designated strictly for

Chicago Lakefront and Boulevard Ramble

0   1   2 km.
0   1   2 mi.

N

Lake Michigan

Peterson Avenue

26.2 Granville Avenue 27.0

Winthrop Avenue

27.6 27.7

Foster Avenue

Lawrence Avenue

Montrose Avenue

Irving Park Road

North

Branch

Ravenswood Avenue

23.0

Addison Street

Montrose Harbor

Wellington Avenue

Wolcott Avenue

22.0

Leavitt Street

Diversey Avenue

Logan Boulevard

21.3

21.2

Kedzie Boulevard

Chicago

Palmer Boulevard

19.1

19.4

Chicago

Lincoln Park Zoo

North Avenue Beach

HUMBOLDT PARK

North Avenue

Western Avenue

Lake Shore Drive

17.8

River

Chicago Lakefront Path

Franklin Boulevard

16.2

16.9

94

90

Navy Pier

GARFIELD PARK

Garfield Park Conservatory

Madison Street

Michigan Avenue

15.2 15.4

Art Institute of Chicago

River

Independence Boulevard

Central Park Avenue

Sacramento Boulevard

290

41

Shedd Aquarium

13.1

Roosevelt Road

Adler Planetarium

14.0

DOUGLAS PARK

Wood Street

10.8

9.5

Field Museum of Natural History

Soldier Field

Douglas Boulevard

18th Street

Chicago

7.7

Marshall Boulevard

21st Street

National Museum of Mexican Art

Northerly Island

Cermak Road

12.5

11.0

8.1

South *Branch*

55

55

elderly residents. The lightly ornamented brick apartment buildings and row houses, the grassy lawns, and the curving riverbank create an atmosphere more pleasant than most city housing projects. Despite pressure from residents and local preservation organizations to save it, a plan is now under way to tear down the Lathrop Homes and redevelop the land.

The route along Ravenswood Avenue takes you between a string of old brick warehouses and a set of train tracks perched on an earthen embankment landscaped with trees, rocks, small gardens, and occasional benches. After reaching the Lakefront Path, you'll pass Foster Avenue Beach and Wilson Skate Park, and then arrive at Montrose Harbor, where the ride started.

Miles and Directions

0.0 Head south on the Lakefront Path as it parallels Lake Shore Drive.

7.7 Turn right on Woldron Drive, which runs along the south end of Soldier Field.

7.9 Bear left on the pathway that goes under Lake Shore Drive. Follow the ramp over the railroad tracks.

8.1 Head west on 18th Street, then take a quick tour of the Prairie Avenue Historic District by going a block south of 18th Street on Prairie and Indiana Avenues.

9.5 Turn right on Halsted Avenue and immediately turn left on 18th Street.

10.8 Turn left on Wood Street.

11.0 Turn right on 21st Street.

12.5 Turn right on Marshall Boulevard.

13.1 Turn left on Douglas Boulevard.

14.0 Turn right on Independence Boulevard.

15.2 Turn right on Music Court Drive.

15.4 At Woodward Drive, bear left toward Central Park Avenue. Head north on the pathway that runs on the left side of Central Park Avenue.

16.2 Turn right on Franklin Boulevard.

16.9 Turn left on Sacramento Boulevard.

17.8 North of Division Avenue, continue north on the path on the right side of Sacramento Boulevard/Humboldt Drive. Use the pathways to explore Humboldt Park's lagoons.

19.1 Turn left on Palmer Boulevard.

19.4 Turn right on Kedzie Boulevard.

19.9 Turn right on Logan Boulevard. Stay on Logan Boulevard as it curves to the left.

21.2 Turn right on Diversey Avenue. Cross the Chicago River.

21.3 Turn left on Leavitt Street.

21.6 Turn right on Wellington Avenue (a one-way street).

22.0 Turn left on Wolcott Avenue.

23.0 Turn right on Grace Street.

23.1 Turn left on Ravenswood Avenue after passing under the train tracks.

25.9 Jog left on Peterson Avenue, then immediately turn right on Ravenswood Avenue.

26.0 Jog right on Ridge Avenue, then immediately turn left on Ravenswood Avenue.

26.2 Turn right on Granville Avenue.

27.0 Turn right on Winthrop Avenue (a one-way street).

27.6 Turn left on Ardmore Avenue.

27.7 Head south on the Lakefront Path.

29.6 Return to Montrose Harbor.

Local Information

Chicago Convention and Tourism Bureau: 2301 South Lake Shore Dr., Chicago; (312) 567-8500; www.choosechicago.com.

Chicago Park District: 541 North Fairbanks, Chicago; (312) 742-PLAY; www.chicagopark district.com.

Local Events/Attractions

The Field Museum: 1400 South Lake Shore Dr., Chicago; (312) 922-9410; www.fieldmuseum .org.

Garfield Park Conservatory: 300 North Central Park Ave., Chicago; (312) 746-5100; www .garfield-conservatory.org.

Glessner House Museum: A stately English Arts and Crafts home that now contains a world-class collection of nineteenth-century decorative arts; 1800 South Prairie Ave., Chicago; (312) 326-1480; www.glessnerhouse.org.

John G. Shedd Aquarium: 1200 South Lake Shore Dr., Chicago; (312) 939-2438; www .sheddaquarium.org.

National Museum of Mexican Art: Perhaps the best small museum in the city; free admission; 1852 West 19th St., Pilsen; (312) 738-1503; www.nationalmuseumofmexicanart.org.

Navy Pier: Contains the Chicago Children's Museum, a 3-D Imax theater, the Chicago Shakespeare Theatre, a concert venue, a museum of stained-glass windows, a monster-size Ferris wheel, and oodles of obnoxious tourist-oriented shops and overpriced mediocre restaurants; 600 East Grand Ave., Chicago; (800) 595-PIER; www.navypier.com.

Restaurants

Joy Yee's: Various types of Asian cuisine; huge menu with pictures; located in Chinatown at 2159 South China Pl., Chicago; (312) 328-0001; www.joyyee.com.

Lula Cafe: One of Chicago's great small neighborhood restaurants; eclectic fare; 2537 North Kedzie Blvd., Chicago; (773) 489-9554; www.lulacafe.com.

Mundial Cocina Mestiza: Latin American cuisine with a Mediterranean influence; 1640 West 18th St., Chicago; (312) 491-9908; www.mun dialcocinamestiza.com.

Oak Street Beachstro: Good selection of sandwiches and salads; seasonally located where Oak Street Beach meets the Lakefront Path; 1001 North Lake Shore Dr., Chicago; (312) 915-4100; www.oakstreetbeachstro.com.

Spacca Napoli Pizzeria: Authentic Neapolitan pizza made in a wood-burning pizza oven; 1769 West Sunnyside Avenue, Chicago; (773) 878-2420; http://spaccanapolipizzeria.com.

Accommodations

Benedictine Bed and Breakfast: Run by a Catholic monastery in the Bridgeport neighborhood on Chicago's south side; 3111 South Aberdeen St., Chicago; (773) 927-7424; www .chicagomonk.org.

J. Ira and Nicki Harris Family Hostel: Huge, clean, affordable hostel located downtown; dorm-style rooms and a limited number of private rooms; 24 East Congress Pkwy., Chicago; (312) 360-0300; www.hichicago.org.

Bike Shops

Boulevard Bikes: Knowledgeable staff and friendly atmosphere; located on the route in

Logan Square; 2535 North Kedzie Blvd., Chicago; (773) 235-9109; www.boulevardbike shop.com.

Irv's Bike Shop: Small neighborhood bike shop; located on the route in Pilsen; 1725 South Racine Ave., Chicago; (312) 226-6330; www .irvsbikeshop.com.

Restrooms
Start/finish: Montrose Beach House has restrooms and water.

Mile 6.2: Restrooms at the north end of Chicago Harbor (just south of the Chicago Yacht Club).

Mile 10.9: Harrison Park Fieldhouse has restrooms.

Mile 13.1: Restrooms are available in the Douglas Park Fieldhouse.

Mile 15.9: Garfield Park Conservatory has restrooms.

Mile 18.1: Humboldt Park Fieldhouse has restrooms.

Maps
USGS: Chicago Loop quad, Jackson Park quad, Englewood quad.

DeLorme: Illinois Atlas & Gazetteer: Page 29.

11 Chicago South Side Ramble

This ride reveals a south side of Chicago that is vast and persistently interesting. Visit four great Chicago south-side parks, follow the Lake Michigan coastline, and explore Pullman, a nineteenth-century planned neighborhood of Victorian row houses. The route also takes you through areas of heavy industry for which the south side is known. While exploring the wetlands of the Lake Calumet area, it's hard to believe that you're still in the city of Chicago.

Start: Jackson Park parking area behind the Museum of Science and Industry, east of the Wooded Island.

Length: 27.7 miles.

Terrain: Flat lakeshore, urban Chicago neighborhoods, wetlands in the Lake Calumet area.

Traffic and hazards: If riding on a weekday, watch for trucks in the vicinity of Lake Calumet. Most of the roads through this area provide an ample shoulder. While riding in any urban area, keep aware of your surroundings.

Getting there: *Automobile:* Take South Lake Shore Drive south to the Science Drive exit (just after the 57th Street exit). Stay left as you enter the parking lot, located south of the lagoon at the backside of the Museum of Science and Industry. *Public transportation:* Take the Metra Electric District Main Line to the 59th Street station. On 59th Street, head east (toward the lake) for 0.3 mile, crossing Stony Island Avenue and Cornell Avenue. Cross the bridge behind the Museum of Science and Industry, and start the ride on the far side of the parking lot. Coordinates for starting point: 16T 451683E 4626270N

The Ride

This ride starts within Jackson Park, home to one of the most important events in Chicago history: the World's Columbian Exposition of 1893. Some of the features of this world-renowned event still exist within the park. South of the parking area

where this ride begins is a lagoon surrounding an island containing a serene Japanese garden. North of the lagoon, the Museum of Science and Industry also serves as a remnant of the event.

In preparation for the enormous fair, a team of the nation's most celebrated architects and sculptors transformed this park on Chicago's south side into the "White City," as it was called, made largely of plaster buildings designed in a classical style. The city included sculptures, fountains, and some 200 buildings exhibiting art, machinery, animals, plants, food, and many other items. The exposition was a huge success: Over 27 million people turned out to celebrate 400 years of post-Columbus civilization. After the exposition, the city converted the ground's 700 acres back to a park.

As you follow the Lakefront Path south of Jackson Park, there are a few landmarks to admire. The elegant 63rd Street Beach House takes full advantage of the lake with its sprawling open-air balconies and grand porticos. At the beach house, look to the right down Hayes Drive to view the impressive shining statue called *The Republic,* a replica of a much larger statue built for the Columbian Exposition. Leaving Jackson Park, the path threads between the park's outer harbor and inner harbor, by Rabida Children's Hospital, and along a golf course that sits behind the South Shore Cultural Center.

At the corner of 83rd Street and US 41 is the towering spire of St. Michael the Archangel, a Gothic-style church built in 1907 by Polish-American steelworkers from the U.S. Steel South Works. The South Works, located on the lakefront east of the church, closed in 1992. During the mill's heyday in World War II, it employed almost 20,000 people and later produced much of the steel used to build Chicago's skyscrapers, including the Sears Tower (now called the Willis Tower) and the John Hancock Center. The closing of the South Works has had a devastating effect on the economic health of its surrounding neighborhood. The city hopes to revitalize the area by transforming the South Works' 650-acre swath of lakefront land into a new residential and retail development.

The drawbridge over the Calumet River offers a bird's-eye view of Calumet Harbor, an intensely industrial port that moves all sorts of cargo, ranging from metals, grains, stone, and ore to food products such as vegetable oil and sugar. Block-long barges motor down the river and then pull alongside the shore so that cranes can offload their freight. There's a boatyard, scrap-metal recycling facility, and vertical lift bridge for trains. Nearby, I-90 follows the Chicago Skyway Bridge high above the river, bypassing the entire industrial area.

South of the Calumet River you'll enter Calumet Park, a quiet expanse of greenery on the shore of Lake Michigan, fringed by a small neighborhood to the east and heavy industry to the north and south.

The route along the Burnham Greenway Trail from Calumet Park to Wolf Lake follows a noisy stretch of US 41 before entering a quiet neighborhood of bungalows.

◀ *The main Pullman factory building still stands in Chicago's Pullman neighborhood.*

At Eggers Woods Forest Preserve, the trail passes through a thickly wooded area dotted with wetlands. Wolf Lake is a customary spot to pull up to a picnic table, break out the sandwiches, and watch the waterfowl. Despite the heavy industry and the expressway visible across Wolf Lake, this park on the lakeshore is still a mighty peaceful spot.

The next lake to the west, Lake Calumet, is surrounded by ponds, wetlands, and more heavy industry. The big mounds are, of course, landfills. On top of the mounds you may catch a glimpse of grazing goats. Local industries and municipalities have been dumping trash at Lake Calumet for nearly seventy years. Recently the landfill mounds had to be re-graded to prevent what the state calls a "garbalanche" from occurring. After re-grading, the state planted prairie grasses to keep the soil in place. The goats have been trained to eat grasses that crowd out the helpful prairie grasses. With continuing cleanup efforts finally under way at Lake Calumet, there are more opportunities to see wildlife such as coyotes, red-tailed hawks, and various waterbirds.

Situated at the western edge of the Lake Calumet area is what's left of a grandiose experiment in town planning and its beautiful old houses and public buildings. In 1881 George M. Pullman, inventor and manufacturer of the Pullman railroad sleeping car, built a town for the employees of his massive manufacturing plant. Rows of simple but elegant row houses extend a few blocks south from 111th Avenue. At Cottage Grove Avenue stands the Hotel Florence opposite the clock tower and the remains of the factory. One of the most attractive buildings in Pullman is the Greenstone Church (112th Street and St. Lawrence Avenue), with its spire and gabled roof.

In 1893 George Pullman reduced his employees' wages while maintaining their rents at the same price. The workers went on strike, and rail workers around the country refused to work on trains with Pullman cars. Eventually, troops came to quell the strikers. In 1894 the Illinois Supreme Court determined that Pullman could not lease houses and apartments to his workers, and the structures were sold off to private owners. More than a century later, nearly all of Pullman's 900 residences remain.

On the return trip to the Hyde Park neighborhood, King Drive passes through an assortment of working-class south-side neighborhoods: Roseland, Chatham, Greater Grand Crossing, Woodlawn, and Washington Park. Before heading east through the Midway Plaisance, a mile-long park that runs along the southern edge of the University of Chicago, you'll take a quick tour of Washington Park and pass the 102-foot-long concrete sculpture by Laredo Taft called *The Fountain of Time*.

Along the Midway Plaisance, architecture fans will enjoy the English Gothic style that characterizes many of the University of Chicago's buildings. During the Columbian Exposition, the Midway Plaisance hosted amusement rides and a collection of re-created villages from around the world; now it's open parkland with statuary and an ice rink that operates in the winter.

At University Avenue, you'll have the opportunity to make a side trip to see the neighborhood where President Barack Obama and his family live when they're not in Washington, D.C. Head north on University Avenue for 9 blocks, then turn left at

Chicago South Side Ramble

WASHINGTON PARK

Museum of Science and Industry

Midway Plaisance Drive

MIDWAY PLAISANCE

63rd Street

JACKSON PARK

Lakefront Path

Lake Michigan

25.4

26.4

11

71st Street

75th Street

Rainbow Park

83rd Street

Burley Avenue

87th Street

South Lake Shore Drive

Martin Luther King Avenue

Chicago

95th Street

100th Street

Calumet Park

ILLINOIS

INDIANA

2.3

4.0

4.4

5.9

7.4

15.9

Stony Island Avenue

Dorty Avenue

Calumet Harbor

19.0

111th Street

Pullman

17.4

18.5

Lake Calumet

122nd Street

13.5

12.7

10.3

William Powers Conservation Area

Burnham Greenway Path

Eggers Wood Forest Preserve

Wolf Lake

Torrence Avenue

126th Street

12.2

11.2

Calumet River

0   1   2 km.
0   1   2 mi.

N

51st Street. The Obamas' handsome redbrick house is near the corner of Greenwood Ave. and 51st Street at 5046 South Greenwood Avenue. Don't get your hopes up, though, if you want to snap a picture of it: The Chicago Police and the U.S. Secret Service have erected a security zone several blocks wide around the residence.

Continuing ahead on the Midway Plaisance, you'll see dozens of outdoor statues of religious figures at the Rockefeller Memorial Chapel, and closer to Jackson Park, you'll pass a large round perennial flower garden. Before crossing the bridge to return to the starting spot, you might consider taking the bridge on the right to visit the Wooded Island's small but beautiful Japanese garden.

Miles and Directions

0.0   Start in the parking area behind the Museum of Science and Industry. From the parking lot, head east toward Lake Michigan on the path that runs on the north side of the marina.

0.2   After passing under Lake Shore Drive, go up the ramp and turn left (south) on the Lakefront Path.

2.3   At the end of the path, follow the bike lane on US 41, heading southeast.

4.0   Turn left on 83rd Street.

4.2   Turn right on Burley Avenue.

4.4   Continue straight ahead and resume following US 41.

5.9   Turn left on 95th Street, then bear left for a tour of Calumet Park. Stay left on the park road. On the way out of the park, the park road turns into 100th Street, which you'll follow through the underpass.

7.4   Just after the underpass, take the Burnham Greenway Path left.

10.3   After entering Eggers Woods Forest Preserve, take the first paved trail left. Then take the park road to the right into the William Powers Conservation Area.

11.2   From the William Powers Conservation Area, head west on 126th Street. Follow the bike path along this street.

12.2   Turn right on Torrence Avenue and cross the Calumet River.

12.7   Turn left on 122nd Street. If riding on a weekday, watch for big trucks for the next couple of miles. Use the ample shoulder along most of this road.

13.5   Turn right on Stony Island Avenue.

15.9   Turn left on Doty Avenue.

17.4   Just after bridge that carries 111th Street over I-94, take a left on the ramp that goes up to 111th Street.

17.7   Turn left on 111th Street and cross I-94.

18.2   Turn left on Champlain Street into Pullman.

18.5   Turn right on 113th Street, then turn right on Saint Lawrence Avenue.

18.7   Turn left on 111th Street.

19.0   Turn right on Martin Luther King Drive.

25.4   Bear right into Washington Park on Best Drive.

25.5   Take the bike path that circles the lagoon to the right. Go around the Washington Park lagoon clockwise.

26.4 Turn left on the Midway Plaisance. Returning to Jackson Park, continue straight ahead over the bridge.

27.7 Return to the parking area where the ride started.

Local Information

Chicago Convention and Tourism Bureau: 2301 South Lake Shore Dr., Chicago; (312) 567-8500; www.choosechicago.com.

Chicago Southland Convention and Visitors Bureau: 2304 173rd St., Lansing; (708) 895-8200 or (888) 895-8233; www.visitchicago southland.com.

Local Events/Attractions

DuSable Museum of African American History: Affordable museum with engaging exhibits; located in Hyde Park; 740 East 56th Pl., Chicago; (773) 947-0600; www.dusablemuseum .org.

Frank Lloyd Wright's Robie House: Just north of the Midway Plaisance; 5757 South Woodlawn St., Chicago; (773) 834-1847; www.wrightplus .org.

Historic Pullman Foundation Visitor Center: Offers tours and exhibits; a tour held the second weekend in October shows off the house interiors; 112th St. and Cottage Grove Ave., Chicago; (773) 821-7031; www.pullmanil.org.

Museum of Science and Industry: Includes an Omnimax theater and a working coal mine; East 57th St. and Lakeshore Dr., Chicago; (773) 684-1414; www.msichicago.org.

Restaurants

Bonjour Bakery and Cafe: Affordable food for breakfast and lunch in Hyde Park; outdoor seating; 1550-52 East 55th St., Chicago; (773) 241-5300.

The Marina Cafe: Mid-priced Creole- and Caribbean-influenced menu; small bar upstairs; located right on the Lakefront Path in Jackson Park; 6401 South Coast Guard Dr., Chicago; (773) 947-0400.

Snail Thai Cuisine: Basic Thai restaurant in Hyde Park; 1649 East 55th St., Chicago; (773) 667-5423; www.snailthai.com.

Accommodations

Benedictine Bed and Breakfast: Run by a Catholic monastery in the Bridgeport neighborhood on Chicago's south side; 3111 South Aberdeen St., Chicago; (773) 927-7424; www .chicagomonk.org.

J. Ira and Nicki Harris Family Hostel: Huge, clean, affordable hostel located downtown; dorm-style rooms and a limited number of private rooms; 24 East Congress Pkwy., Chicago; (312) 360-0300; www.hichicago.org.

Bike Shops

Blackstone Bicycle Works: Provides educational and recreational opportunities to local boys and girls in addition to standard bike shop offerings; located just south of Midway Plaisance; afternoon hours; 100 South Blackstone Ave., Chicago; (773) 241-5458.

Restrooms

Start/finish: Restrooms are located at the east side of the parking area. Water fountains appear regularly along the Lakefront Path.

Mile 0.6: Restrooms and water are available at the 63rd Street Beach House.

Mile 2.3: South Shore Cultural Center has restrooms and water (as well as a restaurant).

Mile 6.0: Calumet Park has restrooms in the beach house.

Mile 11.0: The William Powers Conservation Area has restrooms.

Maps

USGS: Jackson Park quad, Lake Calumet quad.

DeLorme: Illinois Atlas & Gazetteer: Page 29.

12 I&M Canal Challenge

While exploring the Illinois and Michigan Canal on the path once used by mules to pull boats up and down the canal, there's no shortage of scenic areas containing woods, marshes, prairies, and agricultural land. You'll also encounter a couple of interesting small towns that grew up alongside this waterway dug in the mid-1800s. The second half of the ride follows country roads that lead through gently rolling terrain parallel to the Illinois River.

Start: Catch the I&M Canal Trail at Channahon State Park, located about 10 miles southwest of Joliet.
Length: 48.3 miles, with options for extending the route along the I&M Canal Trail.
Terrain: Flat bottomland and gently rolling agricultural land.

Traffic and hazards: Half of this route follows the I&M Canal Trail; the other half follows predominantly quiet rural roads along the canal and the Illinois River. The surface of the I&M Canal Trail is smooth crushed gravel.

Getting there: From Chicago, take I-55 south to exit 248. From this exit, head southwest on US 6. Turn left on Canal Street. The entrance to Channahon State Park is 3 blocks ahead on the right. Coordinates for starting point: 16T 397384E 4586285N

The Ride

In 1848 the Illinois and Michigan Canal provided the final shipping link between the East Coast and the Gulf of Mexico. From Chicago, the canal angled southwest, running beside stretches of the Des Plaines River and the Illinois River halfway across the state. Long abandoned as a transportation route, the canal now enjoys a new life as a recreation spot. People come to see the locks, aqueducts, and lock-tender houses and learn about the history of the I&M, but they also come to soak up the natural beauty along the canal.

One of the most eye-catching stretches along the entire canal appears on the first few miles of this ride as the trail follows a thin sliver of land bordered by the Des Plaines River on one side and the canal on the other. First, though, at the beginning of the trail in Channahon State Park, you'll see a former canal lock and one of only two lock-tender houses remaining along the canal. Lock tenders had to be available day and night to keep the boat traffic moving. They opened the gate for the canal boat to enter the 12-by-100-foot lock, closed the gate, and then filled or drained the lock to raise or lower the boat. Fifteen locks were needed along the I&M Canal for 141 feet of elevation change.

After leaving Channahon State Park, crossing the Du Page River, and passing another lock, the trail follows a 15-foot-wide strip of land between two bodies of water: the 20- to 30-foot-wide canal on the right and the broad and mighty Des

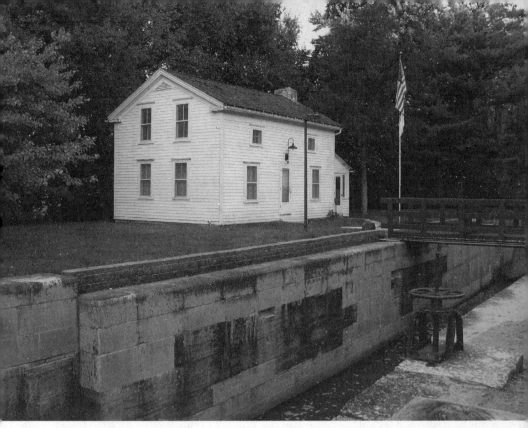

A lock-tender's house sits beside the I&M Canal in Channahon State Park.

Plaines River on the left. The surrounding landscape is wooded and hilly, with bluffs and patches of farmland. During good weather, pleasure boats cruise the Des Plaines. Barges often lumber by, some as long as two city blocks. At McKinley Woods, a pedestrian bridge over the canal leads to hiking trails that go up the park's rugged bluffs.

The bluffs continue beyond McKinley Woods all the way to the Dresden Lock and Dam. Near the dam is the only mule barn left standing along the canal (mule barns were situated every 10 to 15 miles on the canal for the mules and horses to eat and rest before their next haul). Now leaving the shore of the Illinois River, another white wood-frame lock-tender house appears along the path at Aux Sable Creek. This is also where you'll find an aqueduct where the canal is directed over the 40-foot-wide creek.

The Illinois River comes back into view as you brush against Morris's downtown area and whiz past a small riverside park where anglers launch their boats. Beyond Morris, the trail passes Gebhard Woods State Park, a small park with lagoons, a winding creek, and groves of mature oak trees. The trail west of Gebhard Woods offers a gloriously remote experience: This is where bottomland woods take over and the water in the canal is replaced by high stalks of sedge grasses. After crossing a small stream that trickles down toward the Illinois River, you'll duck under the arched wooden supports of the Old Stage Road Bridge. Dense stands of bottomland woods occasionally open up to reveal big sprawling wetlands sprinkled with downed trees and muskrat lodges.

Seneca is where you'll leave the I&M Canal Trail and start heading back to Channahon State Park on quiet country roads. Before leaving the trail, though, you can't miss the Seneca grain elevator—the only one left among dozens of grain elevators that once stood alongside the canal. Built in 1861 and placed on the National Register of Historic Places in 1997, the 80-foot structure reminds us of the main commodity hauled up and down the canal.

In no time after leaving Seneca, you're cutting through grassland and cornfields that tilt gently down toward the wooded banks of the Illinois River on the right. Views of the river come and go along a several-mile stretch of Old Stage Road. Local historians say that Old Stage Road is one of the oldest roads in the area, and was originally a route used by bison herds passing through the tallgrass prairie. After crossing the I&M Canal on the arched bridge you saw earlier, Old Stage Road drifts away from the shore of the Illinois River and then wiggles alongside the hickory- and oak-laden banks of the canal. Approaching Morris, you'll see a gravel-mining operation followed by Mount Caramel Cemetery and Gebhard Woods State Park.

In a region where small towns typically have an equal number of empty and occupied storefronts, Morris's lively downtown clearly runs against the norm. Liberty Street reveals a handsome downtown strip lined with shops, restaurants, and watering holes. Many of the downtown buildings retain their ornate nineteenth-century cornices. The grounds of the Grundy County Courthouse on Washington Street contain several war memorials as well as a 20-foot-high cedar pole, which reportedly marked the burial mound of a local Native American leader named Chief Nucquette. Nineteen burial mounds dating from the Mississippian Period (900–1500 AD) lined the river in Morris but were destroyed for canal construction. The ceremonial pole was saved and installed in the courthouse square in 1925.

On Cemetery Road east of Morris, a large granite boulder in the center of Evergreen Cemetery marks the grave site of one of northern Illinois' most famous American Indian chiefs. Chief Shabbona was a local Potawatomi leader known for befriending white settlers at the time of the Black Hawk War. The Black Hawk War developed when Chief Black Hawk of the Sac tribe refused to relinquish his tribe's ancestral land in the area. Known for his interest in preventing unneeded bloodshed, Shabbona helped convince other Indian leaders in the 1830s that a war against the U.S. government would be a futile undertaking.

A couple more gravel pits appear on the way toward the Aux Sable Aqueduct. You'll also see a smattering of farms and residential developments, and occasional swatches of wetlands. Getting closer to Channahon, you'll leave the Illinois River floodplain and make a steep 100-foot climb up the river bluff. The final several miles take you through flat terrain with clusters of new housing developments.

I&M Canal Challenge

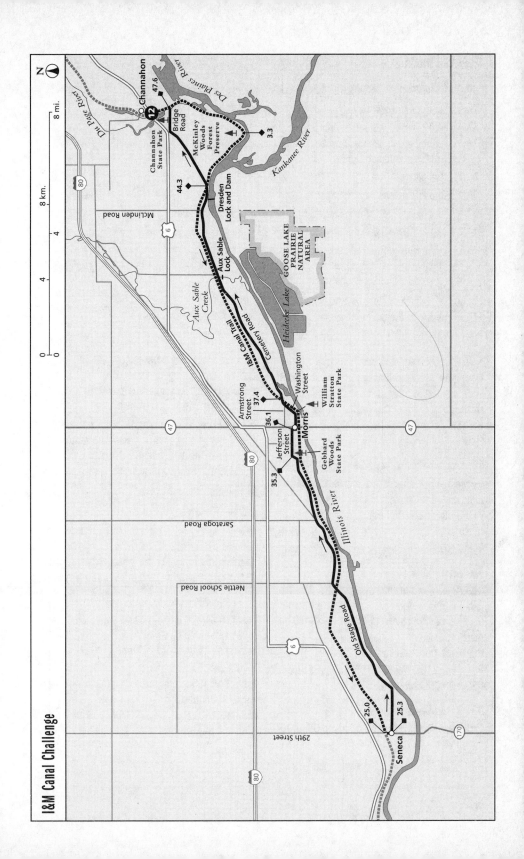

Miles and Directions

0.0 From Channahon State Park, head south (left) on the I&M Canal Trail.

25.0 In Seneca, leave the I&M Canal Trail by turning left on Main Street/SR 170.

25.3 Turn left on Union Street, which soon becomes Old Stage Road.

35.3 Turn right on Freemont Avenue. Getting closer to downtown Morris, Freemont Avenue soon becomes Jefferson Street.

36.1 Turn right on Liberty Street.

36.2 Turn left on Washington Street.

37.4 Turn right on Armstrong Street, which becomes Cemetery Road.

44.3 Just after passing a parking area for the I&M Canal Trail, turn right on Hansel Road.

46.7 When Hansel Road ends, keep straight ahead on the trail. After a quarter mile, the trail ends; resume following Hansel Road ahead. After the trail segment, Hansel Road curves right and becomes Bridge Road.

47.6 After crossing the I&M Canal, turn left on the I&M Canal Trail.

48.3 Return to the start in Channahon State Park.

Local Information

Canal Corridor Association: 201 West 10th St., Lockport; (815) 588-1100; www.canalcor.org.

Heritage Corridor Convention and Visitors Bureau: 339 West Jefferson St., Joliet; (800) 926-2262; www.heritagecorridorcvb.com.

Local Events/Attractions

Goose Lake Prairie State Natural Area: Contains one of the largest tracts of tallgrass prairie in the state; 5010 North Jugtown Rd., Morris; (815) 942-2899; http://dnr.state.il.us/lands/landmgt/parks/i&m/east/goose/home.htm.

Restaurants

Chapin's Restaurant: Steak and seafood; located in downtown Morris; 701 North Liberty St., Morris; (815) 942-1880; www.chapinsrestaurant.us.

Rockwell Inn: Dine among works by Norman Rockwell; 2400 West US 6, Morris; (815) 942-6224; www.rockwellinn.net.

Accommodations

McKinley Woods Forest Preserve: Offers tent camping next to the trail; located west of Channahon on McKinley Rd. south of US 6 and Bridge Rd.; www.fpdwc.org/mckinley.cfm.

Park Motel: Clean and affordable; 1923 North Division St., Morris; (815) 942-1321.

Starved Rock Lodge and Conference Center: Guest rooms and cabins at the state park located at SR 178 and SR 71; P.O. Box 570, Utica, IL 61373; (800) 868-7625; www.starvedrocklodge.com.

Bike Shops

Grand Schwinn Cyclery: 711 Liberty St., Ottawa; (815) 942-1510.

Sumbaum Cycle: 114 North Larkin Ave., Joliet; (815) 744-5333; http://sumbaumcycles.com.

Restrooms and Water

Start/finish: Restrooms and water are available at Channahon State Park.

Mile 3.3: McKinley Woods Forest Preserve has restrooms and water.

Mile 8.8: Restrooms are available at the Aux Sable Aqueduct.

Mile 15.2: Gebhard Woods State Park has restrooms and water.

Mile 25.0: Restrooms, drinks, and snacks are available at the gas station/convenience store next to the trailhead in Seneca.

Mile 36.0: Restrooms are available at the gas stations in downtown Morris at Washington Street and SR 47.

Mile 41.9: Restrooms are available at the Aux Sable Aqueduct.

Maps

USGS: Channahon quad, Minooka quad, Morris quad, Seneca quad.

DeLorme: Illinois Atlas & Gazetteer: Pages 36 and 35.

13 North Shore Cruise

If you're like many cyclists, sometimes the momentum behind a bike ride is generated wholly by the desire to find a scenic spot to relax and enjoy the lunch you packed along. This ride offers great choices for picnicking spots, including roadside prairies, bluffs above Lake Michigan, and several sprawling forest preserves. In addition to the many parks along the way, the second half of the ride takes you through the picturesque campus of Lake Forest University and the historic grounds of Fort Sheridan.

Start: The Glencoe Metra station at the corner of Park Avenue and Green Bay Road in Glencoe.

Length: 35.4 miles.

Terrain: The first half of the ride is flat; the second half is gently rolling.

Traffic and hazards: St. Marys Road has steady traffic, but there's an adequate shoulder for riding. While the traffic on most of these roads is minimal, many North Shore residents have an affinity for buying the largest cars available. Larger cars not only take up more road space, but also render cyclists less visible.

Getting there: *Automobile:* From Chicago, take I-94 north to the Dundee Road exit. Head east on Dundee Road and then turn right on Green Bay Road. Park at or near the Glencoe Metra station on the left. *Public transportation:* Take the Union Pacific North Metra Line to the Glencoe station, where the ride starts. Coordinates for starting point: 16T 437378E 4664870N

The Ride

While the communities of Chicago's North Shore generally aren't regarded as places rich with historic attractions, a few intriguing old landmarks do exist. One of these is Fort Sheridan, an army base established in 1887 at the urging of local businessmen so that troops could respond quickly to labor protests in Chicago. Though troops from Fort Sheridan would respond to labor unrest only once (in 1894 during the Pullman strike), it was a busy place while it served as a training and administrative center from the Spanish-American War through World War II, when over 500,000 military men and women were processed at the fort. The centerpiece of the fort is a 227-foot-tall water tower, originally the tallest structure in the Chicago area. It was shortened by

Sunrise Park in Lake Bluff is just one of the great parks you'll encounter on the North Shore Cruise.

60 feet in 1940 because of structural problems. The long, squat row of buildings on each side of the tower served as troop barracks.

On the way to Fort Sheridan, the first half of the route passes by a series of large wooded parks that invite you to take a break and have a look around. The Heller Nature Center on Ridge Road is the first of these: It features a short network of trails that wind through oak-hickory forests, tallgrass prairie, and wetlands. On St. Marys Road you'll encounter three county-owned forest preserves situated along the Des Plaines River. Wright Woods contains several miles of crushed gravel trails and hundreds of acres of thick bottomland woods along the river. Farther north, you'll pass savanna and stands of hickories, maples, and oaks at MacArthur Woods and eventually come to Old School Forest Preserve, offering more woodland and open prairie.

Just north of Wright Woods Forest Preserve sits a large modern home that belonged to Adlai Stevenson. Born and raised in Bloomington-Normal, Illinois, Stevenson served as Illinois governor, U.S. representative to the United Nations, and two-time presidential candidate. Stevenson didn't linger at this house frequently, but he reportedly enjoyed visiting and used it for entertaining guests such as Eleanor Roosevelt and John F. Kennedy. The Stevenson home is not a museum and is typically open only for special events. Several information panels in front of the house provide some background on Stevenson and the home.

After the bustle of Rockland Road, you'll arrive in the sleepy North Shore community of Lake Bluff. At Sunrise Park, pull up to one of the benches perched on a bluff above our inland sea. The park, located in a tony residential neighborhood, includes a sandy beach at the foot of the bluff.

The winding route of Sheridan Road cuts through the leafy campus of Lake Forest College. The college's stately buildings are surrounded by a series of wooded ravines that bisect much of the area. Young Hall, a yellow brick building built in 1878, dominates the central campus. Behind Young Hall sits Hotchkiss Hall, a red stone structure with small elegant spires.

A few miles south of Lake Forest College, you'll enter the gates of Fort Sheridan to see the hundred or so solidly built and well-maintained administration buildings and houses. The buildings, set within grassy lawns and among patches of woodland, were constructed between 1889 and 1910 of blond-colored bricks made of clay mined from nearby lakefront bluffs. After the base closed in 1993, an extensive environmental cleanup campaign was needed before transforming it into a residential development. An Army Reserve base continues to occupy some of the land, but the majority of it is now privately owned.

Continuing south along Sheridan Road, the landscape is peppered with deep wooded gullies. The thirty or so V-shaped ravines along the North Shore were carved by streams as they twisted from the higher flat ground to the lower level of the lake. While most of the ravines can only be admired from afar, there's one spot along the route where you can explore them more fully. At Moraine Park on Sheridan Road, stairs lead down into a ravine where two streams converge and flow into the lake. Visitors can follow the stone walkway alongside the stream all the way to the beach.

Back on Sheridan Road, you'll soon arrive in the busy downtown area of Highland Park. After passing Ravinia Park, the long-standing outdoor music venue, you'll soon reach the Glencoe Metra station, where the ride began.

Miles and Directions

0.0 Head northwest on Green Bay Road.

2.3 Turn left on Clavey Road.

3.8 Turn right on Ridge Road.

4.8 Turn right on Old Deerfield Road.

4.9 Turn left on Richfield Road.

5.3 Turn right on Ridge Road.

6.6 Turn left on Churchill Lane, which changes to Tennyson Lane as it curves right. Tennyson Lane becomes Ridge Road north of Half Day Road.

8.5 Turn left on Old Mill Road. Continue straight ahead on the pedestrian bridge when Old Mill curves left and becomes Milburne Road. Follow the trail straight ahead to resume the route on Old Mill Road.

10.7 Old Mill Road becomes Fork Drive as it curves to the right. As Fork Drive curves right, it becomes Bowling Green Drive.

11.5 Turn left on Old Barn Lane.

11.6 Turn left on Everett Road. Everett Road becomes St. Marys Road as it curves right.

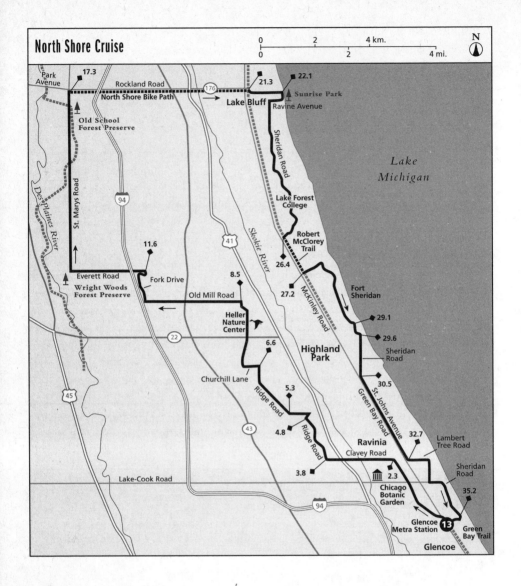

North Shore Cruise

0   2   4 km.
0   2   4 mi.

N

17.3
Park Avenue
Rockland Road
North Shore Bike Path
21.3 **22.1**
Lake Bluff
Sunrise Park
Ravine Avenue
Old School Forest Preserve
St. Marys Road
Des Plaines River
Sheridan Road
Lake Michigan
Lake Forest College
Robert McClorey Trail
11.6
Everett Road
Wright Woods Forest Preserve
Fork Drive
Old Mill Road
8.5
26.4
27.2
Heller Nature Center
Skokie River
Fort Sheridan
29.1
29.6
Highland Park
Sheridan Road
McKinley Road
6.6
Churchill Lane
5.3
30.5
Ridge Road
St. Johns Avenue
Green Bay Road
4.8
Ravinia
Clavey Road
32.7
Lambert Tree Road
3.8
Lake-Cook Road
Chicago Botanic Garden
2.3
Sheridan Road
35.2
Glencoe Metra Station
13
Green Bay Trail
Glencoe

16.7 **Side trip:** Consider taking a 1.6-mile lap around the Old School Forest Preserve—you won't regret it.

17.3 Turn right on the bike path that parallels Park Avenue/SR 176. This street soon becomes Rockland Road.

21.3 After passing under the train tracks, stay left at two successive trail junctions, and cross the bridge over SR 176. Heading north on Sheridan Avenue, turn right on Scranton Avenue.

22.1 Turn right on Sunrise Avenue. Jog right at Prospect Avenue and continue south on Sunrise Avenue.

22.4 Turn right on Ravine Avenue.

22.7	Turn left on Moffet Road. Continue south as Moffet Road merges with Sheridan Road.
26.4	At McCormick Drive, hop on the Robert McClory Path as it parallels Sheridan Road on the right.
27.2	Turn left on Simonds Way.
27.5	Turn left on Leonard Wood North. Continue ahead on Leonard Wood North as it becomes Patten Road.
29.1	Turn left on Walker Avenue.
29.3	Turn right on Oak Street.
29.5	Turn left on Edgecliff Drive.
29.6	Turn right on Sheridan Road.
30.5	In downtown Highland Park, turn right on Central Avenue, then immediately turn left on St. Johns Avenue.
32.7	Bear left on Lambert Tree Road as St. Johns Avenue ends. Merge onto Sheridan Road.
35.2	Turn right on Park Avenue.
35.4	Return to the Glencoe Metra station.

Local Information

Chicago's North Shore Convention and Visitors Bureau: 8001 Lincoln Ave., Suite 715, Skokie; (866) 369-0011; www.cnscvb.com.

Chicago Convention and Tourism Bureau: 2301 South Lake Shore Dr., Chicago; (312) 567-8500; www.choosechicago.com.

Lake County Forest Preserve District: 2000 North Milwaukee Ave., Libertyville; (847) 367-6640; www.lcfpd.org.

Lake County Convention and Visitors Bureau: 5455 West Grand Ave., Suite 302, Gurnee; (847) 662-2700; www.lakecounty.org.

Local Events/Attractions

Chicago Botanic Garden: The garden is free, but there's a fee for parking; 1000 Lake Cook Rd., Glencoe; (847) 835-5440; www.chicago botanic.org.

Heller Nature Center: Large wooded park with trails; 2821 Ridge Rd., Highland Park; (847) 433-6901; www.pdhp.org.

Ravinia Music Festival: Hosts live concerts all summer long; lawn seats are a great deal; 418 Sheridan Rd., Highland Park; (847) 266-5000; www.ravinia.org.

Restaurants

Bluffington's Cafe: Good sandwiches and salads; 113 East Scranton Ave., Lake Bluff; (847) 295-3344.

The Perfect Blend: Inviting coffeehouse in downtown Highland Park; 491 Central Ave., Highland Park; (847) 266-1667.

The Silo: Known for its deep-dish pizzas; 625 Rockland Rd., Lake Bluff; (847) 234-6660; www.silopizza.com.

Yummy Bowl: Chinese and Thai cuisine; 1908 Sheridan Rd., Highland Park; (847) 266-8880.

Accommodations

Margarita European Inn: European-style hotel; rates vary according to rooms; 1566 Oak Ave., Evanston; (847) 869-2273; www.margaritainn .com.

Ravinia Guest House: English Colonial–style B&B within walking distance of Ravinia Park; 264 Oakland Dr., Highland Park; (847) 433-3140.

Sunset Motel: Affordable motel on the route; 511 Rockland Rd., Lake Bluff; (847) 234-4669; www.sunsetmotelroute41.com.

Higher Gear: 1874 Sheridan Rd., Highland Park; (847) 433-2453; www.highergearchicago .com.

Restrooms

Start/finish: Glencoe Metra station has restrooms.

Mile 13.3: Wright Woods Forest Preserve offers restrooms and water.

Mile 16.7: Old School Forest Preserve has restrooms and water.

Mile 29.8: Moraine Park has restrooms.

Maps

USGS: Highland Park quad, Libertyville quad, Waukegan quad, Wheeling quad.

DeLorme: Illinois Atlas & Gazetteer: Page 29.

14 Salt Creek Ramble

After following the Salt Creek Trail through a series of forest preserves straddling Cook and DuPage Counties, you'll explore quiet residential neighborhoods within a handful of western suburbs that grew up alongside the railroad between Chicago and Aurora. Plan to spend some time gawking at the attractive public buildings and many historic homes in Riverside, a village designed by the great landscape architect Frederick Law Olmstead. Wrap up the ride with a loop through Oak Park and a brief tour of the oldest Jewish cemetery in the region.

Start: Brookfield Woods Forest Preserve on 31st Street in Brookfield.
Length: 30.2 miles.
Terrain: The western half of this ride—including the Salt Creek Trail—includes many areas that are gently rolling. The rest is flat.

Traffic and hazards: Most of these streets have little traffic. There are a few short sections on busier roads, such as Des Plaines Avenue, 31st Street, and Cermak Road. About 7 miles of the route follow the paved Salt Creek Trail. A short section of the ride follows a crushed gravel trail through Fullersburg Forest Preserve.

Getting there: *Automobile:* Take I-290 to SR 171 (South 1st Avenue). Head south on SR 171, then turn right on 31st Street. Look for Brookfield Woods Forest Preserve on the right. Park at the back of the lot where the Salt Creek Trail starts. *Public transportation:* Take the BNSF Metra Line to the Brookfield station. From the station, follow Prairie Avenue north for about 1 mile to 31st Street. At 31st Street, turn right, cross Salt Creek, and pick up the path at the far back parking area of Brookfield Woods. Coordinates for starting point: 16T 430272E 4631788N

The Ride

For most of its 50-mile-long route, Salt Creek winds through a series of densely populated western Chicago suburbs. The section of the creek that accompanies the first 10 miles of this ride, however, runs through a handful of county-operated forest preserves that feature gently rolling topography and lush bottomland woods.

Starting at the east end of the Salt Creek Trail in Brookfield Woods, the path takes you on a curving route through a small savanna before arriving at the creek. While tracing the route of the creek, you'll see that this 40-foot-wide waterway occupies a shallow ravine that is wide in some places, narrow in others. After the first road crossing, one of Salt Creek's only major tributaries, Addison Creek, merges with Salt Creek from the north.

Now on the south side of Salt Creek, the trail wiggles back and forth between the creek bank and the nearby floodplain densely tangled with shrubs, deadfall, and small trees. Of course, better views of the creek and the surrounding landscape are granted when the trees are bare. After crossing 31st Street, the terrain acquires a gently rolling character. This is where the trail mounts a few small bluffs overlooking bends in the creek. If you look closely when the trees are bare, you'll notice a couple of sharp bends in the process of getting cut off from the rest of the creek.

Before entering Fullersburg Forest Preserve, consider a stop at the Graue Mill and Museum. Check out the grinding demonstrations on the first floor, then head down to the basement to learn about the mill's history with the Underground Railroad. The mill also contains a collection of doodads and antiques from the late 1800s, such as room settings, farm implements, and a re-created general store.

Within Fullersburg Forest Preserve, you'll again follow Salt Creek as it meanders beneath small bluffs, around a couple of islands, and under footbridges. Saying goodbye to the forest preserve, you'll ascend a modest-size hill and then pass a string of large, lavish homes along Spring Road and Madison Street. One of the more adventurously designed houses is a triangular-shaped dwelling with slanted sides.

As you make your way along the quiet residential streets in Hinsdale, Western Springs, La Grange, and Brookfield, you'll see parks, schools, churches, and plenty of well-kept yards. This series of quiet, leafy suburban communities grew up along the Chicago, Burlington & Quincy Railroad line (now a Metra line) that ran between Chicago and Aurora.

Crossing the Des Plaines River, you'll arrive at one of the more well-known communities situated alongside this train line: the historic suburb of Riverside. Designed by Frederick Law Olmstead, who designed New York's Central Park and the grounds of the Chicago Columbian Exposition, Riverside was one of the first planned communities in the nation. Chosen for its pleasant location along the Des Plaines River and rail access, the village claims an impressive collection of historic homes. Also eye-catching are the public buildings in the downtown area, such as the water tower, the library, and the village hall topped with a clock tower. Even the schools were elegantly designed: The redbrick Central School at 61 Woodside Road may be the only school in the Chicago area with gargoyles on its facade. Behind the village hall is a pedestrian suspension bridge over the Des Plaines River that leads into one of the many swaths of local parkland.

Longcommon Road features an assortment of historic homes built in a variety of styles. Many of them are large, rambling, wood-frame Victorian homes; some are

clearly inspired by the Prairie style; and interestingly enough, others are rather modest brick ranch houses. After the elegant Prairie-style structure at 135 Longcommon, which houses a church, look for 225 Longcommon Rd., a huge three-story Victorian home built for John F. Palmer, inventor of the pneumatic tube first used in bicycle tires and then used in car tires.

In Berwyn, the 2.5-mile ride on East Avenue starts off with several blocks of 1920s bungalows—all uniform except for minor variations in color and ornamentation. Entering Oak Park, the monolithic Ascension Catholic Church appears on the left. Built of limestone in a Romanesque style, the church is topped with a tiled roof and a dome. Large Victorian homes decorate the sides of East Avenue as you get closer to Oak Park's downtown. After brushing against the south edge of downtown Oak Park, you'll roll into Forest Park.

In Forest Park, you'll encounter Waldheim Jewish Cemeteries, the largest Jewish graveyard in the Chicago area, containing about 240 smaller, separate cemeteries and totaling over 175,000 individual plots. The smaller cemeteries—some of which still have their own gates of stone or brick, sometimes with iron doors facing in various directions—are composed of individuals from family groups, synagogues, and various Jewish organizations. Heading south on Hannah Avenue, the cemeteries on the left contain newer grave sites, many of them established after the 1940s. Turning on Greenberg Road takes you alongside older plots, many bordered by small roads named for biblical figures such as Abraham, Isaac, Jacob, Sarah, and Rebecca.

The 200-acre Waldheim Jewish Cemeteries is just one of the several large cemeteries that together occupy the majority of the land in Forest Park. After encountering another cemetery and a massive mausoleum on Des Plaines Avenue, you'll pass five different forest preserves on the banks of the Des Plaines River. Once the Brookfield Zoo comes into view on 31st Street, you'll know you've arrived back at the starting point.

Miles and Directions

0.0 Shortly after picking up the trail in Brookfield Woods, follow the signs pointing left on McCormick Avenue for a short on-street section. After the on-street section, you'll reconnect with the Salt Creek Trail and follow it for the next 7 miles.

7.0 After passing under I-294, follow the path to the right through a small nature sanctuary to Canterberry Lane. Turn left on Canterberry Lane.

7.5 Turn left on York Road and follow the bike path on the left side of the road.

8.1 Turn right on the crushed gravel path into Fullersburg Forest Preserve before crossing Salt Creek. But first, consider a stop at the Graue Mill on the other side of the creek at York Road.

9.5 In Fullersburg Forest Preserve, cross Salt Creek on the second bridge on the left. Stay to the left to reach the visitor center. Follow the park driveway out to Spring Road.

◀ *An attractive water tower sits in downtown Riverside.*

Salt Creek Ramble

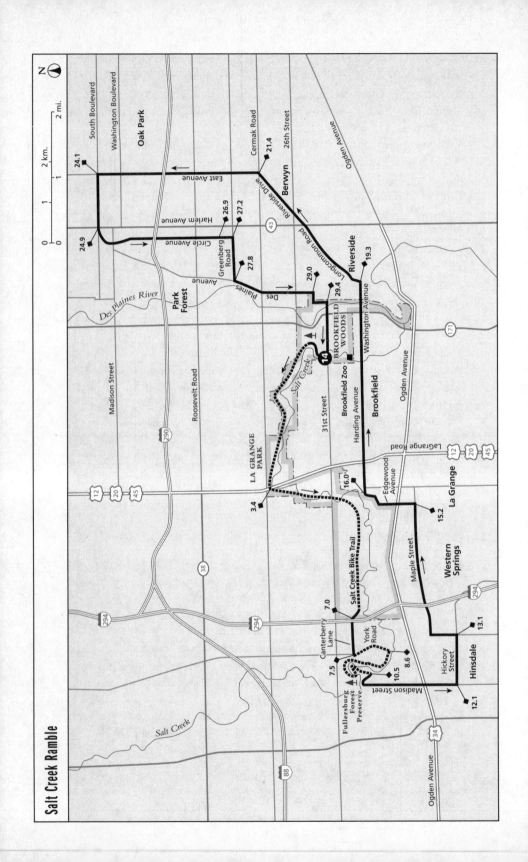

N

0   1   2 km.
0   1   2 mi.

South Boulevard
Washington Boulevard

Oak Park

24.1

24.9

Cermak Road

26th Street

Berwyn

21.4

East Avenue

Harlem Avenue

Circle Avenue

Greenberg Road

26.9

27.2

27.8

Riverside Drive

43

Longcommon Road

Ogden Avenue

Riverside

19.3

29.0

29.4

Des Plaines Avenue

Park Forest

Des Plaines River

Madison Street

Roosevelt Road

290

BROOKFIELD WOODS

14

Salt Creek

Brookfield Zoo

Brookfield

Washington Avenue

Harding Avenue

31st Street

Ogden Avenue

171

LA GRANGE PARK

3.4

Salt Creek Bike Trail

16.0

Edgewood Avenue

LaGrange Road

La Grange

12
20
45

15.2

12
20
45

38

Maple Street

Western Springs

294

Canterberry Lane

7.0

7.5

York Road

Fullersburg Forest Preserve

Salt Creek

8.6

10.5

12.1

13.1

Hickory Street

Hinsdale

Madison Street

Ogden Avenue

34

294

88

294

10.5 Turn right on Spring Road.

10.8 Turn left on Madison Street.

12.1 Turn left on Hickory Street.

13.0 Turn left on Oak Street.

13.3 Turn right on Minneola Street.

13.6 Take the pedestrian bridge over I-294. Continue straight ahead on Maple Street.

14.4 At Wolf Road, take a slight jog to the left and continue east on 41st Street.

15.2 Turn left on Edgewood Avenue.

16.0 Edgewood Avenue curves right and turns into Harding Avenue.

17.1 Harding Avenue becomes Washington Avenue. At the roundabout, continue straight ahead on Washington Avenue.

18.6 In Brookfield, Washington Avenue turns into Ridgewood Road and then turns into Forest Avenue.

19.3 Turn left on Longcommon Road. Longcommon is a diagonal road with lots of streets merging with it at various angles—let the street signs guide the way. First, though, take a tour of Riverside's handsome downtown area.

20.5 Longcommon Road turns into Riverside Drive.

21.4 Turn right on Cermak Road. Watch for traffic; this is a busy road.

21.6 Turn left on East Avenue.

24.1 Turn left on South Boulevard.

24.9 At Harlem Avenue, take a slight jog to the left and then continue ahead on Circle Avenue.

26.9 Turn right on 15th Street and then immediately turn left at the dead end, which is Hannah Avenue but has no street sign.

27.2 Turn right where Hannah Avenue ends at Greenberg Road; no street sign is posted at this intersection.

27.8 Turn left on Des Plaines Avenue. This street can be busy, but it is wide.

29.0 Turn right at the sign for National Grove Forest Preserve. The street is 29th Street, but there is no street sign. Follow 29th Street as it curves left.

29.4 Turn right on 31st Street. Proceed with care; this street can be busy.

30.1 Turn right to enter Brookfield Woods Forest Preserve.

30.2 Return to the parking area.

Local Information

Chicago Convention and Tourism Bureau: 2301 South Lake Shore Dr., Chicago; (312) 567-8500; www.choosechicago.com.

Cook County Forest Preserve District: 536 North Harlem Ave., River Forest; (800) 870-3666; www.fpdcc.com.

DuPage County Convention and Visitors Bureau: 915 Harger Rd., Suite 240, Oak Brook; (630) 575-8070; www.dupagecvb.com.

DuPage County Forest Preserve District: 3S580 Naperville Rd., Wheaton; (630) 933-7200; www.dupageforest.com.

Oak Park Area Convention and Visitors Bureau: 1118 Westgate, Oak Park; (708) 524-7800; www.visitoakpark.com.

Local Events/Attractions

Brookfield Zoo: One of the largest zoos in the world with more than 2,500 animals, including frolicking dolphins and big apes; First Avenue and West 31st Street, Brookfield; (708) 485-2200; www.brookfieldzoo.org.

Fullersburg Forest Preserve Visitor Center: Displays a 13,000-year-old wooly mammoth skeleton uncovered locally in 1977; in April or May, ask for the wildflower guide; 3609 Spring Rd., Oak Brook; (630) 850-8110; www.dupageforest.com.

Graue Mill and Museum: A National Historic Landmark, now a living-history museum; 3800 York Rd., Oak Brook; (630) 655-2090; www.grauemill.org.

Riverside Historic District: Enjoy the gaslit street lamps, winding streets, and attractive historic neighborhoods; start your visit at the Riverside Historical Museum, 10 Pine Ave., Riverside; (708) 447-2574.

Restaurants

Benjarong Thai Restaurant: Well-regarded Thai restaurant located yards from the Salt Creek Trail near the LaGrange Road crossing; 2138 Mannheim Rd., Westchester; (708) 409-0339; http://benjarong.us.

Grumpy's Coffee and Ice Cream: A comfortable atmosphere to pursue your fix; 1 Riverside Rd., Riverside; (708) 443-5603.

Khyber Pass: This Indian restaurant is a local favorite; delicious lunch buffet; 1031 Lake St., Oak Park; (708) 445-9032; www.khyberpassrestaurant.com.

Little Bohemian Restaurant: Hearty fare of pierogies, Cornish hen, and potato pancakes; 25 East Burlington St., Riverside; (708) 442-1251.

York Tavern: Reliable spot for burgers and beer; next to Fullersburg Forest Preserve; 3702 York Rd., Oak Brook; (630) 323-5090.

Accommodations

Colony Motel: Basic, very affordable rooms; 9232 West Ogden Ave., Brookfield; (708) 485-0300; www.colonymotelbrookfield.com.

Under the Gingko Tree Bed and Breakfast: Affordable rooms with private baths; 300 North Kenilworth Ave., Oak Park; (708) 524-3237; www.undertheginkgotreebb.com.

Bike Shops

Oak Park Cyclery: Rentals available; 1113 Chicago Ave., Oak Park; (888) 371-2453; www.oakparkcyclery.com.

Westchester Wheels: Rentals available; located right next to the trail; 10411 Cermak Rd., Westchester; (708) 562-0330.

Restrooms

Start/finish: A portable restroom is available in Brookfield Woods.

Mile 3.0: Brezina Woods has restrooms.

Mile 6.2: Bemis Woods North has restrooms.

Mile 10.0: Water and restrooms are available at the Fullersburg visitor center.

Mile 14.9: Gilbert Park has restrooms and water.

Maps

USGS: Berwyn quad, Hinsdale quad, River Forest quad.

DeLorme: Illinois Atlas & Gazetteer: Page 29.

15 Woodstock Ramble

After a lap around Woodstock's celebrated town square, the route takes you through the rolling terrain of northern McHenry Country. At Glacial Park, one of the most attractive parks in northern Illinois, you'll come across a fine picnicking spot at the edge of a gurgling creek that runs through a large grassland. On the return trip to Woodstock, the hills increase, as do long-range views of the surrounding landscape sprinkled with farms and houses.

Start: Parking area 1 block east of the Woodstock town square at Jefferson Street and Jackson Street.
Length: 33.7 miles.

Terrain: Much of the ride is gently rolling. Hills do appear along the way, but none are steep.
Traffic and hazards: While traffic is minimal on most of these roads, use caution because cars tend to move briskly.

Getting there: *Automobile:* From I-90 northwest of Chicago, head north on SR 47. In Woodstock, turn left on Calhoun Street, then turn right on Jefferson Street. Park in the lot near the train tracks at the northwest corner of Jefferson Street and Jackson Street. *Public transportation:* The Union Pacific Northwest Metra Line offers service from Chicago to Woodstock. From the train station, catch the route by heading 1 block east to Clay Street. Coordinates for starting point: 16T 380852E 4685538N

The Ride

By all accounts, Woodstock has the most charming town square in the entire state. Hollywood reinforced this impression by shooting most of the 1993 film *Groundhog Day* in Woodstock's downtown area. The town square is composed of a leafy park and a bandstand surrounded by a series of Victorian buildings containing an assortment of restaurants and inviting shops focusing on antiques, art, handicrafts, and sweets. Visitors often stop at the galleries at the Old Courthouse Arts Center to see artwork by local and national artists. They also come to admire the historic opera house. Since it opened in 1890, the opera house has hosted luminaries one would hardly expect to appear in a small-town venue. The list includes speakers such as Jane Addams and Leo Tolstoy and actors like Paul Newman and Orson Welles.

After soaking up the atmosphere in downtown Woodstock, it's time to start meandering north through Woodstock's residential neighborhoods. The residential areas give way to farmland and open countryside upon reaching Queen Anne Road at mile 3. On Thompson Road, the gently rolling roadway drops into a shallow ravine to cross Nippersink Creek.

After grazing the shoreline of Wonder Lake and logging about a dozen miles of riding, don't miss the picnic area alongside Nippersink Creek at Glacial Park (turn

right on Keystone Road). For those with an interest in learning how glaciers sculpted the landscape in northeastern Illinois, Glacial Park is a geologic jewel. Rising in the distance, just beyond the big swath of prairie that borders the picnic area, is a series of glacially created mounds called kames. Kames are formed when glacial meltwater deposits large quantities of sand and gravel in depressions in the ice or at the edge of the glacier. The 100-foot-high Camelback Kame, located directly east, is said to have formed at the edge of a glacier as it receded some 15,500 years ago.

Glacial Park's bog and marshes also offer a link to the area's geologic past. These wetlands began to take shape when large chunks of ice detached from a receding glacier; as ice melted, a pond formed in the depression and, eventually, vegetation overtook the pond. Some visitors arrive at Glacial Park via the Prairie Trail, a 25-mile multiuse path that stretches from the Wisconsin border south to Algonquin.

Now turning to the west, you'll make a gradual climb up Barnard Mill Road and then take in long views to the north as you follow Vander Karr Road. At SR 47, picnic shelters and a sign offering a rough sketch of Illinois history serve as a welcome for visitors from Wisconsin, which borders Illinois 3 miles north. Farms come and go as you turn onto Johnson Road and catch views of the wide, shallow valley containing Nippersink Creek to the east. The agricultural landscape is speckled with houses, silos, barns, and patches of woodland.

On St. Patrick Road, you'll pass a country church of the same name and an accompanying cemetery. If the season permits, an apple farm on this stretch of roadway invites you to select fruit from a roadside stand or straight from the tree. Returning to Woodstock on Rose Farm Road, the rolling, wooded terrain continues to offer long views of woodland and hills to the south. Closing in on Woodstock, a series of minor hills are mixed with a sprinkling of ponds. Once in the town, handsome wood-frame homes escort you back to the parking area.

Miles and Directions

0.0 From the parking lot at the corner of Jackson Street and Jefferson Street in Woodstock, head west on Jackson Street.

0.1 At the town square, turn right on Benton Street. Continue ahead as Benton Street becomes Clay Street.

1.4 Keep straight ahead on Locust Street as Clay Street turns left.

1.5 Turn right on SR 47/Seminary Road, then immediately turn left on St. Johns Road.

2.3 Jog left on Raffel Road, then immediately turn right on Banford Road.

3.0 Turn left on Queen Anne Road.

6.1 Turn right on Aavang Road.

7.0 Turn left on Greenwood Road.

The old opera house is one of the many attractive buildings that border the town square in Woodstock.

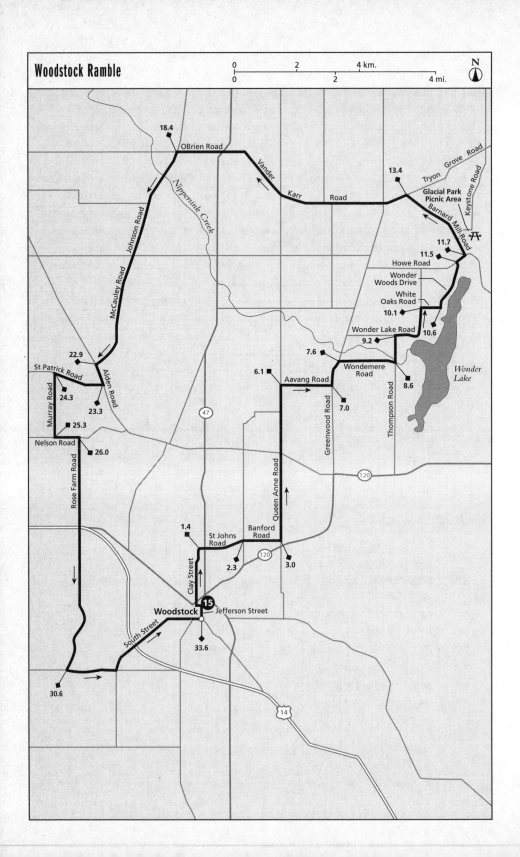

Woodstock Ramble

0   2   4 km.

0   2   4 mi.

N

18.4

OBrien Road

Vander

Karr   Road

13.4

Tryon Grove Road

Keystone Road

Glacial Park Picnic Area

Barnard Mill Road

Nippersink Creek

Johnson Road

11.7

11.5

Howe Road

Wonder Woods Drive

White Oaks Road

10.1

10.6

Wonder Lake Road

9.2

7.6

Wondemere Road

Wonder Lake

McCauley Road

22.9

St Patrick Road

Alden Road

24.3

23.3

6.1

Aavang Road

7.0

Greenwood Road

8.6

Thompson Road

Murray Road

25.3

Nelson Road

26.0

47

Rose Farm Road

120

Queen Anne Road

1.4

St Johns Road

Banford Road

2.3

120

3.0

Clay Street

Woodstock **15** Jefferson Street

33.6

30.6

South Street

14

7.6 Turn right on Wondermere Road.

8.6 Turn left on Thompson Road.

9.2 Turn right on Wonder Lake Road.

10.1 Turn right on White Oaks Road.

10.6 Turn left on Wonder Woods Drive.

11.5 Turn right on Howe Road.

11.7 Turn left on Barnard Mill Road.

12.0 **Side trip:** Take a brief side trip to the Glacial Park picnic area by turning right on Keystone Road.

13.4 Turn left on Tryon Grove Road. Continue ahead as Tryon Grove Road becomes Vander Karr Road. Vander Karr Road becomes OBrien Road after crossing SR 47.

18.4 Turn left on Johnson Road, which soon becomes McCauley Road.

22.9 Turn left on Alden Road.

23.3 Turn right on St. Patrick Road.

24.3 Turn left on Murray Road.

25.3 Turn left on Nelson Road.

26.0 Turn right on Rose Farm Road.

30.6 Turn left on South Street (there is no sign identifying this road).

33.6 Turn left on Jefferson Street.

33.7 Return to the parking area where the ride started.

Local Information

McHenry County Convention and Visitors Bureau: 5435 Bull Valley Rd., Suite 324-B, McHenry; (815) 363-6177; www.visitmchenry county.com.

Woodstock: The city's Web site has a handy walking tour of the town square; 121 West Calhoun St., Woodstock; (815) 338-4300; www .woodstock-il.com.

Local Events/Attractions

Lake Geneva: Charming—if somewhat touristy— town situated on a beautiful lake just across the Wisconsin border about 20 miles north of Woodstock; Walworth County Visitors Bureau, 9 West Walworth St., Elkhorn, WI; (262) 723-3980; www.visitwalworthcounty.com.

McHenry County Conservation District: Operates Glacial Park Conservation Area and the 25-mile Prairie Trail; 18410 US 14, Woodstock; (815) 338-6223; www.mccdistrict.org.

Royal Oak Orchard: In addition to the orchard, there's a bakery, gift shop, and restaurant; located west of Hebron; 15908 Hebron Rd., Harvard; (815) 648-4141; www.royaloakfarm orchard.com.

Woodstock Farmers Market: Held in the town square Tuesday and Saturday mornings, May through October; www.woodstockfarmers market.org.

Restaurants

La Petite Creperie and Bistro: Crepes and wine on the town square; 115 North Johnson St., Woodstock; (815) 337-0765; www.lapetite creperie.net.

Pirro's Restaurante: Traditional Italian menu, including a great selection of pizzas; 228 Main St., Woodstock; (815) 337-7341; http://pirros restaurante.com.

Accommodations

Bundling Board Inn: Affordable and close to downtown; 220 East South St., Woodstock;

(815) 338-7054; www.bundlingboard.com.

Days Inn Woodstock: 990 Lake Ave., Wood-stock; (815) 338-0629.

Bike Shops

Village Pedaler: 470 West Virginia St., Crystal Lake; (815) 459-1833; www.villagepedaler.com.

Restrooms and Water

Mile 1.0: Olson Park has a portable toilet in the northwest corner of the park.

Mile 12.0: Restrooms are available at the Gla-cial Park picnic area.

Maps

USGS: Hebron quad, Marengo North quad, Richmond quad, Woodstock quad.

DeLorme: Illinois Atlas & Gazetteer: Pages 19 and 20.

Central Illinois

L ike much of the state, central Illinois was once covered by a vast prairie, broken only by wooded areas around rivers, streams, and hills. The prairie is now long gone, having been overturned by generations of farmers' plows. Thousands of years of tallgrass prairie growing and dying created some of the most fertile cropland in the nation. Instead of high stands of prairie grass in late summer and early fall, now you'll see rows of corn 7 feet high, forming living walls on both sides of the road. You'll also see plenty of soy fields, as well other crops such as hay, alfalfa, wheat, and fruit.

The western side of central Illinois is defined by rivers: the Illinois River to the east, the Mississippi River to the west, and the Spoon River through the middle. A handful of the rides in this section are focused around Peoria, central Illinois' largest city, which sits on the shore of the Illinois River. Both the Illinois and the Mississippi run between a series of high wooded bluffs that offer excellent cycling opportunities. In the river valleys, you'll encounter sprawling wetlands and big river pools, sometimes several miles across. You'll see enormous barges hauling grain and coal up and down the rivers, and you'll get to know historic river towns.

In central Illinois, especially the eastern half, long-distance bike riders will revel in the wide-open terrain, where they can rack up many miles with little traffic in sight. These central Illinois farm roads are known for being straight, flat, and quiet. Arthur, which hosts one of the largest Amish communities in the nation, is a great riding destination. Cyclists will feel at home within this low-tech community of horse and buggy traffic, horse-drawn farm implements, and a steady stream of Amish cyclists.

While it's the rural land that this part of Illinois is most known for, you'll have the opportunity to get acquainted with an assortment of cities and towns, too. If you've never visited these places, now's your chance to get to know cities that sprouted up on the central Illinois prairie. Expect to see leafy parks, residential neighborhoods, and historic downtowns. On the Charleston Cruise, you'll encounter a charming town square and the campus of Eastern Illinois University; on the Allerton Park–Monticello Cruise, you'll see mansions built by patent medicine bigwigs; and on the Lewistown Ramble, you'll pass the boyhood home of Edgar Lee Masters, who wrote *Spoon River Anthology* about life in a fictionalized version of the town. In Peoria, you'll see a surprising mix of public sculptures and historic architecture on an urban ride that starts and ends at the city zoo.

16 Allerton Park-Monticello Cruise

After exploring the sprawling mansion and stunning sculpture gardens in Robert Allerton Park, the gentle bluffs of the Sangamon River provide many miles of unsurpassed local riding. Cyclists from Decatur and Champaign love these roads because they're scenic, quiet, and winding. Along the way, you'll pass through the vibrant little town of Monticello, home to a few art galleries and a historic district featuring a surprising collection of nineteenth-century mansions.

Start: The main parking area at Robert Allerton Park, located about 25 miles west of Champaign.
Length: 45.7 miles.
Terrain: Expect rolling woodland, occasional hills, and some flat agricultural land.

Traffic and hazards: Pay close attention to the Miles and Directions because this ride contains many turns and a few of the junctions are missing street signs. The 1-mile stretch on SR 10 will be busy.

Getting there: From I-72 west of Champaign, take exit 164 south toward Monticello. Turn right at Old Route 47 (CR 1625 North). Turn left on CR 625 East, then turn right onto County Farm Road. Look for the park entrance on the left. Coordinates for starting point: 16T 359498E 4429542N

The Ride

In 2007 the Illinois tourism office decided to promote travel in the Prairie State by coming up with the Seven Wonders of Illinois. When the list was released, state residents were familiar with most of the honorees, but many people hadn't heard of one of the chosen attractions, Robert Allerton Park. The 1,500-acre park was the personal estate of Robert Allerton, the son of an extremely wealthy businessman who made his fortune in banking and the Chicago stockyards. The park contains a mansion surrounded by a series of formal sculpture gardens and walkways. There are also bluffs, upland woods, and floodplain forest along the Sangamon River. In 1946, after Allerton moved to Hawaii, he donated the estate to the University of Illinois Champaign-Urbana.

The formal gardens, for the most part, are situated along Old Timber Road heading west from the main parking area (be sure to walk your bike through the gardens). This is where you'll see a beautiful brick-walled garden with vines growing in careful patterns, a Chinese maze garden, a sunken garden, and several other striking gardens, each accompanied by classical sculptures.

After the garden walk, you'll be pedaling west along Old Timber Road under a canopy of outsize oak and hickory trees. As Old Timber Road veers to the right through the gate, be sure to take the short side trip straight ahead to see the magnificent *Sun Singer* sculpture, which depicts a male figure—set high on a pedestal on a large grassy lawn—reaching toward the sun.

This stretch of roadway outside of Monticello is lined with pine trees.

For the next 10 miles before Monticello, the route leads you through agricultural land and over several streams. After crossing the Sangamon River, the road dips and bobs along the river's bluffs, heavy with maple and hickory trees. CR 1450 North runs along the south edge of Allerton Park; concerts are held during the summer in the big red barn that appears on this road.

In Monticello, be sure to take a tour of the compact downtown area, which contains a handful of interesting shops, art galleries, and a county courthouse. Heading out of town along State Street, you'll pass a string of impressive mansions built in neoclassical, Italianate, and Victorian styles. This part of Monticello reportedly possessed the highest income per capita of any place in the United States before the turn of the century. These grand houses, known as Millionaire's Row, in many cases were financed by a boom in 1893 when a local doctor invented and started producing a laxative called Pepsin Syrup.

North of Monticello, you'll pass a city park with a playground and ball fields, and Valentine Park, a quiet wooded county park with picnic tables and a short hiking trail.

Heading north parallel to the Sangamon River, the route is varied and scenic. The gentle river bluffs sometimes serve up minor hills, but most often the terrain rolls gradually along, offering a steady mix of forest and cropland. Take a breather at one

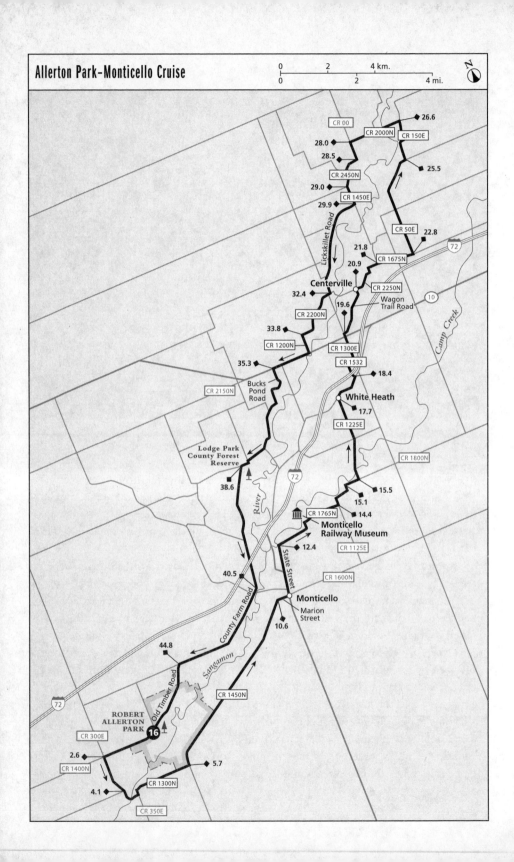

Allerton Park–Monticello Cruise

of the occasional creek crossings or pull off the road at one of the two Piatt County forest preserves on the west side of the Sangamon (neither of these preserves offer restrooms or water).

The west side of the river is much like the east. A series of curving, mostly quiet roads lead you over minor river bluffs and occasionally down into the floodplain. After crossing SR 10, the terrain picks up more of a roll, and more small streams and dense woods appear.

Returning to Allerton Park, wrap up the ride with a visit to the Fu Dog Garden, one of several places in the park where couples hold marriage ceremonies. This dramatic garden features a corridor guarded by two opposing lines of cobalt-blue ceramic Fu Dogs on pedestals. Head back to the parking area by walking through the 100-yard-long vine walk.

Miles and Directions

0.0 From the main parking area at Allerton Park, turn left on Old Timber Road.

1.0 Stay on Old Timber Road as it veers right and passes through the gate, then immediately turn left on CR 1400 North. **Side trip:** Continue straight for 0.7 mile to see the *Sun Singer* sculpture.

2.6 Turn left on CR 300 East.

4.1 Turn left on CR 1300 North.

5.7 Turn left on CR 1450 North. (The road sign at this junction is unclear, but you've made the correct turn if you immediately cross a river after making the turn.) This road takes you all the way to Monticello, where it turns into Allerton Road.

10.6 Turn right on Marion Street in Monticello.

11.0 Turn left on State Street.

12.4 Turn right on CR 1750 North.

14.4 Turn left on CR 1125 East.

15.1 Turn right on CR 1800 North.

15.5 Turn left on CR 1225 East. This road soon turns into Meridian Street.

17.7 Turn right on Old Highway 47. No road sign at this intersection, but it should be clear.

18.4 Turn left on CR 1532. Again, no road signs for this junction, but you can't miss it because you can see that the road crosses over I-72. This road soon turns into CR 1300 East.

19.6 Turn right on Wagon Trail Road.

20.9 Turn right at CR 2250 North. Just ahead, stay left on CR 2250 North at the junction with Welch Cobb Circle.

21.8 Turn right on CR 1675 North.

22.8 Turn left on CR 50 East.

25.5 Turn left on CR 150 East.

26.6 Turn left on CR 2000 North.

28.0 Turn left on CR 00.

28.5 Turn right on CR 2450 North.

29.0 Turn left CR 1450 East.

29.9 Turn right on Lickskillet Road.

32.4 Turn right on CR 2200 North. No road sign at this junction, but it's the only right turn in Centerville.

33.8 Turn left on CR 1200 East.

34.3 Turn right on SR 10. This 1-mile stretch on SR 10 is likely to be busy.

35.3 Turn left on Bucks Pond Road.

38.6 Stay left on Bucks Pond Road (CR 1965 North).

40.5 Turn left on County Farm Road. Continue straight ahead on North Fisler Road as you cross Old Highway 47. Soon, the road mysteriously turns back into County Farm Road. This road turns into CR 1550 North.

44.8 Turn left on Old Timber Road (look for the signs for Allerton Park).

45.7 Return the Allerton Park main parking area.

Local Information

Central Illinois Tourism Development Office: 700 East Adams St., Springfield; (217) 525-7980; www.visitcentralillinois.com.

Monticello Tourism and Chamber of Commerce: Visit the Web site for historic walking tour guides; P.O. Box 313, Monticello, IL 61856; (217) 762-7921; www.monticellotourism.org.

Local Events/Attractions

Allerton Park and Retreat Center: 515 Old Timber Rd., Monticello; (217) 333-3287; www.continuinged.uiuc.edu/allerton.

Monticello Railway Museum: Displays a variety of old locomotives and offers train rides into Monticello; located near the junction of I-72 and SR 105; (217) 762-9011; www.mrym.org.

Restaurants

Brown Bag Deli Restaurant: Salads and over-stuffed sandwiches; 212 West Washington St., Monticello; (217) 762-9221; www.monticellobrownbag.com.

Montgomery's: Fine dining with an emphasis on seasonal fare; 108 South Charter St., Monticello; (217) 762-3833; www.montgomerysdining.com.

Pies by Inge: Homemade pies, cakes, and brownies; 212 West Washington St., Monticello; (217) 762-9221.

Steeple Gallery Coffee House: 102 East Lafayette, Monticello; (217) 762-2924.

Accommodations

Best Western Monticello Gateway Inn: Indoor pool; 805 Iron Horse Pl., Monticello; (217) 762-9436; www.bestwestern.com/monticello gatewayinn.

Foster's Inn: Clean and affordable; 1414 North Market St., Monticello; (217) 762-9835; www.fosterinn.com.

Friends Creek Regional Park: County-owned park with a small campground, hiking trails, and a historic schoolhouse; located about 15 miles west of Monticello; (217) 423-7708; www.maconcountyconservation.org.

Bike Shops

Durst Cycle and Fitness: 1201 South Mattis Ave., Champaign; (217) 352-3300; www.durstcycle.com.

Restrooms

Start/finish: Water and restrooms are located next to the main Allerton parking lot.

Mile 11.0: Various restaurants and gas stations can be found in Monticello.

Maps

USGS: Mahomet quad, Cerro Gordo quad, Monticello quad.

DeLorme: Illinois Atlas & Gazetteer: Pages 53 and 63.

17 Amish Country Ramble

Taking a spin through the largest Amish community in Illinois and the fourth-largest in the nation, you may come to realize that Amish country is best explored on a bike. On a bike you're seeing the landscape at about the same speed as someone riding in an Amish horse and buggy, and you're less likely to feel as though you're intruding upon the Amish low-tech way of life. You're also more likely to stop and chew the fat with someone at the Amish schools, Amish businesses, and dozens of small Amish farms that you'll pass. Reinforcing the kinship between cyclists and the Amish is the realization that many Amish people ride bikes, too.

Start: Arthur/Amish Country Visitors Center, located at the intersection of Vine Street and Progress Street in downtown Arthur.
Length: 31.6 miles. (Since the roads resemble a checkerboard grid, it's a snap to expand or shorten this route.)
Terrain: The roads are straight and flat.

Traffic and hazards: You'll encounter two short stretches along SR 133, which is quite busy. Don't sweat it, though—SR 133 has wide paved shoulders to accommodate the horse and buggy traffic. When you inevitably hit a pile of horse dung, keep the wheel pointed straight and keep pedaling.

Getting there: From I-57, take exit 203 heading west on SR 133. In Arthur, turn right on Vine Street. Park at the Arthur/Amish Country Visitors Center at the intersection of Vine Street and Progress Street. Coordinates for starting point: 16S 373803E 4397135N

The Ride

Many of the 4,000 or so Amish people living around the little town of Arthur reside on small farms 80 to 100 acres in size. Others operate and work at small businesses that focus on goods and services such as woodworking and furniture, buggy and harness repair, and clothing. There are also businesses that sell a slew of different food items, such as cheese, baked goods, and produce. While some Amish crafts and foods are sold in shops in downtown Arthur, the authentic Amish shops are in the countryside outside of town, where you're headed.

Within the first few miles outside of Arthur, you'll pass a panoply of these Amish-owned businesses focusing on quilts, sewing machine repair, wooden gazebos, shoes, and tools. Feel free to stop in: These stores are open to everyone. You may feel especially drawn to Homestead Bakery on CR 2000 North for a tasty cinnamon roll to fuel the ride. If you're riding near harvest time, check out the Great Pumpkin Patch next door: It has 400 varieties of squashes, pumpkins, and gourds (one annual display features a collection of squashes shaped like every letter of the alphabet).

After a few miles, you'll get a feel for the sights and rhythms of the Amish farms located along these roads. Typically, beautiful flower and vegetable gardens adorn the yards, buggies sit in the driveways or inside one of the outbuildings, and bicycles are

Horse and buggy serves as a popular mode of transportation around Arthur.

often propped on kickstands out front. People may be hanging laundry or working on farming equipment near the barn. In the adjoining fields, you may see men or women driving teams of horses pulling the same type of farming equipment in use for generations. What you won't see at the farms are cars, satellite TV dishes, and power lines running from the telephone poles to the houses. Amish houses tend to be simple, colored white, and fairly large, with several rooms opening to one big room, where they may hold church services (services rotate among the households in this Amish community). When you encounter people working on their farms or passing by in buggies, they all offer a friendly greeting.

On the way into Arcola, you'll find a few more businesses focusing on items such as buggies, cabinetry, and lawn furniture. A couple of Amish schools also appear along the way. On the trip to downtown Arcola, the route passes some attractive Victorian homes, as well as the town library that was built with money donated by industrialist Andrew Carnegie. (In the early twentieth century, Carnegie funded the construction of some 2,500 libraries worldwide. Illinois hosts 106 of them.) In downtown Arcola, you'll see antiques stores, an unusual museum dedicated to Raggedy Ann and Andy, and the Illinois Amish Interpretive Center, where you can learn more about the Amish in Illinois. Returning to Arthur from Arcola, fewer formal Amish businesses dot the countryside, but plenty of Amish farms still appear along the way.

Halfway between Arcola and Arthur, the route crosses the Kaskaskia River three times in about as many miles. The longest river in Illinois, the Kaskaskia was dammed

Amish Country Ramble

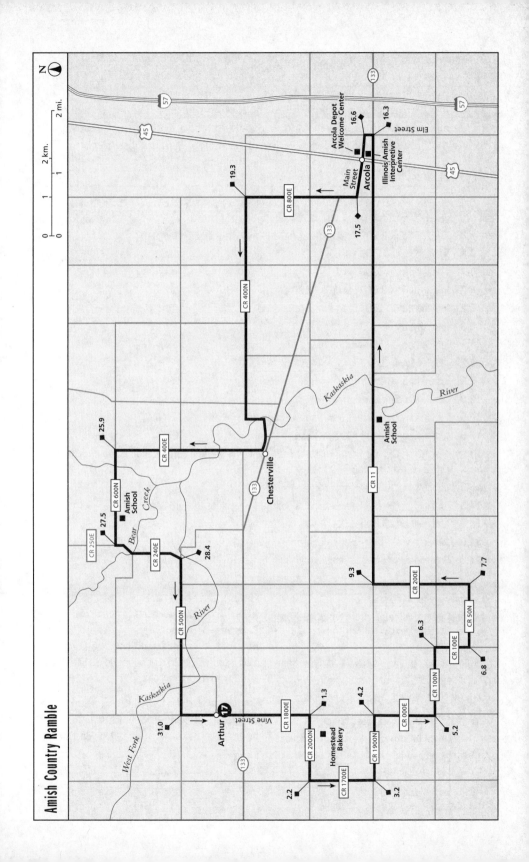

to create Carlyle Lake—the largest lake in the state—and Lake Shelbyville, the state's third-largest lake. The Kaskaskia River flows south into Lake Shelbyville just 10 miles downstream and enters Carlyle Lake about 75 miles to the south.

Back in Arthur, take the opportunity to explore this attractive little town that was founded by the Amish. Since Amish people live in Arthur and frequently pass through, you'll often hear the clippity-clop of horse hooves in the distance.

Miles and Directions

0.0 Start on Vine Street in Arthur, near the crossing of Progress Street. Vine Street turns into CR 1800 East (CR 000 East).

1.3 Turn right on CR 2000 North. (Homestead Bakery is ahead on the left.)

2.2 Turn left on CR 1700 East.

3.2 Turn left on CR 1900 North.

4.2 Turn right on CR 000 East (CR 1800 East).

5.2 Turn left on CR 100 North.

6.3 Turn right on CR 100 East.

6.8 Turn left on CR 50 North.

7.7 Turn left on CR 200 East.

9.3 Turn right on CR 11.

16.3 Turn left on Elm Street.

16.6 Turn left on Main Street, Arcola's downtown strip.

17.5 Turn right on SR 133 (CR 800 East).

19.3 Turn left on CR 400 North. Follow the road left as it becomes CR 26, then follow it to the right as it becomes CR 400 East.

25.9 Turn left on CR 600 North.

27.5 Turn left on CR 250 East. Stay left as this road becomes CR 240 East.

28.4 Turn right on CR 500 North.

31.0 Turn left on CR 000 East.

31.6 Return to the corner of Vine and Progress Streets.

Local Information

Arcola Depot Welcome Center: 135 North Oak St., Arcola; (217) 268-4530; www.arcola chamber.com.

Arthur/Amish Country Visitors Center: 106 East Progress St., Arthur; (800) 722-6474; www.illinoisamishcountry.com.

Local Events/Attractions

Illinois Amish Interpretive Center: Great place to learn more about the Amish in Illinois; includes a gift shop; 111 South Locust St., Arcola; (888) 452-6474; www.amishcenter.com.

Rockome Gardens: Sort of an Amish theme park, with buggy rides and homemade candy; 125 North CR 425 East, Arcola; (217) 268-4106; www.rockome.com.

Restaurants

The Dutch Kitchen: Good Amish-style food on the route in downtown Arcola; 127 East Main St., Arcola; (217) 268-3518.

Roselen's Coffees and Delights: Claims to be the only Amish-owned coffee shop in Illinois and possibly the world; 1045 East Columbia St. (SR 133), Arthur; (217) 543-3106.

Accommodations

Flower Patch Bed and Breakfast: 225 East Jefferson St., Arcola; (217) 268-4876; www .arcolaflowerpatch.com.

Bike Shops

Schlabach's Bike Shop and Discount Store: Amish-owned bike shop; rentals available; 109 East CR 500 North, Arthur; (217) 543-3493.

Restrooms

Start/finish: The Arthur/Amish Country Visitors Center at the corner of Vine and Progress Streets has restrooms and water. (Also, a gas station is located north on Vine Street.)

Mile 16.6: The Illinois Amish Interpretive Center has restrooms and water.

Mile 16.7: Arcola Depot Welcome Center has restrooms and water.

Maps

USGS: Arcola quad, Arthur quad.

DeLorme: Illinois Atlas & Gazetteer: Pages 63 and 64.

18 Bloomington Classic

This ride offers a delicious mix of small rural towns and scenic countryside northwest of Bloomington—much of it in the hilly landscape surrounding the Mackinaw River. The route also follows miles of long, straight, quiet farm roads that run by old farmhouses and barns. The first section of this ride takes you along Old Peoria Road, a local favorite among cyclists because of its rolling terrain and winding progression.

Start: West Route 9 Wayside, the western parking area for the section of the Constitutional Trail that runs west from Bloomington.
Length: 64.2 miles.
Terrain: The first 40 miles are dominated by rolling terrain, with occasional steep hills; the remainder is mostly flat farmland.

Traffic and hazards: At mile 25.7, use caution while riding for 0.4 mile on SR 117: This is a busy road with a narrow shoulder. Short stretches of busy roadway also occur along SR 9 and Dee-Mac Road; both of these roads have ample shoulders. At mile 36, you'll encounter 1.2 miles of dirt road.

Getting there: From I-55/74, exit at 160B and head west on US 150/SR 9. Park in the West Route 9 Wayside 2 miles ahead on the left. Coordinates for starting point: 16T 325124E 4483675N

The Ride

One of the highlights of this ride is the wooded hills and bluffs surrounding the Mackinaw River. At about 15 miles into the ride, north of Congerville, the hills begin to swell and multiply as you enter an area known as the Eureka Moraine. A moraine takes shape when an ice sheet advances at the same pace that it melts. As a result, the glacier acts as a conveyor belt, dropping off its load of rock, dirt, and debris—the stuff

Rolling hills, some of them sizable, appear near the Mackinaw River on the Bloomington Challenge.

of hills. The Eureka Moraine is part of a series of central Illinois moraines that ice sheets deposited between 15,000 and 20,000 years ago.

Before arriving at the Eureka Moraine, however, you'll enjoy the winding, rolling route along Old Peoria Road. Never straight for long, this one-time connector road between Bloomington and Peoria runs by agricultural land, patches of woodland, and rural homes. Just after the town of Danvers, the route leaves Old Peoria Road and heads north toward hillier scenery. After ducking under I-74 and climbing a small hill, you'll pass through the microscopic community of Congerville, which lays claim to the Prairie State's coldest recorded temperature of -36 degrees Fahrenheit on January 5, 1999.

North of Congerville, as you glide downhill toward the bridge over the Mackinaw River, look for the wetlands on the left and a herd of grazing elk on the hillside on the right. The bridge over the Mackinaw River offers a fine view of the serene 60-foot-wide, tree-lined river. A couple more turns brings you to CR 1625 East. This road cuts through a savanna and patches of grassland before offering up stunning views of the wooded hills to the south as you whiz down the hill to cross Walnut Creek.

The next highlight of the ride comes south of Deer Creek as you follow Cook Road down the steep, 150-foot wooded bluff into the Mackinaw River floodplain. At the bottom of the bluff, you'll pass by an idyllic farm set within an expanse of cropland cradled by hills. Leaving the cornfields, the road hugs the Mackinaw River for nearly a half mile within the Mackinaw River State Fish and Wildlife Area. Here

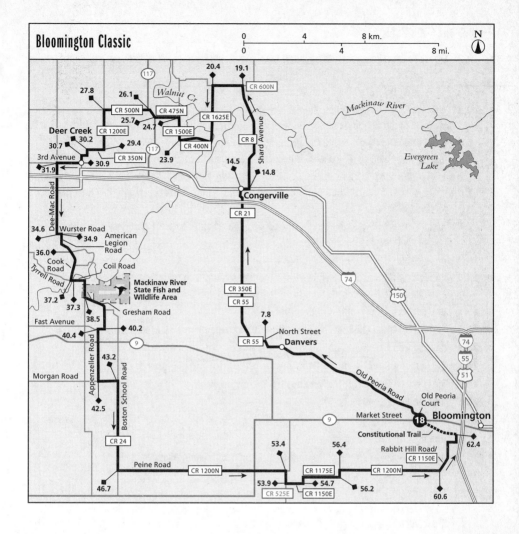

Bloomington Classic

you'll see big maples hanging over the river and great blue herons waiting for a meal in the rocky-bottom shallows. In some places you may want to hop off the bike to get a closer peek at this lush riparian landscape. The remainder of the passage through the fish and wildlife area brings you through grassland and savanna mixed with game fields used by hunters.

After this final encounter with the Mackinaw River, the route follows farm roads that run straight as rows of corn. Turning east toward Bloomington on CR 1200 North, watch for picturesque old barns and farmhouses sprinkled among the fields. These roads are so quiet, it may seem like you could take a nap in the middle of the road with little fear of getting roused. In other words, these roads are perfect for opening up the gates and riding hard with no worries about traffic. Traffic picks up some, but never gets too busy, as you get closer to Bloomington.

Miles and Directions

0.0   From the West Route 9 Wayside, head to the right on SR 9 (Market Street). Use the ample shoulder for the short stretch on this busy road.

0.3   Turn left on US 150/Mitsubishi Motorway.

0.5   Turn left on Old Peoria Court. There is no road sign, but the road is easy to locate because it's the first left heading north from SR 9.

1.1   Turn left on Old Peoria Road. Old Peoria Road is also given a long list of various numbered road names. While it may seem confusing, it's not. Just keep an eye out for the Old Peoria Road signs, and keep following the main curvy roadway as it angles northwest.

7.6   In Danvers, Old Peoria Road becomes Main Street. As Main Street curves right, it becomes Madison Street.

7.8   Turn left on CR 55 (North Street). Stay on CR 55 as it turns onto CR 350 East. This road eventually becomes CR 21.

14.5   Turn right on US 150 (Kaufman Street).

14.8   Turn left on CR 8 (Shard Avenue). Keep your senses tuned in on this road. While the traffic is minimal, the few vehicles tend to be big, fast-moving trucks.

19.1   Turn left on CR 600 North.

20.4   Turn left on CR 1625 East (becomes CR 400 North as the road curves right).

23.9   Turn right on CR 1500 East.

24.7   Turn left on CR 475 North.

25.7   Turn right on SR 117. This short stretch will likely be busy.

26.1   Turn left on CR 500 North.

27.8   Turn left on CR 1200 East.

29.4   Turn right on CR 350 North.

30.2   Turn left on CR 1125 East. This road turns into CR 325 North as it curves right.

30.7   Turn left on Camp Road.

30.9   Turn right on 3rd Avenue. Continue 2 more blocks on Camp Road to reach a gas station/convenience store; this is the final store for the remainder of the journey. Take a break at the small municipal park located on Main Street.

31.9   Turn left on Dee-Mac Road.

34.6   Continue straight ahead on Wurster Road as Dee-Mac Road curves right. The road sign is confusing because it looks like Dee-Mac Road continues straight. It does not.

34.9   Turn right on American Legion Road.

36.0   Turn right on Cook Road. Be careful: It's a steep descent on a gravel road.

37.2   Turn left on Tyrrell Road.

37.3   Turn left on Coil Road after crossing the bridge.

38.5   Turn left on Gresham Road.

40.2   Turn right on Fast Avenue.

40.4   Turn left on Appenzeller Road.

42.5   Turn left on Morgan Road.

43.2   Turn right on Boston School Road.

46.7	Turn left on Peine Road/CR 1200 North.
53.4	Turn right on CR 525 East.
53.9	Turn left on CR 1150 North.
54.7	Turn left on CR 600 East. This road becomes CR 1175 North as it curves to the right.
56.2	Turn left on CR 750 East.
56.4	Turn right on CR 1200 North.
60.6	Turn left on Rabbit Hill Road/CR 1150 East.
62.4	Turn left on the Constitutional Trail.
64.2	Return to the West Route 9 Wayside.

Local Information

Bloomington-Normal Area Convention and Visitors Bureau: 3201 CIRA Dr., Suite 201, Bloomington; (309) 665-0033 or (800) 433-8226; www.bloomingtonnormalcvb.org.

Local Events/Attractions

David Davis Mansion State Historic Site: Take a tour of this posh historic home once owned by a U.S. Supreme Court judge; 1000 East Monroe Dr., Bloomington; (309) 828-1084; http://daviddavismansion.org.

Upper Limits Rock Climbing Gym: Creatively makes use of five 65-foot-high grain silos; 1304 West Washington St., Bloomington; (309) 829-8255; www.upperlimits.com/bloomington.

Restaurants

The Garlic Press Market Cafe: Restaurant adjoins a cooking/gift store; heavy emphasis on fresh, healthy ingredients; 106 North St., Normal; (309) 852-0987; www.thegarlicpress.com.

Accommodations

Burr House Bed and Breakfast: Located across the street from Franklin Park; 210 East Chestnut St., Bloomington; (309) 828-4182; http://home.comcast.net/~leighton.cook/BurrHouse.

Chain hotels: Can be found along SR 9/US 150 between I-74/55 and the West Route 9 Wayside, where the ride starts.

Comlara County Park: Offers the best camping in the area; located 15 minutes north of Bloomington; 13001 Recreation Area Dr., Hudson; (309) 726-2025; www.mcleancountyil.gov/Parks/Camping.htm.

Bike Shops

Bloomington Cycle and Fitness: Knowledgeable staff; located on the Constitutional Trail in Bloomington; 712 East Empire St., Bloomington; (309) 820-8036; www.bloomingtoncycleandfitness.com.

Vitesse Cycle Shop: 206 South Linden St., Normal; (309) 454-1541; http://vitessecycle.com.

Restrooms

Start/finish: Portable restroom located at the parking area.

Mile 7.4: A water spigot and restrooms are in the municipal park in Danvers.

Mile 14.8: The gas station/convenience store in Congerville has restrooms.

Mile 31.0: Gas station/convenience store in Deer Creek on 1st Street and Camp Road.

Maps

USGS: Bloomington West quad, Danvers quad, Eureka quad, Mackinaw quad, Normal West quad, Stanford quad, Secor quad.

DeLorme: Illinois Atlas & Gazetteer: Pages 52, 42, 41, and 51.

19 Charleston Cruise

This ride takes you south of Charleston along quiet roads winding through the beautiful hilly woodlands that accompany the scenic Embarras River. After a bit of Lincolnia on the first leg of the ride, you'll zigzag through gently rolling farmland, cross a handful of creeks, and encounter prairie, bottomland, and plenty of hills. The final part of this tour explores Charleston, a pleasant historic town that hosts the campus of Eastern Illinois University.

Start: Sister City Park on the southeastern edge of Charleston. Charleston is located about 50 miles south of Champaign.
Length: 38.1 miles.

Terrain: Hilly areas mixed with gently rolling farmland.
Traffic and hazards: Most of these roads are very quiet. Closer to Charleston, traffic picks up a bit.

Getting there: Coming from the north or south along I-57, exit at SR 16 heading east (exit 190A). In Charleston, turn right on SR 130. Sister City Park is on the right. Coordinates for starting point: 16S 399849E 4369277N

The Ride

Charleston has a rich history for a town of only 20,000 or so souls. On the north side of Charleston, the fairgrounds have hosted the Coles County Fair continuously since 1854—making it the oldest county fair in the state. In its early years, the fairgrounds hosted speakers such as William Jennings Bryan, the evangelist preacher Billy Sunday, and one of the historic debates between Abraham Lincoln and Stephen Douglas in their campaign for the U.S. Senate. Adding to Charleston's charm is an impressive old courthouse located in the downtown historic district. Two other Charleston-area attractions that have contributed much to the local flavor—both of which you'll encounter on this ride—are the campus of Eastern Illinois University and a farm south of town once owned by Abraham Lincoln's father and stepmother.

As you make your way toward the Lincoln Log Cabin State Historic Site on the first quarter of this ride, you'll roller-coaster over a series of hills and bluffs that accompany the Embarras (pronounced *EM-brah*) River south of Charleston. The fun starts right away as you head south on 18th Street: Ravines on the left side of the road plunge 100 feet down toward the Embarras. The small cemetery on the left marks the beginning of a long downhill that carries you into the river valley and over Kickapoo Creek. Beyond the creek's banks of elm and walnut are big open spaces decorated with swaths of goldenrod and other prairie plants.

After the creek, get ready for a hearty climb out of the valley through thick, shadowy oak-hickory woodland that looks like it was created by the Brothers Grimm. Descend again and look for the Embarras River on the left as it winds through the

The rusting remains of an abandoned bridge appear on the way into Charleston.

pastureland. Plainview Road grows narrow as it cuts between the flat cropland on the left and the wooded bluff on the right.

The next part of the ride brings you by a couple of Lincoln-oriented historic spots that are less about Old Abe and more about his family and their community. The first site you'll encounter is the Moore House, a modest wood-frame house that belonged to Lincoln's stepsister, Matilda Johnson Hall Moore, and her husband. Another mile down the road sits the farm where Lincoln's father and stepmother lived and worked. Lincoln never lived in the area, but he visited regularly. Now the farm's got all the trappings of a living-history museum: There's a new visitor center with exhibits, a gift shop, picnicking areas, and costumed staff hanging out in a replica of the Lincolns' cabin (the original cabin was lost after being moved to Chicago's Columbian Exposition in 1892). A stone's throw from the Lincoln farm and cabin, the state opened up a neighboring historic farm to visitors. Fortunately, many of the exhibits within the park veer away from the Lincoln-slept-here brand of presidential hagiography and instead focus on the more engaging topic of Illinois rural life in the mid-1800s.

A few miles down the road, you'll cross a bridge over the Embarras River, followed by crossings of a handful of Embarras tributaries—Clear Creek, Opossum

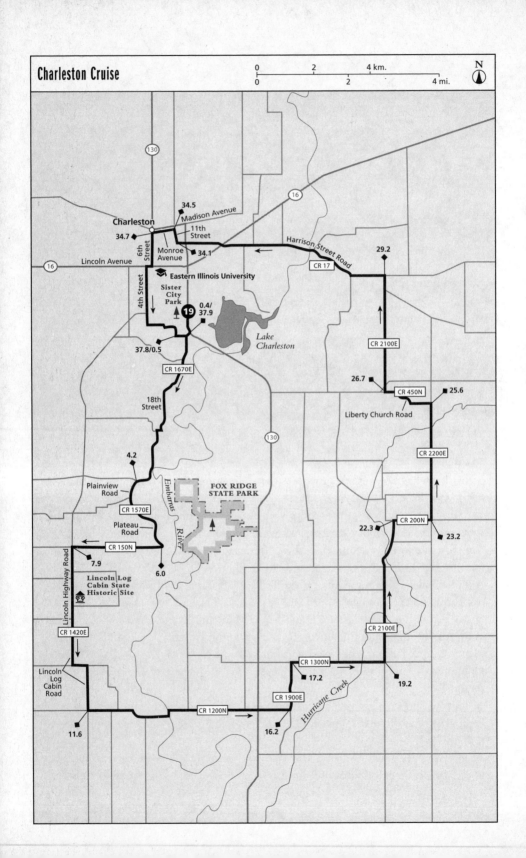

Charleston Cruise

0   2   4 km.

0   2   4 mi.

N

130

16

34.5 Madison Avenue

Charleston

34.7 11th Street

6th Street

34.1 Monroe Avenue

Harrison Street Road

29.2

CR 17

Lincoln Avenue

16

4th Street

Eastern Illinois University

Sister City Park

19 0.4/ 37.9

Lake Charleston

CR 2100E

37.8/0.5

26.7

CR 450N

25.6

CR 1670E

Liberty Church Road

18th Street

CR 2200E

130

4.2

Embarras River

FOX RIDGE STATE PARK

Plainview Road

CR 1570E

CR 200N

Plateau Road

22.3

23.2

CR 150N

7.9

6.0

Lincoln Log Cabin State Historic Site

Lincoln Highway Road

CR 2100E

CR 1420E

Lincoln Log Cabin Road

CR 1300N

17.2

19.2

CR 1900E

CR 1200N

Hurricane Creek

11.6

16.2

Creek, and Hurricane Creek—and their accompanying bottomlands. Heading north on CR 2100 East, the climbs start to grow in size. After crossing the West Branch of Hurricane Creek, the road leads you between an attractive stretch of prairie and a small ravine containing the creek. (To get closer to the creek, look for the hunters parking area on the left.)

The final leg of the ride takes you on a twisting scenic road that again crosses the wide, tree-lined Embarras. An attractive steel-trestle bridge now out of commission sits just north of the current bridge. Arriving in downtown Charleston, take a lap around the main square and enjoy the old courthouse, the historic district, and the folksy murals depicting the town's history.

Heading south from downtown, you'll pass Victorian houses and the occasional fraternity or sorority house as you ride toward the front door of the castlelike Old Main building at Eastern Illinois University. Heading through campus on the sidewalk to the right of Old Main brings you by a handful of residential buildings, the science building, the gymnasium, and the library—as well as some pleasant grassy lawns. The last couple of miles lead you through residential areas on your way back to SR 130 and Sister City Park.

Miles and Directions

0.0 Head right on SR 130 from Sister City Park.

0.4 Turn right on CR 610 North (Nursery Road).

0.5 Turn left on 18th Street (CR 1670 East).

4.2 Turn left on Plainview Road (CR 1570 East). Stay on the paved road as Plainview Road turns into Plateau Road.

6.0 Climb the hill and bear right on CR 150 North. There is no sign identifying CR 150 North.

7.9 Turn left on Lincoln Highway Road (CR 1420 East). The Moore Home State Memorial is on the right. Soon, this road turns into Lincoln Log Cabin Road.

9.0 The Lincoln Log Cabin State Historical Site is on the left.

11.6 Turn left on CR 1200 North.

16.2 Turn left on CR 1900 East.

17.2 Turn right on CR 1300 North.

19.2 Turn left on CR 2100 E. On some signs, this road is identified as CR 5.

22.3 Turn right on CR 200 North.

23.2 Turn left on CR 2200 East.

25.6 Turn left on CR 450 North (Liberty Church Road).

26.7 Turn right on CR 2100 East.

29.2 Turn left on Harrison Street Road (CR 17).

34.1 Turn right on 11th Street.

34.5 Turn left on Monroe Avenue.

34.7 Turn left on 6th Street.

35.4 At Lincoln Avenue, 6th Street runs into Eastern Illinois University's Old Main Building. Take the sidewalk to the right of the building and head south through campus. After a half mile of cutting through campus on the sidewalk, make your way to the right over to 4th Street and keep heading south.

36.7 As the road curves left, 4th Street turns into Nursery Road.

37.8 Turn left on SR 130.

38.1 Return to Sister City Park.

Local Information

City of Charleston: 520 Jackson Ave., Charleston; (217) 348-0430; www.charlestontourism.org.

Local Events/Attractions

Charleston historic downtown: Plenty of shops are located around the courthouse; (217) 348-0430; www.charlestontourism.org.

Lincoln-Douglas Debate Museum: Small museum at the Coles County Fairgrounds exploring the debates; 126 E St., Charleston; (217) 345-7919.

Lincoln Log Cabin State Historic Site: 400 South Lincoln Highway Rd., Lerna; (217) 345-1845; www.lincolnlogcabin.org.

Restaurants

Bangkok Thai: Good food and a pleasant atmosphere; 1140 Lincoln Ave., Charleston; (217) 348-1232; www.bangkokthaicharleston.com.

Jackson Avenue Coffee: Serves up the good stuff in a great downtown location; 708 Jackson Ave., Charleston; (217) 345-5283; www.jacksonavenuecoffee.com.

Accommodations

Days Inn Charleston: Clean and affordable; 810 West Lincoln Ave., Charleston; (217) 345-7689.

The Osage Inn: Guests stay in a 1860s log home; 13444 East CR 720 North, Charleston; (217) 345-2622.

Bike Shops

Bike and Hike: 959 18th St., Charleston; (217) 345-1316; www.bikeandhikeweb.com.

Restrooms

Start/finish: Sister City Park has restrooms and water.

Mile 9.0: The Lincoln Log Cabin State Historic Site has flush toilets, water, and picnic areas.

Mile 33.0: An assortment of restaurants and gas stations are available in Charleston.

Maps

USGS: Charleston South quad, Westfield West quad, Toledo quad, Union Center quad.

DeLorme: Illinois Atlas & Gazetteer: Page 72.

20 Crow Creek Ramble

Looking for a short, scenic ride in central Illinois? Want minimal hills? How about a ride where you're likely to see more people sitting on their porches than driving in their cars? Well, the roads through the gentle hills and bluffs in the Illinois River Valley northeast of Peoria should fit the bill. A great ride for beginners, it follows peaceful winding roads through farm country and large swaths of scenic woodland.

Start: The parking lot for the Marshall State Fish and Wildlife Area hiking trails, located 5 miles south of Lacon.
Length: 16 miles.

Terrain: Rolling hills, floodplain, and flat farmland.
Traffic and hazards: Particularly at the beginning and end of this ride, watch for farm equipment on the road.

Getting there: From I-74 in Peoria, take US 150/SR 116 north to SR 26. Turn left on SR 26 and follow it to Richland Road. Turn right on Richland Road, then take another right on Blue Heron Road. Park in the lot on the right for the Marshall State Fish and Wildlife Area hiking trails. To reach the starting point from I-39 to the east, exit at SR 17 and head west. In Lacon, turn left on SR 26. Turn left on Richland Road, then turn right on Blue Heron Road. Coordinates for starting point: 16T 296511E 4536904N

The Ride

As the Illinois River cuts through central Illinois, wooded bluffs sporadically rise up on each side of the river, creating a series of dramatic valleys. At times the bluffs rise within a stone's throw of the river; in other places, the bluffs appear a mile or two away from the water. This ride starts a half mile from the river on a bluff that nearly meets the river's edge. While you won't see the Illinois River on this ride, you can enjoy the fact that its tributaries helped shape the lovely rolling hills and valleys you'll be exploring.

The low mileage and quiet roads on this ride makes it perfect for beginners or riders more interested in a jaunt than an expedition. Still, the ride's not without its challenges. You can put your legs to the test on three short but steep uphill sections. Since the traffic is very light on these roads, riders should feel comfortable hopping off the bike and walking uphill if they so desire. The only downside of this ramble is the lack of roadside amenities. No bother, though—the ride is short enough to make the lack of services a minor issue.

After a pokey start that leads you through a couple of miles of flat farmland, the route picks up speed and sends you on a steep, scenic descent. At the bottom of the hill, you'll see some facilities owned by the Sun Foundation, an organization that offers art and science programs to local children and families. The next couple of miles of pedaling lead you through some remarkably pretty bottomlands surrounding Crow

Creek: You'll see wetland grasses swaying in the breeze, cottonwood trees wrapped with vines, and oak- and maple-clad bluffs swelling up around you.

Continuing along Washburn Road, the road is flanked by a wooded bluff on the left and Snag Creek on the right. After crossing the rocky-bottomed Snag Creek and passing a few stately old barns, you'll leave the bottomlands and head up one of the few steep climbs on the route. On the way, keep an eye out for bluebirds: They're drawn to pastures and open areas along these lightly traveled roadsides.

The route north from Washburn Road takes a couple of pleasant dips in the process of making a second crossing of both Snag Creek and Crow Creek. The crossing of Crow Creek occurs at a scenic spot where gravelly tongues of land reach into the widening creek. If you're looking for a rest stop, this would be a nice place to linger. After making both of these creek crossings, the road winds upward. The climb after Crow Creek is a steep one, and may prompt beginners to walk their bikes.

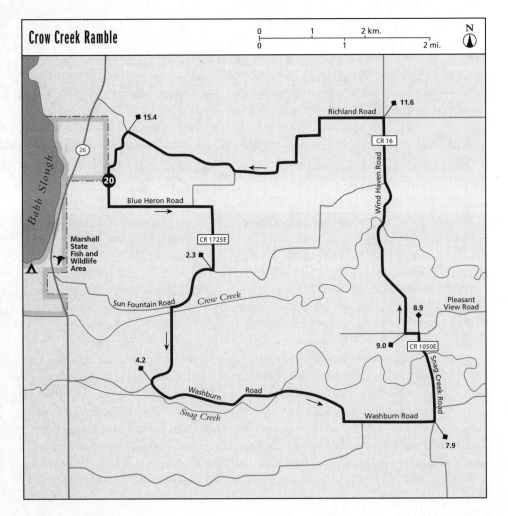

A couple of miles after turning on Richland Road, the road traces a lovely ravine as it descends a bluff. This is one of those exhilarating downhill stretches where you may have trouble deciding how to proceed. Do you squeeze the brakes so that you can fully appreciate the maple- and oak-laden bluffs rising from the edge of the road? Or do you let the wheels spin, crouch over the bars, and allow gravity to have its way? Either way, keep in mind that as soon as you round the base of the bluff and turn onto Blue Heron Road, you've got a hearty climb.

While climbing nearly 200 feet on Blue Heron Road, a stunning ravine opens up at the edge of the pavement on the left. Unless you have bionic legs, you needn't worry about slowing your speed to appreciate the view. A couple of quick turns at the top of the bluff bring you back to the starting point.

Miles and Directions

0.0 From the parking lot for the Marshall State Fish and Wildlife Area hiking trails, turn right on Blue Heron Road. After a couple of turns, Blue Heron Road turns into CR 1725 East.

2.3 Turn right on Sun Fountain Road.

3.1 Turn left on Washburn Road; cross the railroad tracks and Crow Creek.

4.2 Take Washburn Road to the left as it splits. Cross Snag Creek.

7.9 Turn left on Snag Creek Road/CR 1050 East. Cross Snag Creek again.

8.9 Turn left on Pleasant View Road.

9.0 Turn right on Wind Haven Road/CR 16. Cross Crow Creek.

11.6 Turn left on Richland Road.

15.4 Turn left on Blue Heron Road.

16.0 Return to parking lot.

Local Information

Peoria Area Convention & Visitors Bureau: 456 Fulton St., Suite 300, Peoria; (800) 747-0302; www.peoria.org.

Local Events/Attractions

Marshall State Fish and Wildlife Area: The starting point for this ride is the trailhead for more than 3 miles of hiking along the bluffs overlooking the Illinois River; camping is available in the main section of the wildlife area on SR 26; RR 1, Box 238, Lacon; (309) 246-8351; http://dnr.state.il.us/lands/landmgt/parks/r1/marshall.htm.

Metamora Courthouse State Historic Site: The 1845 courthouse is where Abraham Lincoln practiced law and handled more than seventy cases; located on the town square; 113 East Partridge St., Metamora; (309) 367-4470; www.metamorail.org.

Restaurants

Aztekita Restaurant: Good Mexican food on the town square; 128 North Davenport St., Metamora; (309) 367-2600.

Accommodations

Mission Oak Inn Bed and Breakfast: On the spendy side but quite nice; 1108 CR 930 East, Henry; (309) 470-4083; www.missionoakinn.com.

Woodford State Fish and Wildlife Area: Best nearby camping option; on the shore of the Illinois River, the area attracts waterfowl and anglers; RR 1, Low Point; (309) 822-8861; http://dnr.state.il.us/lands/landmgt/parks/r1/woodford.htm.

Bushwhacker: Combination bike, outdoors, and patio furniture shop has a loyal following in the area; 4700 North University in the Metro Centre, Peoria; (309) 692-4812; http://bush whacker.com.

Restrooms

No restrooms or water are on this route, but you can find them at the Marshall State Fish and Wildlife Area campground a couple of miles south of Richland Road on SR 26. Also, services are available in the town of Lacon, just 5 miles north on SR 26.

Maps

USGS: Chillicothe quad, Washburn quad
DeLorme: Illinois Atlas & Gazetteer: Page 41.

21 Evergreen Lake–Lake Bloomington Cruise

While exploring the shoreline of two lakes north of Bloomington, plan for a picnic at any one of a handful of attractive parks along the way. The quiet rural roads between the lakes are decorated with small farms, old barns, and big spreads of cropland.

Start: The beach house parking area at Comlara County Park, located 10 miles north of Bloomington.
Length: 35.3 miles.

Terrain: You'll encounter lake shoreline farmland that is flat and gently rolling.
Traffic and hazards: While traffic is minimal on all of these roads, be cautious on the winding road that loops around Lake Bloomington.

Getting there: North of Bloomington-Normal, exit I-39 on CR 2500 North and drive west. Turn left on Comlara Park Road; the entrance to the park is on the right. Follow the signs to the beach. Coordinates for starting point: 16T 328013E 4500231N

The Ride

Just north of the twin cities of Bloomington–Normal are a pair of scenic lakes called Evergreen Lake and Lake Bloomington. As with nearly every other lake in central and southern Illinois, these two were created by damming streams and rivers. Now the lakes serve the dual purpose of recreation spot and municipal water source. Lake Bloomington was constructed in 1929 and has a water treatment plant on its shore. Evergreen Lake was constructed in the 1960s; water from Evergreen is pumped to Lake Bloomington for treatment. Each lake claims a unique atmosphere: Lake Bloomington hosts a mixture of residences (many of them fairly upscale), summer camps, parks, and nature preserves. Evergreen Lake, on the other hand, is surrounded by 2,200 acres of rolling wooded terrain and wetlands that comprise Comlara County Park.

Starting to ride counterclockwise around the lake from Comlara Park's main recreation area, you'll soon have big views of the lake's wooded shoreline. While riding along the shoreline, watch for hawks perched in trees above the roadside, as well as rafts

Denman Cemetery is named after an early settler from the area.

of waterbirds in the lake. A grassy picnic area appears as you reach the earthen dam that blocks outflow of the lake via Sixmile Creek. (The dam was elevated 5 feet in 1995, increasing the lake's storage capacity by 36 percent.) Before leaving Comlara Park and Evergreen Lake, you'll pass several trailheads for hiking and mountain biking.

After a few turns, suddenly it seems you're deep into Illinois corn country. If traveling these roads in late summer, the high stalks and narrow road create the effect of passing through a tunnel of corn. On the way to Lake Bloomington, the agricultural landscape is broken up now and then with points of interest. Before turning onto East 2250 Road North, you'll pass the postage-stamp-size Denman Cemetery, named after one of the county's early settlers. A couple of turns later, on the way into the village of Hudson, the road accompanies a pleasant stretch of grassland and oak savanna. On the other side of Hudson, large barns of various shapes pepper the roadside.

On CR 2250 North, Lake Bloomington is visible through the trees before the road drops down to cross a bridge over one of the lake's fingers. Mostly wetland surrounded by lush bottomland woods, this is a great spot to look for herons and other waterbirds. Up ahead, the road winds through a dense grove of hickory and walnut trees and then passes dozens of small wood buildings that comprise East Bay Camp, a Christian camp that's been around since the beginning of Lake Bloomington. The camp's white chapel on the right was built in a different spot in 1869 and then moved to its present location ninety-five years later.

Evergreen Lake–Lake Bloomington Cruise

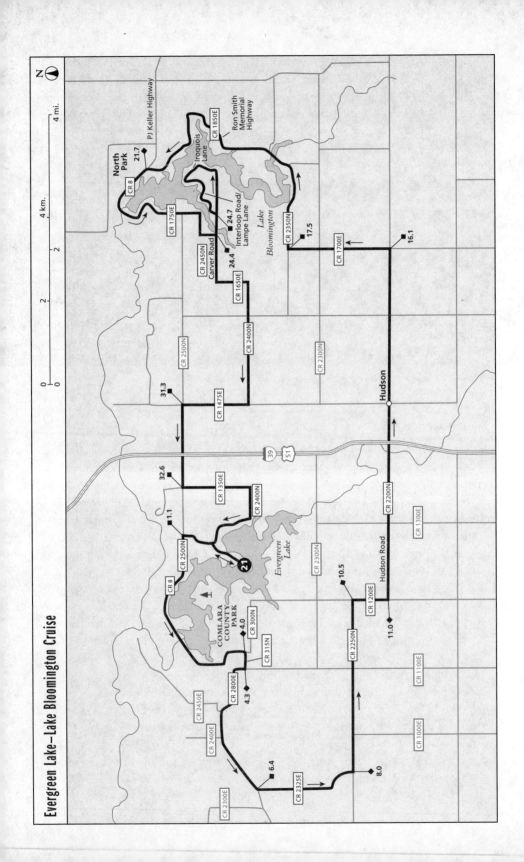

Turning left on PJ Keller Highway and crossing one of the lake's dams leads you by two lovely parks. At North Park, stately oak trees rise above rolling grassy lawns. Closer to the shore, stellar picnicking spots are located on a small bluff above the water. After crossing the pedestrian bridge over the Money Creek Spillway, you'll pass over a large dam, turn left after the water treatment facility, and enter the impressive gates of Hubbard Park. The castlelike water plant purifies water from Lake Bloomington and pumps it 14 miles to the city reservoir. A small bluff, located between the boat launch on the left and a marina on the right, offers pleasant views of the lake.

Down the road, you'll pass a 75-foot steel structure that looks like a fire tower, but it was actually used to direct night flights between Chicago and Saint Louis. In operation for only eleven years, it was built in 1939 as part of a string of seven beacon towers between Joliet and Springfield.

After crossing another arm of the lake and turning onto Lampe Lane, you'll embark on a short and scenic road that snakes along the hilly, densely wooded shoreline of the lake. This mile-long stretch through protected land has several trails on the left leading to the shoreline of the lake. Many picnicking spots also appear along the way. Turning on to Iroquois Lane and then Carver Road brings you by a swath of tallgrass prairie that has been restored by a local organization that works to preserve and restore open land.

The route back to Comlara Park takes you along peaceful farm roads to the I-39 overpass. As you approach Evergreen Lake, Deer Island appears just offshore. Sprinkled throughout this section of the lake are dead trees—likely the remnants of the most recent boost in the lake's water level. If you're riding on a hot summer day, the beach awaits your return.

Miles and Directions

0.0 Start at the beach house parking area in Comlara County Park.

0.6 Turn left on Comlara Park Road/CR 1275 East.

1.1 Turn left on CR 8/CR 2500 North.

4.0 Turn right on Township Road 315 North.

4.3 Turn right on CR 2800 East.

6.4 Turn left on CR 2325 East.

8.0 Turn left on CR 2250 North.

10.5 Turn right on CR 1200 East.

11.0 Turn left on CR 2200 North/Hudson Road.

13.8 Pass through the town of Hudson.

16.1 Turn left on CR 1700 East.

17.5 Turn right on CR 2350 North.

21.7 Turn left on PJ Keller Highway. Follow the road through North Park as it parallels the highway, then cross the pedestrian bridge over the spillway. After crossing the bridge, turn left into Hubbard Park and stay to the left to reach CR 1750 East.

24.4	Turn left on CR 2450 North/Carver Road.
24.7	Turn left on Interloop Road/Lampe Lane. Stay to the right as Interloop Road turns into Iroquois Lane and then becomes CR 2450 North/Carver Road. CR 2450 North curves left and becomes CR 1650 East, curves right and becomes CR 2400 North, and then curves right again to become CR 1475 East.
31.3	Turn left on CR 2500 North/Lake Bloomington Road.
32.6	Turn left on CR 1350 East.
34.7	Turn left into Comlara County Park.
35.3	Return to the beach parking lot.

Local Information

Bloomington-Normal Area Convention and Visitors Bureau: 3201 CIRA Dr., Suite 201, Bloomington; (309) 665-0033 or (800) 433-8226; www.bloomingtonnormalcvb.org.

Local Events/Attractions

David Davis Mansion State Historic Site: Take a tour of this posh historic home once owned by a U.S. Supreme Court judge; 1000 East Monroe Dr., Bloomington; (309) 828-1084; http://david davismansion.org.

Mud, Sweat, and Gears: Annual mountain bike race held in early September on the extensive biking trails at Comlara County Park; www.comlara mtb.com.

Restaurants

Green Gables: Bar/restaurant with standard food and friendly staff; 17485 East 2500 North Rd., Hudson; (309) 747-2496.

Accommodations

Burr House Bed and Breakfast: Located across the street from Franklin Park; 210 East Chestnut St., Bloomington; (309) 828-4182; http:// home.comcast.net/~leighton.cook/BurrHouse.

Chain hotels: A few have set up shop along SR 9/US 150 near I-74/55.

Comlara County Park: Bounty of campsites; the best are the walk-in sites located right on Evergreen Lake; 13001 Recreation Area Dr., Hudson; (309) 726-2025; http://www.mclean countyil.gov/Parks/Camping.htm.

Bike Shops

Bloomington Cycle and Fitness: Knowledgeable staff; shop is located on the Constitutional Trail in Bloomington; 712 East Empire St., Bloomington; (309) 820-8036; www.blooming toncycleandfitness.com.

Vitesse Cycle Shop: 206 South Linden St., Normal; (309) 454-1541; http://vitessecycle.com.

Restrooms

Start/finish: Comlara County Park beach house has restrooms and water.

Mile 3.8: A vault toilet is available at the mountain bike staging area.

Mile 13.8: A gas station/convenience store in Hudson has restrooms.

Mile 22.0: North Park and Hubbard Park have restrooms.

Maps

USGS: Gridley quad, Normal East quad, El Paso quad, Normal West quad.

DeLorme: Illinois Atlas & Gazetteer: Page 42.

22 Illinois River Cruise

One of the highlights of this ride is a generous stretch of roadway that offers outstanding views along a wide swath of the Illinois River. Another attraction—just after the ride's halfway point—is the choice of baked goods, sandwiches, fruits, and other tasty items available at Tanners Orchard, a local institution that combines an orchard with a bakery, a restaurant, and a sort of kiddie theme park. Sprinkled between these landmarks are wooded bluffs, prairies, twisting streams, and pleasantly rolling farmland.

Start: Shore Acres Park, located at the south end of Chillicothe.
Length: 42.7 miles.
Terrain: The majority of this route is flat or gently rolling. You will do some climbing in the vicinity of the bluff that runs parallel to the Illinois River.

Traffic and hazards: While riding near the Caterpillar Technical Center on Cloverdale Road, be ready for traffic if work shifts are changing. Watch for large farm machinery, especially on the long stretch of Anderson Road and CR 1700 East. SR 17 does not contain heavy traffic but it moves fast, so keep to the right.

Getting there: From I-74 in Peoria, head north on SR 29 and follow it all the way to Chillicothe. Turn right on Cloverdale Road, then take the first right on 2nd Street (unmarked). The entrance to Shore Acres Park is just ahead on the left. The park clubhouse building is straight ahead; park to the left of it. From I-39, take SR 17 east to Lacon. Cross the Illinois River, then turn left on SR 29. In Chillicothe, turn left on Cloverdale Road. Coordinates for starting point: 16T 290301E 4530952N

The Ride

People who enjoy following the routes of rivers will be thrilled for the first 5 miles of this ride as it accompanies one of the state's major waterways, the Illinois River. But this stretch of the Illinois offers little resemblance to a typical river: At about 1.5 miles wide, it looks more like a big lake slowly flowing through a wide valley south to Peoria.

The starting point for this ride, Shore Acres Park, occupies a stretch of river shoreline located opposite a long, thin island that runs parallel to the shore. The position of the island conceals the river's full size. But a mile or so south of Shore Acres Park, when the road begins to closely trace the river's shoreline on River Beach Road, stunning views open up, revealing the river's full dimensions. While admiring the wooded bluffs on the opposite shore, you'll likely see motorboats and the occasional river barge pushed by a tug. Along the road, small patches of woodland are mixed in with modest residential dwellings.

As you leave the river and turn west, you'll pass by the Caterpillar Technical Center, where the heavy equipment manufacturer performs research, development, and testing of its diesel engines. (Headquartered in the Peoria area, Caterpillar is by far the area's largest local employer.)

The Illinois River Cruise hugs the shore of the Illinois River for about 5 miles.

Once on Sante Fe Road, the route starts climbing the bluff. As it flows through central Illinois, much of the Illinois River is accompanied by nearby bluffs. In some places, such as Peoria, the bluffs sit right next to the river, but in this area, the bluffs are situated several miles back. Reaching the top of this bluff, occasional openings in the woodland reveal expansive views on each side of the road. The undulations of the landscape become gentler and farmland reappears as you approach the hamlet of Edelstein. As you continue north along Anderson Road, there are several spots that grant pleasant views of the gently rolling pastoral landscape speckled with farms and trees.

The goat and llama pasture on the right marks your arrival at Tanners Orchard, which offers a smorgasbord for the hungry cyclist. Members of the Illinois Valley Wheelm'n, a local cycling club that has been pedaling this route for a number of years, say Tanners is unsurpassed as a destination for carb-loading on baked goods. "My favorite is the apple bread pudding topped with nuts and drizzled caramel," reports Wheelm'n member Cathy Wilber.

From Tanners Orchard the route heads back toward Chillicothe and down the bluff through scenic stretches of woodland and prairie. Since the rest of the route offers little in the way of parks and roadside businesses at which to take a break, you may consider pulling off at one of the pleasant creek crossings. A particularly nice spot is the bridge over Little Senachwine Creek on CR 550 North. At the bottom of the bluff, it's a short, flat ride back to Chillicothe.

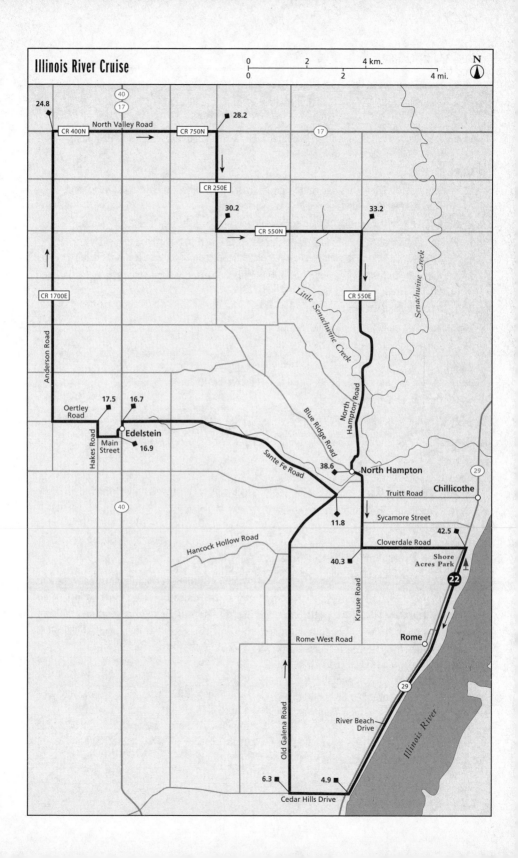

Miles and Directions

0.0 From Shore Acres Park, turn left on River Beach Drive.

4.9 Turn right on SR 29 and then immediately left on Cedar Hills Drive.

6.3 Turn right on Old Galena Road.

11.8 Stay right as Old Galena Road becomes Truitt Road, then turn left on North Hampton Road. Follow Sante Fe Road to the left.

16.7 Turn left on SR 40.

16.9 Turn right on Edelstein Road and follow it through Edelstein as it turns into Main Street. Pass a small community park with a picnic shelter.

17.5 Turn right on Hakes Road, which curves left and becomes Oertley Road.

18.8 Turn right on Anderson Road. This intersection is not marked but is easy to identify because there's an airstrip at the intersection. Anderson Road soon becomes CR 1700 East.

24.8 Turn right on North Valley Road (CR 400 North). Just ahead the road changes to SR 17/CR 750 North.

26.1 Reach Tanners Orchard.

28.2 Turn right on CR 250 East/CR 13.

30.2 Turn left on CR 550 North/CR 18.

33.2 Turn right on CR 550 East/North Hampton Road.

38.6 Stay left on Blue Ridge Road, which turns into Krause Road.

40.3 Turn left on Cloverdale Road.

42.5 Take the first right after crossing SR 29 (the street—2nd Street—is unmarked). Fifty yards ahead on the left, follow the sidewalk into Shore Acres Park.

42.7 Return to the parking area.

Local Information

City of Chillicothe Marketing and Tourism: 908 North 2nd St., Chillicothe; (309) 274-5056; www.ci.chillicothe.il.us.

Peoria Area Convention & Visitors Bureau: 456 Fulton St., Suite 300, Peoria; (800) 747-0302; www.peoria.org.

Local Events/Attractions

Tanners Orchard: Lures in people from all around for the fresh fruit, preserves, bakery, U-pick orchards, and plenty of kid-oriented attractions, including a goat and llama pasture; open July 16 to November 30; 740 SR 40, Speer; (309) 493-5442; www.tannersorchard.com.

Three Sisters Park: Located just south of Chillicothe, this park hosts a handful of annual events including a bluegrass music festival in June, Farm Heritage Days in August, and a haunted house in October; 17189 SR 29, Chillicothe; (866) 278-8837; www.threesisterspark.com.

Restaurants

Grecian Gardens: Standard American fare with some Greek dishes mixed in; not so inviting on the outside, but the food is good and the staff is friendly; 304 South Plaza Park, Chillicothe; (309) 274-6616.

River Beach Pub and Eatery: Bar food on the Illinois River; 13637 North River Beach Dr., Chillicothe; (309) 579-2535; www.riverbeachpub.com.

Tanners Orchard Bakery: Sells sandwiches and, of course, pies; see contact info above.

Accommodations

Jubilee College State Park: Many campsites; 13015 West Fussner Rd., Brimfield; (309) 446-3758; http://dnr.state.il.us/lands/landmgt/parks/r1/jubilee.htm.

Old Church House Inn: Bed-and-breakfast located in a restored church; 1416 East Mossville Rd., Mossville; (309) 579-2300.

Super 8: Convenient location is very close to the start of the ride; 615 South 4th St., Chillicothe; (309) 274-2568.

Bike Shops

Bushwhacker: Combination bike, outdoors, and patio furniture shop has a loyal following in the area; 4700 North University in the Metro Centre, Peoria; (309) 692-4812; http//bushwhacker.com.

Restrooms

Start/finish: Shore Acres Park has restrooms in the water park building.

Mile 26.1: Restrooms are available at Tanners Orchard.

Maps

USGS: Rome quad, La Prairie Center quad, Castleton quad, Edelstein quad, Spring Bay quad.

DeLorme: Illinois Atlas & Gazetteer: Pages 41 and 33.

23 Jubilee College Challenge

This classic central Illinois ride provides a thorough introduction to the pastoral landscape of western Peoria County. Memorable hills and vales greet you in the first and final miles of the ride. In between, the gently undulating farmland is broken up by creeks, small towns, and abandoned strip mines now covered in grassland and filled with occasional small lakes and ponds.

Start: Park at the picnic shelter on the left as you enter Jubilee College State Historic Site.

Length: 44.8 miles.

Terrain: Gently rolling farmland dominates this route, but there are enough hills at the beginning and the end to make it a challenge for many beginning riders.

Traffic and hazards: US 150 at the beginning of the ride and Brimfield-Jubilee Road at the end are both busy roads.

Getting there: From I-74 in Peoria, head northwest to exit 82. Turn right on Kickapoo-Edwards Road, then left on US 150. Turn right on Princeville-Jubilee Road (follow the signs for the Jubilee College State Historic Site). Turn left on Jubilee College Road and follow it into the historic site. Park in the first lot on the left at the picnic shelter. Coordinates for starting point: 16T 265595E 4521979N

The Ride

It's for good reason that Peoria–area cycling groups have been happily turning their pedals along these roads for more than thirty years. The route offers a taste of the rural bliss that keeps many central Illinoisans firmly rooted in the area: In between pleasant little towns, you'll encounter generous helpings of wooded hills and grasslands mixed with peaceful rolling farmland. Topping it off is an interesting starting point at the historic grounds of Jubilee College State Park.

The historic building that housed Jubilee College from 1840 to 1871 is a stone's throw from the parking area where this ride begins. Set within rolling grassy grounds studded with large old oaks is the two-story Gothic Revival building that has been thoroughly restored by the state. The school was founded as a seminary for Episcopal ministers heading westward, but it ended up primarily serving as a boarding high school. Philander Chase, founder of Jubilee (as well as Kenyon College in Ohio), drew up plans to build an elaborate campus, but they never came to fruition for lack of funding. Chase exerted tight control over all the goings-on at the college, and after his death is 1852, the school steadily declined.

The ride starts with a brief tour of this attractive state park. Immediately upon leaving the historic site, the park road drops steeply—a 13 percent grade—through dense woodland on its way down to Jubilee Creek. While following the winding road through the southern section of the 3,200-acre park, you'll pass a series of picnicking spots and the entrance to the park's camping area.

After contending with traffic along a brief stretch of US 150 and then ducking under I-74, you'll encounter a ribbony stretch of Kickapoo Creek followed by a short, steep hill that appears from a distance to be a vertical wall of pavement. At the top, claim the reward: an expansive view of the hilly, wooded landscape to the east.

The road takes a big dip before crossing SR 8; after SR 8, watch your speed on a couple of sharp turns on short downhill sections. The many ponds, long narrow lakes, and accompanying mounds on the way to Elmwood reveal the area's strip-mining past. Surface mining for coal was widespread in this area from the 1950s to the 1970s (the last Peoria-area strip-mining operation closed in 1996). Underground coal mines also operated locally: Hanna City hosted an active underground mine during the early twentieth century. Now only a handful of surface and underground coal mines exist in Illinois, mostly in the southern part of the state.

Elmwood hosts a pleasant town square containing a bandstand and a sculpture by Laredo Taft, who was born in the town in 1860. Taft was perhaps the most prominent sculptor in Illinois in the early twentieth century. His most well-known works are the 100-foot-long *Fountain of Time* at the University of Chicago and the 50-foot-tall Black Hawk statue near Oregon, Illinois. His sculpture in Elmwood, *The Pioneers,* unveiled in 1928, honors the men and women who "bridged the streams, subdued the soil and founded a state."

On the way out of Elmwood, you'll pass a small Laredo Taft museum situated within one of the spacious Victorian houses just off Magnolia Street. Outside of Elmwood on Tiber Creek Road, watch for the rambling lawn on the right that has been adorned with an array of carefully arranged plants, trees, and flowers.

After Brimfield, you'll have the pleasure of roller-coasting along a 5.5-mile stretch of Brimfield-Jubilee Road that takes you back to Jubilee College State Park. The hills

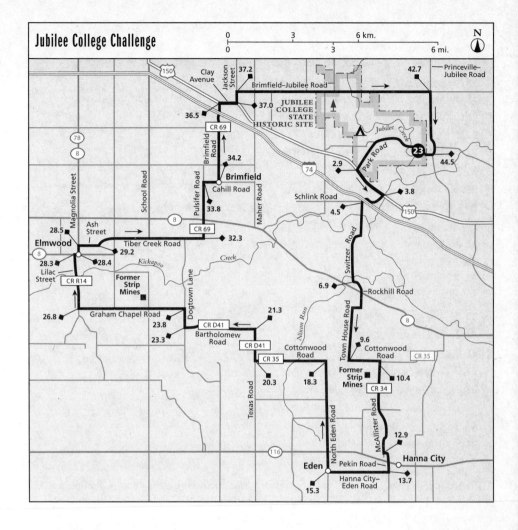

Jubilee College Challenge

0   3   6 km.

0   3   6 mi.

N

are steep and intense, but not very high: If you gather some steam on the way down one hill, you can usually make it halfway up the next one without much effort.

Miles and Directions

0.0   In Jubilee College State Historic Site, turn left on the road that drops down the hill and heads through the park.

2.9   Leaving the state park, turn left on US 150. Watch for traffic.

3.8   Turn right on Schlink Road.

4.5   Turn left on Switzer Road.

6.9   Turn left on Rockhill Road. South of SR 8, this road turns into Town House Road. Watch your speed on the sharp turns.

9.6   Turn left on West Cottonwood Road/CR 35.

10.4	Turn right on McAllister Road/CR 34. No road sign is posted at this intersection—it's the first right turn after turning onto West Cottonwood Road.
12.9	Turn left on Pekin Road. This turn comes at the bottom of a dip—watch your speed.
13.7	Turn right on Hanna City–Eden Road.
15.3	Turn right on North Eden Road (the road sign is difficult to read because it has faded).
18.3	Turn left on West Cottonwood Road/CR 35.
20.3	Turn right on Texas Road/CR D41.
21.3	Turn left on Bartholomew Road/CR D41.
23.3	Turn right on Dogtown Lane.
23.8	Turn left on Graham Chapel Road.
26.8	Turn right on CR R14 (name changes to Lilac Street in Elmwood).
28.3	Turn right on Main Street (SR 8/78).
28.4	Turn left on Magnolia Street (SR 8/78).
28.5	Turn right on Ash Street.
29.2	Turn left on Tiber Creek Road
32.3	Turn left on Pulsifer Road/CR 69.
33.8	Turn right on Cahill Road.
34.2	Turn left on Brimfield Road/CR 69.
36.5	Turn right on Clay Avenue.
37.0	Turn left on Jackson Street.
37.2	Turn right on Brimfield-Jubilee Road.
42.7	Turn right on Princeville-Jubilee Road.
44.5	Turn right on Jubilee College Road.
44.8	Return to the parking lot.

Local Information

Peoria Area Convention & Visitors Bureau: 456 Fulton St., Suite 300, Peoria; (800) 747-0302; www.peoria.org.

Local Events/Attractions

Christ Orchard: Pick your own apples, cherries, plums, pumpkins, and squashes, and purchase jam, jelly, honey, cider, and Indian corn; 4313 North Texas Rd., Elmwood; (309) 446-9751; www.christorchardonline.com.

Elmwood Historical Society/Laredo Taft Museum: 302 North Magnolia St., Elmwood; (309) 742-7791 or (309) 742-2431.

Illinois Valley Wheelm'n: In September the club hosts the No Baloney Ride on this route, which brings in several hundred people and boasts the "best and most plentiful food of any ride in the area"; 6518 North Sheridan Rd., Suite 2, Peoria; www.ivwheelmn.org.

Jubilee College State Historic Site: The state pulled out all the stops in rehabbing this building; free tours offered; 11817 Jubilee College Rd., Brimfield; (309) 243-9489.

Restaurants

Ludy's Kickapoo Creek Saloon: Serves up highly celebrated burgers with a special mix of seasoning; 9828 US 150, Edwards; (309) 692-6446.

Accommodations

Hotels/motels: You'll find several chain establishments on War Memorial Drive (US 150) on the way into Peoria.

Jubilee College State Park: The park has several camping areas, including a spot for walk-in tent camping; 13015 West Fussner Rd., Brimfield; (309) 446-3758; http://dnr.state.il.us/lands/landmgt/parks/r1/jubilee.htm.

Wildlife Prairie State Park: This zoo/park with a pioneer farmstead offers several lodging options, most notably a set of train cabooses; 3826 North Taylor Rd., Hanna City; (309) 676-0998; www.wildlifeprairiestatepark.org.

Bike Shops

Bushwhacker: Combination bike, outdoors, and patio furniture shop has a loyal following in the area; 4700 North University in the Metro Centre, Peoria; (309) 692-4812; http://bushwhacker.com.

Restrooms

Start/finish: Restrooms located across from parking area.

Mile 13.3: Turn right on SR 116 to reach the gas station/convenience store in Hanna City.

Mile 28.5: Restrooms are available at the gas station and Tastee Freez on Main Street in Elmwood.

Mile 36.6: Turn right on US 150 to reach the gas station/convenience store in Brimfield.

Maps

USGS: Oak Hill quad, Hanna City quad, Elmwood quad.

DeLorme: Illinois Atlas & Gazetteer: Page 40.

24 Kickapoo State Park Ramble

It's hard to believe that all the scenic lakes and wooded hills at Kickapoo State Park were once home to an extensive strip-mining operation. After marveling at this enormous reclamation project, you'll tour the quiet country roads that border the Middle Fork State Fish and Wildlife Area and ride through the valley carved out by a scenic river.

Start: Begin at Kickapoo State Park in the Clear Lake parking area between the canoe launch and Kickapoo Park Road.
Length: 25.8 miles.
Terrain: Gently rolling terrain dominates, but a few steep hills crop up along the way.
Traffic and hazards: The first mile on Newton Road may have steady truck traffic. Trucks will diminish after crossing CR 2150 North.

Getting there: Take exit 206 from I-74 west of Danville. Head north on Oakwood Street. Turn right on Glenburn Creek Road and follow it into Kickapoo State Park. Just after crossing the Middle Fork of the Vermillion River, park in the small lot on the left, adjacent to Kickapoo Landing. Coordinates for starting point: 16T 436919E 4443143N

The Ride

What was once considered a forsaken blight on the land is now one of the most popular parks in central Illinois. Located 6 miles west of Danville, the land at Kickapoo State Park was strip-mined for coal for nearly a hundred years. Strip mines were big business within Vermilion County, and according to the State of Illinois, these

All the ponds at Kickapoo State Park were strip mines at one time.

mines were the first in the country to use mechanized strip-mining techniques. In 1939 the state began acquiring land at Kickapoo from United Electric Coal Co. and restoring the barren moonscape made up of spoil piles and mine pits to prairie, ponds, and hilly woodland. The result was the first park in the nation created on the site of a former strip mine.

On this ride you'll see hills and mounds created by mining spoils in addition to a handful of the twenty-two ponds and lakes that were once mining pits. North of the park, the route runs through prairies and along quiet farm roads. You'll cross a picturesque stretch of the Middle Fork of the Vermilion River and pass by the Middle Fork State Fish and Wildlife Area and Kennekuk County Park.

The first section of the ride runs through a dense hardwood forest that looks like a smaller version of the Great North Woods. Look for the rocky outcropping on the right as you head up the hill on CR 1000 East and ascend about 100 feet out of the river valley. The landscape soon levels out and an attractive tallgrass prairie with goldenrod and black-eyed Susans replaces the thick stands of maple and cottonwood. After passing the turnoff for Sportman's Lake, the road follows the top edge of a steep bluff that plummets down more than 100 feet to the right. The route along the edge of the bluff is followed by more grassland sprinkled with trees.

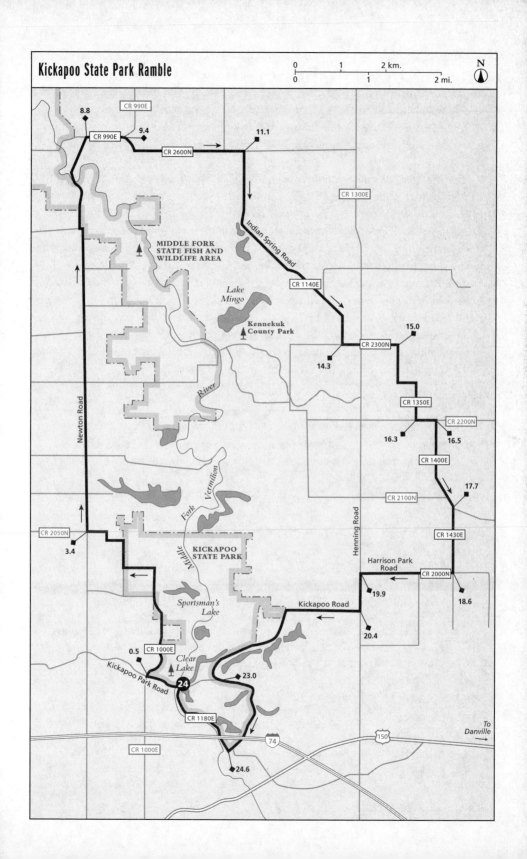

Kickapoo State Park Ramble

0   1   2 km.
0   1   2 mi.

N

8.8

CR 990E

9.4

CR 990E

11.1

CR 2600N

CR 1300E

Indian Spring Road

CR 1140E

MIDDLE FORK
STATE FISH AND
WILDLIFE AREA

Lake
Mingo

Kennekuk
County Park

15.0

CR 2300N

14.3

CR 1350E

CR 2200N

16.3   16.5

River

CR 1400E

Fork Vermilion

CR 2100N

17.7

Newton Road

CR 2050N

3.4

Middle

KICKAPOO
STATE PARK

CR 1430E

Henning Road

Harrison Park
Road

CR 2000N

19.9

18.6

Sportsman's
Lake

Kickapoo Road

20.4

0.5

CR 1000E

Clear
Lake

Kickapoo Park Road

24

23.0

CR 1180E

74

150

To
Danville

CR 1000E

24.6

As you get closer to the Middle Fork of the Vermilion River, the woodland thickens and the road descends toward the river along a deep ravine on the left. The federal government identified the Middle Fork as one of the most pristine and beautiful rivers in the Midwest in 1990 when it was named a National Wild and Scenic River, the only Illinois river with this status. Turning right on CR 990 East takes you on a gentle downhill through swaths of grassland and across a small tributary of the Vermilion River.

For the next 10 miles, you'll zigzag along level farm roads on your way back to Kickapoo State Park. (About halfway through this section, consider a quick detour to Kennekuk County Park—see the side trip at mile 14.3 below.) Returning to the woodland of Kickapoo, you'll have a chance to visit Emerald Pond on one of the park roads branching to the right. As you get into the southern part of the park, you'll pass several large picnic areas and Allhands Cemetery, and then shoot down a steep road leading to more ponds. The bridge over I-74—which is bracketed by short, steep hills—offers an expansive view of Long Lake and its accompanying wetlands on the right. As the park road curves back to the parking area, you will pass several more ponds and accompany the Middle Fork of the Vermilion, located on the left beyond the small bluff. During the summer, leaves hide the river, but you can get closer to it by taking one of the hiking trails that appear along the way.

Miles and Directions

0.0 From Kickapoo State Park, head to the right (west) on Kickapoo Park Road.

0.5 Turn right on CR 1000 East. (**Side trip:** At 1.4 miles, consider taking the park road to the right down a steep road to see Sportsman's Lake.) CR 1000 East becomes CR 200 North and CR 950 East as it zigzags to Newton Road.

3.4 Turn right on Newton Road (CR 900 East). Be alert for truck traffic during the first mile on this road.

7.5 Follow CR 900 East as it quickly turns right and then left.

8.8 Turn right on CR 990 East.

9.4 Turn right on CR 2600 North.

11.1 Turn right on Indian Spring Road (CR 1140 East). There is no sign for this road, but it's easy to find because it's the first paved road on the right after turning onto CR 2600 North.

14.3 Turn left on CR 2300 North. **Side trip:** To visit Kennekuk County Park, turn right on Henning Road; the park entrance is less than a mile ahead. The park offers many miles of trails, lots of picnicking spots, and shoreline along Lake Mingo.

15.0 Turn right on CR 1350 East.

16.3 Turn left on CR 2200 North.

16.5 Turn right on CR 1400 East.

17.7 Turn right on CR 1430 East.

18.6 Turn right on Harrison Park Road (CR 2000 North).

19.9 Turn left on Henning Road.

20.4 Turn right on Kickapoo Road.

23.0 Turn left where the road ends and follow the sign to EAST AREAS.

24.6 Turn right and follow the sign to CLEAR POND.

25.8 Return to the parking area near the park concessions.

Local Information

Danville Convention and Visitors Bureau: 100 West Main #146, Danville; (217) 442-2096; www.danvillecvb.com.

Local Events/Attractions

Middle Fork of the Vermilion River: Considered one of Illinois' best paddling rivers in spring and early summer; rent your gear and arrange a shuttle at Kickapoo Landing; (217) 446-8399.

Vermilion County Museum and Fithian Home: Displays a variety of exhibits, some related to Abe Lincoln's time in the area; 116 North Gilbert St., Danville; (217) 442-2922; www.vermilion countymuseum.org.

Restaurants

Dockside Cafe at Kickapoo Landing: Offers sandwiches and other types of simple fare; seasonal; located in Kickapoo State Park, 50 yards from the start of the ride; (217) 446-8399; http://kickapoolanding.com.

Java Hut: Serves sandwiches, quiche, and a few entrees in downtown Danville; 13 North Ver-milion St., Danville; (217) 443-6808; www.the javahut.biz.

Accommodations

Hotels/motels: A variety can be found near where I-75 crosses US 150.

Kickapoo State Park: Has two campgrounds within a half mile of the beginning of the ride; 10906 Kickapoo Park Rd., Oakwood; (217) 442-4915; http://dnr.state.il.us/lands/landmgt/parks/r3/kickapoo.htm.

Bike Shops

Cycles Plus: 12 West Woodbury St., Danville; (217) 442-3214.

Restrooms

Start/finish: A vault toilet and water spigot are located at the start.

Maps

USGS: Danville NW quad, Collison quad.

DeLorme: Illinois Atlas & Gazetteer: Page 55.

25 Lewistown Ramble

This short ride explores the pleasant countryside surrounding Lewistown, the former home of Edgar Lee Masters, a famous Illinois literary figure. West of Lewistown, you'll follow an established on-street bike route through patches of woodland and sections of rolling landscape. The ride begins and ends at the Dickson Mounds Museum, one of the best on-site archeological museums in the country.

Start: Dickson Mounds Museum, located between Lewistown and Havana.
Length: 21.8 miles.
Terrain: While most of this route is flat and gently rolling, it encounters some mildly hilly terrain outside of Lewistown and near the Dickson Mounds Museum.

Traffic and hazards: Traffic can be steady on SR 100. Traffic is not heavy heading out of Lewistown on Avenue L, but it moves fast. Be especially careful on the curves; local residents say drivers will occasionally cross the center-line on the curves.

Getting there: From I-74 in Peoria, take US 24 south. Just before reaching Lewistown, turn left on Dickson Mounds Road. Park in the museum lot located on the top of the bluff at the right. From Chicago, take I-55 south to US 136 and follow it west. After crossing the Illinois River, turn right on SR 97/78, then turn left on CR 31. The museum is on the left. If your car is in the museum lot after 5:00 p.m., make arrangements with the museum to leave the gates open, or just park nearby at the Dickson Mounds picnic area instead. Coordinates for starting point: 15T 744962E 4470650N

The Ride

Lewistown is a place where two cemeteries figure prominently in the local landscape. One of these is the Lewistown town cemetery, which you'll pass near this ride's halfway point. This cemetery played a central role in the magnum opus of Edgar Lee Masters, a Lewistown native and one of Illinois' most famous authors. The starting point of this ride, however, marks the location of a much older cemetery. Southeast of Lewistown on a bluff overlooking the wide, flat valley where the Spoon River joins the Illinois River is a cemetery with burial plots that go back to AD 200. Remains of some 800 individuals have been uncovered within the local burial mounds. The burials occurred over a span of about 400 years—more recent burials are from about AD 1250.

The ride begins and ends at this burial site, which now hosts the Dickson Mounds Museum, an archeological museum operated by the State of Illinois. The study of the ancient past at the burial site began in 1927 when chiropractor Don Dickson conducted excavations on the family farm. Instead of removing the bones from the graves he excavated, he removed only the dirt, leaving the bones and associated objects in place. Eventually, he built a structure over the excavation and opened it as a private museum.

Over the years Dickson Mounds has become a focal point in the study of the pre-history of the Illinois River Valley, one of the richest archaeological regions in the country. After the Dickson burial site was bought by the state, the Dickson Mounds Museum opened in 1972, and underwent a major renovation in the early 1990s. In response to changing attitudes, new legislation regarding burial remains, and pressure from Native American groups, the museum closed access to the remains as part of the renovation.

From the Dickson Mounds Museum, this ride takes you through gently rolling farmland on the way to Lewistown. After looping around and heading south into Lewistown on SR 100, you can't miss the 150-year-old Oak Hill Cemetery, made famous by Edgar Lee Masters' *Spoon River Anthology*. In the book, the dead in an Illinois graveyard relay in matter-of-fact but haunting tones the unvarnished details of their lives. Many of the characters and their experiences are drawn from former residents of Lewistown and Petersburg, Illinois. Masters used his childhood experiences in these two communities as a basis for the poems.

After turning right on Milton Avenue, you'll pass by Edgar Lee Masters' former home (now privately owned and not open to the public). The Masters family moved to Lewistown from Petersburg in 1880 when Edgar Lee was eleven. Masters stayed in Lewistown until reaching his early twenties, when he left for Chicago and eventually became a law partner of the famous lawyer Clarence Darrow. Although he published over fifty books, Masters' only great literary success was *Spoon River Anthology,* which appeared in 1915. Masters died in 1950 and is buried in Petersburg, which is located near Springfield.

For the next 7 miles, the route follows the Milton Hillside Loop Trail, a well-marked bike route along a series of quiet roads. Following the arrows for the bike route guides you west of town on a curvy rolling road, and then south through an area with occasional houses and ponds dropped among the cornfields. The route back into town leads you through a small wooded ravine, past a modest pig farm, and through a Lewistown residential area.

In Lewistown, you'll pass the stately Lewistown courthouse, and then just down the street, Rasmussen Blacksmith Shop and Museum. The blacksmith shop, operated by the same family from 1882 to 1969, now has an array of old smithy tools on display, as well as antique farm equipment.

The final section of the ride offers a pleasing series of dips and rises along a curvy road that twice crosses East Creek. As you admire the sprawling wetlands of the flat river valley in front of you at the corner of CR 9 and Dickson Mounds Road, look for the Indian mound in the field to the right: It's a small rise with some trees growing on it. Unfortunately, many of the other mounds in the area have been plowed under or are no longer recognizable. Wrapping up the ride, be sure to stop at the Dickson Mounds Museum to learn more about local Native American life in the Illinois River Valley. (You may also want to visit one of the largest Indian mounds in the area: It covers nearly two acres, stands 14 feet high, and now serves as a town park in nearby Havana. Follow the signs to the mound as you pass through Havana on US 136.)

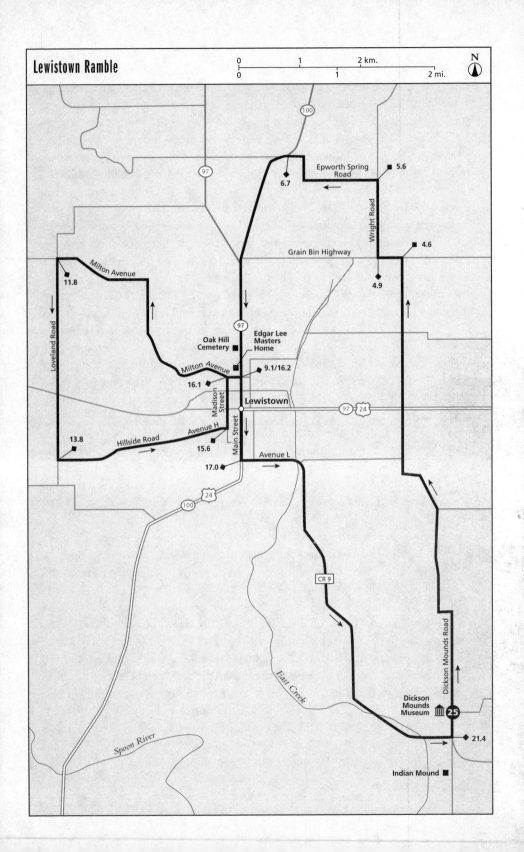

Lewistown Ramble

0   1   2 km.
0   1   2 mi.

N

100

97

Epworth Spring
Road

6.7

5.6

Wright Road

Grain Bin Highway

4.6

4.9

Milton Avenue

11.8

Loveland Road

97

Oak Hill
Cemetery

Edgar Lee
Masters
Home

Milton Avenue

9.1/16.2

16.1

Madison
Street

Lewistown

97 24

Hillside Road

Avenue H

Main Street

13.8

15.6

Avenue L

17.0

24

100

CR 9

Dickson Mounds Road

East Creek

Dickson
Mounds
Museum

25

21.4

Spoon River

Indian Mound

Miles and Directions

0.0 From the Dickson Mounds Museum, turn left on Dickson Mounds Road.

4.6 Turn left on Grain Bin Highway.

4.9 Turn right on Wright Road.

5.6 Turn left on Epworth Spring Road.

6.7 Turn left on SR 100 after crossing the train tracks. The brief stretch on SR 100 will likely have traffic: Stay single-file if you're with a group. As you enter Lewistown, SR 100 becomes Main Street.

8.8 **Side trip:** Take a brief spin through the scenic grounds of Oak Hill Cemetery on the right.

9.1 Turn right on Milton Avenue. Follow the sign for Milton Hillside Loop trail, and let the arrows lead the way for the next 7 miles.

11.8 Turn left on Loveland Road.

13.8 Turn left on Hillside Road. This road becomes Avenue H as you approach Lewistown.

15.6 Turn left on Madison Street.

16.1 Turn right on Milton Avenue.

16.2 Turn right on Main Street.

17.0 Turn left on Avenue L. This road soon becomes CR 9.

21.4 Turn left on Dickson Mounds Road.

21.8 At the top of the hill, turn left into the Dickson Mounds parking lot.

Local Information

Fulton County Tourism Council: 700 East Oak St., Room 307, Canton; (309) 647-6074 or (309) 293-2741; www.fultoncountytourism.org.
Havana Area Chamber of Commerce: P.O. Box 116, Havana, IL 62644; (309) 543-3528; www.scenichavana.com.

Local Events/Attractions

Dickson Mounds Museum: Free archeological museum; don't miss the view from the observation deck; 10956 North Dickson Mounds Rd., Lewistown; (309) 547-3721; www.museum.state.il.us/ismsites/dickson.
Rasmussen Blacksmith Shop and Museum: Family-operated horseshoe and wagon-wheel maker from 1882 and until 1969; 396 South Main St., Lewistown; (309) 547-4306.

Restaurants

The Palm Cafe: Upscale, contemporary cuisine; located in the historic Canton House Hotel; 101 East Elm St., Canton; (309) 647-2233; www.cantondowntown.com/PalmCafe.

Accommodations

Dale Roberts Lodging: Clean and affordable; 301½ West Main St., Havana; (309) 543-4156.
Landmark Inn Bed and Breakfast: 1060 North Main St., Canton; (309) 647-9746; www.landmarkinnofcanton.com.

Bike Shops

The Bike Shop: 137 Columbia St., Macomb; (309) 833-5748; www.bikeshopmacomb.com.
Bushwhacker: Combination bike, outdoors, and patio furniture shop has a loyal following in the area; 4700 North University in the Metro Centre, Peoria; (309) 692-4812.

Restrooms

Start/finish: Dickson Mounds Museum has restrooms and water.

Mile 9.1: Gas station in Lewistown has restrooms.
Mile 16.1: Gas station in Lewistown has restrooms.

Maps
USGS: Havana quad, St. David quad, Lewistown quad, Duncan Mills quad.
DeLorme: Illinois Atlas & Gazetteer: Pages 50 and 49.

26 Nauvoo Ramble

Nauvoo, one of the most fascinating historic towns in the Midwest, contains an impressive collection of preserved houses, businesses, and public buildings constructed from 1839 to 1846 when the Mormon Church called the town home. In addition to exploring this richly historic area, the ride leads you on a series of quiet farm roads outside of Nauvoo and alongside a couple of stunning stretches of the Mississippi River shoreline.

Start: Nauvoo State Park, in the town of Nauvoo. Nauvoo is located about 85 miles southwest of the Quad Cities.
Length: 25.5 miles.
Terrain: Mostly flat or gently rolling. One steep hill to climb at mile 4.9.

Traffic and hazards: While returning to Nauvoo on SR 96, watch for traffic. Most of this stretch of roadway offers an ample riding shoulder, but in some places the shoulder disappears.

Getting there: From Galesburg, head west on US 34. After Biggsville, turn left on SR 94. When SR 94 turns to the left, continue straight ahead on SR 96 into Lomax. After passing through downtown Nauvoo on SR 96, the state park is on the left. From Macomb, head west on US 136. In Hamilton, turn right on SR 96. Enter Nauvoo State Park on the right on the way to downtown Nauvoo. Park at the Frank Stevenson Shelter House located next to the historical museum. Coordinates for starting point: 15T 398604E 4672193N

The Ride

Nauvoo holds a special place in the history of the Mormon Church. Because of this, it has become something of a Mormon mecca, drawing people from all over the world to see this remote Illinois town founded by Mormons in 1839. Once the town was established, Mormon missionaries such as Brigham Young converted thousands in England and elsewhere, prompting people to migrate to the area. Business and industry flourished, and by 1844 Nauvoo's population surpassed Chicago's, making it Illinois' largest city.

As the city grew in size, its power grew as well. Neighboring communities took a dim view of the powerful Mormon voting bloc exercised in local politics and the heavy concentration of power in the hands of one man. Joseph Smith, the founder of

The beginning and end of the Nauvoo Ramble will treat riders to expansive views of the Mississippi River.

Mormonism, was not only the leader of the church, but also the mayor of Nauvoo, the head of the municipal court, and the general of the city's militia. Tensions between Mormons and surrounding communities soon erupted into violence. In 1844, Smith was shot and killed while jailed in the nearby town of Carthage.

After Smith's death, Nauvoo continued to serve as headquarters of the Mormon Church for another couple of years until the members saw that the problems with neighboring communities were too great. In 1846, under the leadership of Brigham Young, the Mormons left for Utah. A few, including the family of Joseph Smith, remained in Nauvoo and formed the Reorganized Church of Jesus Christ of Latter-day Saints, now called the Community of Christ. While much of the town has disappeared—particularly the wood-frame houses—several dozen structures have been preserved as exhibits, including a collection of handsome brick houses and businesses.

Before starting the ride, consider a visit to the Nauvoo State Park Museum, which occupies a house built by Mormons in the 1840s. The restored home has a wine cellar and a collection of artifacts from all periods of Nauvoo's history. The seemingly out-of-place wine cellar and attached vineyards were established by a French Socialist commune called the Icarians that came to Nauvoo shortly after the Mormons left.

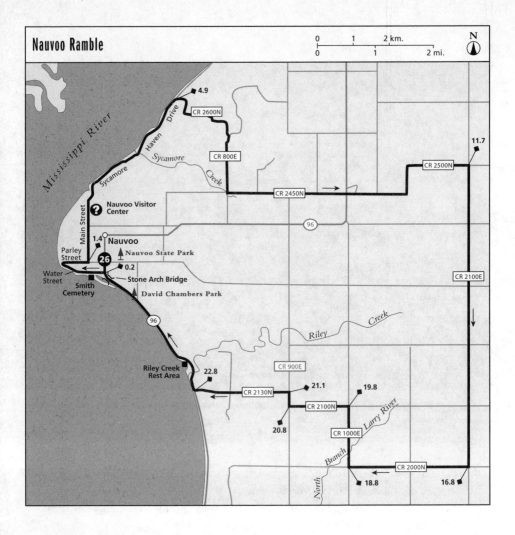

After crossing SR 96, you'll pass a large brick hotel called the Nauvoo House; the Mansion House, which was Smith's main residence; and Smith's first local homestead. Next to the homestead is the cemetery where Smith is buried. It should be apparent why Smith chose to live in this spot: The views of the 1-mile-wide Mississippi River are entrancing. On Parley Street a series of roadside signs feature journal entries from church members as they journeyed west from Nauvoo in 1846. Just beyond the stately meeting hall and the blacksmith shop, you'll round the corner onto Main Street and pass a series of historic buildings that hosted businesses such as a boot shop, a printer, a tinsmith, and a bakery. Many of the shops invite visitors inside to watch period demonstrations.

With the historic streets of Nauvoo now in the rearview mirror, you'll begin riding alongside the mighty Miss-sip' on Sycamore Haven Drive. While tracing the wooded shoreline, stunning views emerge, revealing the full scale of this nearly

2-mile-wide section of the river. Near the shore, swallows wheel over great fields of lily pads. A sprinkling of homes is squeezed between the river and the wooded bluffs rising nearly 150 feet on the right.

After a steep climb up the bluff on a short stretch of gravel road, be sure to pause and turn around at the top for an expansive view of the river. A few turns later, the landscape is now flat and covered with corn. While touring the cropland, a handful of winding creeks pass under the roads. Every so often, the open stillness of the land is interrupted by the turning blades of old windmills and barking dogs at farmhouses. A few farmhouses are built of brick or stone; some have collapsed roofs and overgrown driveways.

At about 22 miles into the route, you'll leave the farmland, descend a bluff nearly 100 feet, and return to the shore of the Mississippi River. Several riverside parks appear on the short trip back to Nauvoo. First is the Riley Creek Rest Area, which contains picnic tables overlooking many acres of lily pads in an eddy in the river. Just up the road, a scenic turnout called Davids Chamber contains a trickling stream flowing over a 10-foot rocky waterfall. Another waterfall appears just up the road at a tiny wayside park called Stone Arch Bridge. From the wayside's parking area, follow a short trail down to the creek and peer into the opening of the stone bridge to see the 5-foot waterfall at the other end.

Before wrapping up the ride, consider a quick visit to the new Mormon Temple, built in 2002 on the site of the town's first temple. The building sits on a spot that presents breathtaking views of the old village and the river as it bends around a promontory. To reach the temple from Nauvoo State Park, head north on SR 96 and turn left on Wells Street.

Miles and Directions

0.0 From the Frank Stevenson Shelter House located next to the historical museum in Nauvoo State Park, head out to the park entrance on SR 96 (North County Road) and turn left.

0.2 Turn right on Water Street. Follow Water Street as it takes a sharp curve right and becomes Parley Street.

1.4 Turn left on Main Street. Stay to the right on Main Street as it becomes Sycamore Haven Drive.

4.9 Turn right on CR 2600 North.

7.2 Turn left on CR 2450 North. Stay on this road as it curves and becomes CR 2500 North.

11.7 Turn right on CR 2100 East.

16.8 Turn right on CR 2000 North.

18.8 Turn right on CR 1000 East.

19.8 Turn left on CR 2100 North.

20.8 Turn right on CR 900 East.

21.1 Turn left on CR 2130 North.

22.8 Turn right on SR 96.

25.5 Arrive back at Nauvoo State Park.

Local Information

Historic Nauvoo Visitors Center: Corner of Partridge St. and Hubbard St., Nauvoo; (888) 453-6434; www.historicnauvoo.net.

Western Illinois Tourism Development Office: 581 South Deere Rd., Macomb; (309) 837-7460; www.visitwesternillinois.info.

Local Events/Attractions

Historic Nauvoo: Check out the free demonstrations and displays at the brick maker, bakery, school, post office, tin shop, and blacksmith; most shops are located on Main Street in old Nauvoo.

Nauvoo State Park Museum: Open summer afternoons; located in the state park; P.O. Box 426, Nauvoo, IL 62354; (217) 453-2512; http://dnr.state.il.us/lands/landmgt/parks/r4/nauvoo.htm.

Nauvoo Wagon Tours: During the summer, these hour-long free tours start every half hour from the visitor center; see Historic Nauvoo Visitors Center contact information above.

Restaurants

Hotel Nauvoo: Known for its dinner buffet; 1290 Mulholland St., Nauvoo; (217) 453-2211; www.hotelnauvoo.com.

Nauvoo Mill and Bakery: Sandwiches, sweets, and bread for sale; 1530 Mulholland St., Nauvoo; (888) 453-6734.

Accommodations

Hotel Nauvoo: Historic building in old Nauvoo; owners also operate a nearby motel; see contact information above.

Nauvoo State Park: Has a couple of pleasant camping areas; see contact information above; http://dnr.state.il.us/lands/landmgt/parks/r4/nauvoo.htm.

Bike Shops

Madison-Davis Bicycles: 912 South 8th St., Quincy; (217) 222-7262; www.madison-davisbicycles.com.

Restrooms

Start/finish: Water and restrooms are available at the picnic shelter where the ride begins.

Mile 2.1: Water and restrooms are available at the Historic Nauvoo Visitors Center.

Mile 23.4: Riley Creek Rest Area has restrooms.

Maps

USGS: Hamilton quad, Nauvoo quad, Niota quad.

DeLorme: Illinois Atlas & Gazetteer: Pages 56 and 47.

27 Peoria Sculpture and Architecture Ramble

Peoria is a perfect place for an urban bike tour: As the oldest city in Illinois, there's much to see, and the city itself is not large enough to make traffic a problem. You'll get a taste of Peoria's history, architecture, and public sculptures by taking this trip through the city neighborhoods, into downtown, along the river pathway, and past the city zoo.

Start: Glen Oak Park in Peoria at the parking lot near the amphitheater.
Length: 10.6 miles.
Terrain: A 100-foot bluff runs through Peoria parallel to the Illinois River. The route takes a trip down and then up this steep bluff.

Traffic and hazards: Most of the streets on this route are quiet, with just a few busy patches. In any case, these are all urban streets and drivers are accustomed to cyclists.

Getting there: From I-74 in Peoria, exit on University Avenue and head north. Turn right on McClure Avenue and continue straight ahead into Glen Oak Park. Inside the park, stay to the right and park in the large parking area on the right near the playground and amphitheater. Coordinates for starting point: 16T 282367E 4510007N

The Ride

What better way to get to know a city than to hop on a bike? On a bicycle, you can cover a lot of ground and it's easy to stop to gawk at the sights. A bike also allows you to become fully acquainted with the terrain along the way. Sheldon Schafer, the vice president of education at Peoria's Lakeview Museum, is well aware of the advantages of seeing a city such as Peoria on a bike. This urban Peoria ride is drawn from one of the many free group rides that he's been leading in Peoria for a number of years.

Starting out from the Glen Oak Zoo brings you through several residential neighborhoods. One neighborhood that's particularly interesting is along Columbia Terrace: The street is lined with large Victorian wood-frame homes with inviting front porches and lawns decorated with flowers and plants.

Entering Bradley University, you won't fail to notice Bradley Hall, an impressive building from 1897 that has a statue of the school's founder in front. Within the Bradley Campus Quad, there are a half-dozen sculptures that are worth taking a peek at. A large geometric sculpture to the right by Linda Howard (*Centerpeace*) seems to change its shape and patterns as you ride around it (and through it!). Don't miss the two figurative sculptures at the far end of the quad by Nita Sunderland, a Bradley alum and teacher who is considered to be Peoria's greatest living female artist. The art and architecture, as well as the manicured lawns, gardens, and stately trees, make Bradley's quad a very pleasant spot to hang out.

Ronald Bladen's sculpture Sonar Tide *sits in front of Peoria City Hall.*

Heading south from the campus, look for the Frank Lloyd Wright house that was built for a local utility company executive at the northwest corner of Institute Place and Moss Avenue (1505 West Moss Ave.). Continuing along Moss Avenue reveals a string of historic homes that were built on this bluff. Another notable house is the Pettengill-Morron House, built in 1868 by a boot and shoe manufacturer and now a museum owned by the Peoria Historical Society.

A handful of the impressive houses on the street are locally known as "whiskey mansions" because they were built by the owners and managers of the many distilleries that once operated in Peoria. Access to grain, coal, clean water, and river transportation allowed Peoria to become the whiskey capital of the world in the late 1800s. So great was Peoria's share of whiskey taxes paid to the federal government that it was larger than any other district in the entire United States. The final drop of booze was fermented in Peoria in the 1980s, when a Hiram Walker distillery was bought and converted to an ethanol production facility.

Turning off Moss Avenue takes you on a short, steep ride down the bluff, through a new housing development, and to the foot of the life-size bronze statue of Jean Baptiste Pointe DuSable at the corner of Richard Pryor Place and John H. Gwynn Jr. Avenue. DuSable, born of a French father and an African slave mother, lived in Peoria before and after he built the first permanent homestead in Chicago.

The street the sculpture is on commemorates another important African American from Peoria. Richard Pryor grew up in his grandmother's brothel in Peoria and stayed in the city long enough to launch his comedy career. Many comedians call Pryor the most influential comic of the past fifty years. Sadly, the Peoria City Council argued for months about whether it was fitting to name this half-mile-long street in honor of Pryor.

Arriving downtown, you'll pass Peoria City Hall, a handsome building built of red stone in 1899. In front of city hall is *Sonar Tide,* a 16-ton minimalist sculpture by Ronald Bladen. At Fulton Street and Jefferson Avenue is another figurative sculpture by Nita Sunderland called *Cedric the Sea Dragon.* In the vicinity of the county courthouse at the corner of Main Street and Jefferson Avenue there are a couple of sculptures of human figures from the Works Progress Administration; there is a life-size statue of Abraham Lincoln and a large Civil War memorial in the sunken courtyard behind the courthouse.

Dropping down to the Riverfront Path, you'll find several sculptures by Peoria-based artist Preston Jackson. Seeing Jackson's playful work sprinkled along the riverfront, one wouldn't have guessed they were done by the same artist who sculpted the realistic DuSable statue up the road.

For nearly 2 miles you'll follow the Riverfront Path as it runs by touristy restaurants, past the bandstand, and under the Baker Bridge. Before arriving at the marina, the route takes you through a pleasant collection of landscaped flower gardens. A few quick turns later take you to Abington Street and back toward Glen Oak Park and the zoo.

Near the entrance to Glen Oak Park stands a statue of Robert Ingersoll, a former Peoria resident and Illinois attorney general who was reportedly the most popular orator in the nation during the late nineteenth century. At a time when oratory was a form of public entertainment, Ingersoll traveled the country and spoke on an array of topics, including science, religion, literature, and history. An early popularizer of Charles Darwin, Ingersoll was a strong advocate of science and reason, and often argued for the rights of women and African Americans.

From the Ingersoll statue, the park road climbs the steep wooded bluff and then winds through a picnic area. Stay to the right past the zoo entrance to arrive back at the parking area near the amphitheater.

Miles and Directions

0.0 From the southwest parking area at Glen Oak Park, head south through the gates toward the pond and turn right on Republic Street.

0.8 Turn left on Peoria Avenue.

1.0 Turn right on Nebraska Avenue, then immediately left on Dechman Avenue.

1.2 Turn right on Richmond Avenue.

1.6 Turn left on North Street.

1.9 Turn right on Columbia Terrace.

2.9 Turn left on Glenwood Avenue.

3.2 Take the first left (sidewalk between the buildings) after crossing West Main Street and enter the Bradley University Quad.

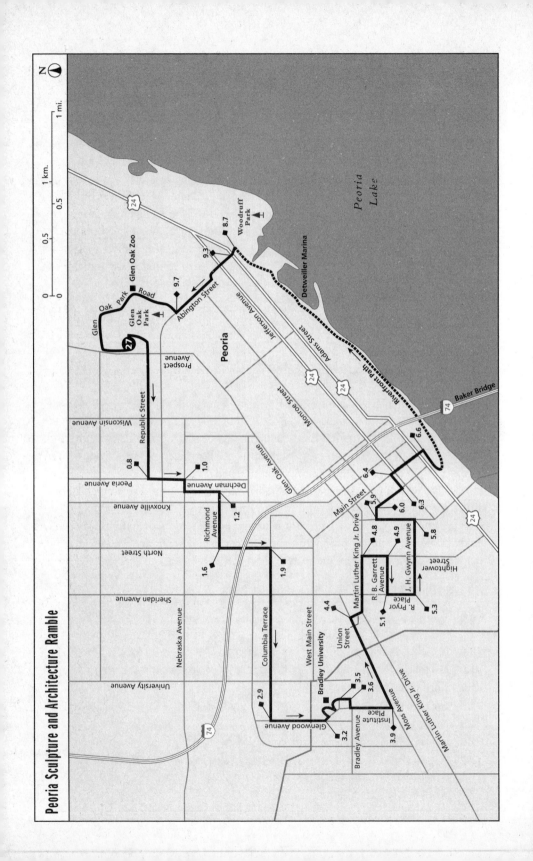

Peoria Sculpture and Architecture Ramble

N

1 mi.

1 km.

0.5   0.5

0   0

24

Glen Oak Zoo

Glen Oak Park Road

Glen Oak Park

9.7

27

Prospect Avenue

Peoria

Abington Street

9.3

8.7

Woodruff Park

Detweiller Marina

Peoria Lake

Jefferson Avenue

Adams Street

Republic Street

Wisconsin Avenue

Monroe Street

24

24

Riverfront Path

74 Baker Bridge

0.8

Peoria Avenue

1.0

Dechman Avenue

6.6

Knoxville Avenue

Glen Oak Avenue

Main Street

6.4

5.9

6.0

6.3

Richmond Avenue

1.2

North Street

Martin Luther King Jr. Drive

4.8

4.9

5.8

1.6

1.9

Sheridan Avenue

R. B. Garrett Avenue

J. H. Gwynn Avenue

Highwater Street

24

Nebraska Avenue

Columbia Terrace

R. Pryor Place

5.1

5.3

University Avenue

West Main Street

Union Street

4.4

Bradley University

2.9

Glenwood Avenue

3.5

3.6

Institute Place

3.2

Bradley Avenue

3.9

Moss Avenue

Martin Luther King Jr. Drive

3.5 Turn right on Elmwood Avenue (this street looks like a long parking lot).

3.6 Turn right on Bradley Avenue, then make a quick left on Institute Place.

3.9 Turn left on Moss Avenue.

4.4 Turn right on Union Street, descend this short steep hill, and then take a quick left turn onto Dr. Martin Luther King Jr. Drive.

4.8 Turn right on Hightower Street.

4.9 Turn right on Romeo B. Garrett Avenue.

5.1 Turn left on Richard Pryor Place.

5.3 Turn left on John H. Gwynn Jr. Avenue.

5.8 Turn left on William Kumpf Boulevard.

5.9 Turn right on Monroe Street.

6.0 Turn right on Fulton Street.

6.3 Turn left on Jefferson Avenue. Since this road contains one-way traffic coming at you, walk your bike on the sidewalk for this 1 block.

6.4 Turn right on Main Street.

6.6 Turn right on the bike/pedestrian path at the end of Main Street. Just after the River Station building, turn left toward the river and then take the path to the left as it runs alongside the river. After the Riverplex building, stay to the right on the path. In the marina parking lot, continue straight ahead. After the marina, take the path to the right for a brief side trip out on the breaker.

8.7 Turn left on Grant Street, then immediately turn left on Adams Street. This street is one-way going in the opposite direction, so you may want to walk your bike or ride on the sidewalk.

9.3 Turn right on Abington Street.

9.7 Turn right on Glen Oak Park Road.

10.6 Stay to the right on the park road to return to the parking lot.

Local Information

Peoria Riverfront Visitors Center: 110 Northeast Water St., Peoria; (800) 747-0302; www.peoria.org.

Local Events/Attractions

Glen Oak Zoo: 2218 North Prospect Rd., Peoria; (309) 686-3365; www.peoriazoo.org.

Pedal Peoria: A series of free, casual group rides focusing on themes such as local history, city gardens, and soft-serve ice cream; www.ivwheelmn.org or www.lakeview-museum.org.

Peoria Riverfront Market: Offers goods from local farmers, artists, and musicians on Saturdays until noon, June through September; Liberty Park, Peoria; (309) 671-5555.

Pettengill-Morron House Museum: 1212 West Moss Ave., Peoria; (309) 674-1921.

Restaurants

Thanh Linh Vietnamese Restaurant: Located next to Bradley University; 1223 West Main St., Peoria; (309) 495-0179.

Accommodations

Hotels/motels: You'll find several upscale hotels in Peoria's downtown area. More affordable digs can be found on War Memorial Drive and across the river in East Peoria.

Jubilee College State Park: Contains many campsites; located 20 minutes north of town; 13015 West Fussner Rd., Brimfield; (309) 446-3758; http://dnr.state.il.us/lands/landmgt/parks/r1/jubilee.htm.

Randolph Terrace Historic Bed and Breakfast: 201 West Columbia Terr., Peoria; (309) 688-7858; www.randolphterrace.com.

Bike Shops

Bushwhacker: Combination bike, outdoors, and patio furniture shop has a loyal following in the area; 4700 North University in the Metro Centre, Peoria; (309) 692-4812; http://bushwhacker.com.

Restrooms

Start/finish: Restrooms are near the amphitheater on the east side of the parking area.

Mile 7.0: The Gateway Building on the riverfront has restrooms and water.

Maps

USGS: Peoria East quad.

DeLorme: Illinois Atlas & Gazetteer: Page 41.

28 Sand Ridge State Forest Ramble

This ride is full of scenic pleasures. At Sand Ridge State Forest, you'll encounter rolling terrain covered with oak-hickory woods, plantations of pine, open grasslands, and unique sand prairies. After a tour of the state forest, the route passes a state-run fish hatchery and then traces the shoreline of enormous Spring Lake for several miles.

Start: Eagle Bluff Access Area at the Chautauqua National Wildlife Refuge, located north of Havana.

Length: 30.1 miles.

Terrain: Except for the flat sections near Spring Lake, most of the route rolls gently.

There are occasional hills, but none very steep or long.

Traffic and hazards: A couple of miles of this route follow gravel roads. Use caution on the gravel section of Fornoff Road; the surface is fairly loose.

Getting there: From Chicago and Bloomington-Normal, take I-55 south to US 136. Head west on US 136 until you reach CR 3 (CR 2400 East), 16 miles after passing through the town of San Jose. Take CR 3 to the right and continue through Topeka. Turn left on Manito Road (CR 2000 North), then turn right on CR 15 (CR 1950 East). The Eagle Bluff Access Area is 2.3 miles ahead on the left. Coordinates for starting point: 16T 246999E 4473274N

The Ride

At 7,200 acres, Sand Ridge is not only Illinois' largest state forest, it's also one of its largest state-operated natural areas. Most of the forest is blanketed with thick groves of oak, hickory, and pine; there are also large swaths of land that contain fields and sand prairies. Fifteen thousand years ago the floodwaters of the most recent glaciers receded down the Illinois River Valley, leaving a vast deposit of sand in the area. Shifting winds sculpted the 100-foot-high sand dunes evident today as the wooded ridges for which the forest is named. Today Sand Ridge State Forest remains one of few places in Illinois that support an intriguing variety of plants and animals more associated with the Southwest than the Midwest.

After enjoying the expansive views along the shore of Spring Lake on the Sand Ridge State Forest Ramble, the route heads up a 100-foot wooded bluff.

Starting the ride from the Eagle Bluff Access Area, the route traces the top of the 40-foot-high sandy bluff that runs along the east edge of Lake Chautauqua. During much of the year, the oak and hickory trees growing at the top of the bluff allow only the occasional peek at the mile-wide lake. In the 1920s this 5-square-mile lake was diked, drained, and converted to agricultural land; however, the Illinois River, which runs on the other side of the lake, had other plans. In only two years, the river flooded and reclaimed the land.

The Chautauqua refuge is one of more than a half-dozen large swaths of woodland, marsh, lake, and backwater areas along this section of the Illinois River. This impressive string of preserves, managed by both state and federal agencies, starts north of Peoria and follows the river south for about 100 miles. This part of the Illinois River is situated in the middle of what's called the Mississippi Flyway, an important link in the chain of resting and feeding areas for waterfowl and other migratory birds. In the flyway areas, it's common to see nesting and transient bald eagles, as well as thousands of wading birds, shorebirds, and waterfowl. According to the U.S. Fish and

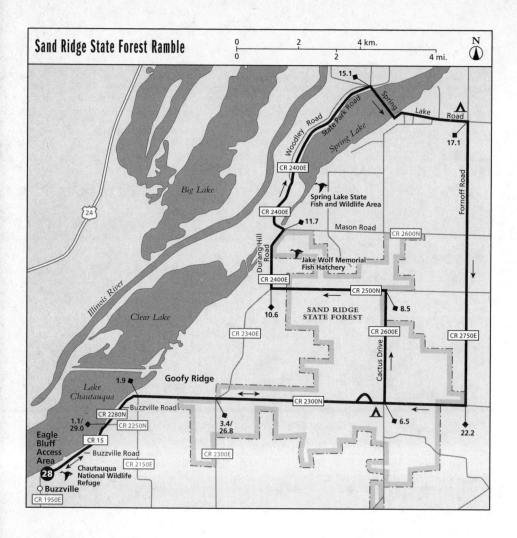

Sand Ridge State Forest Ramble

0   2   4 km.
0   2   4 mi.

N

Wildlife Service, an astounding number of ducks and geese—as many as 250,000—can gather at one time on Lake Chautauqua.

As you penetrate deeper into the state forest, the woods grows thicker and the terrain becomes more rolling. On the roadside, look for flowering plants such as thistles and black-eyed Susans. Before turning on Cactus Drive, the road passes a couple of state forest campgrounds, one of which is for equestrian use only. Cactus Drive lives up to its name: Keep an eye in the roadside ditch for prickly pear cactuses. The cactuses thrive in the forest's sandy soils—as do pine trees, which cover nearly one-third of the forest. Unlike the cactuses, the conifers do not grow here naturally; they were planted by the Civilian Conservation Corps in the 1930s. The cactuses become especially thick on the side of the road approaching the Jake Wolf Fish Hatchery.

The largest of four state-operated fish hatcheries, Jake Wolf is unique because it can rear the greatest variety of fish—sixteen different species. This variety is possible because it draws water from a large aquifer underneath the hatchery. The ground water is 54 degrees Fahrenheit—cold enough to raise trout and salmon. The visitor center, located on the upper level of the hatchery, overlooks the pools used in the different stages of fish production.

The best part of this ride comes with a delightfully scenic spin on the levee beside Spring Lake. For nearly 3 miles the road hugs the shoreline of this large lake containing acres of lily pads and water lilies, along with clusters of waterfowl and wading birds. Wooded bluffs rise above the opposite shore.

After climbing the bluff on the other side of Spring Lake, you'll pass another campground and then head south through pleasantly rolling farmland on your way back to the state forest and toward your starting point. At the end of your ride, don't miss the expansive views of Lake Chautauqua from the Eagle Bluff boat ramp and from the viewing platform at the south end of the parking lot.

Miles and Directions

0.0 Head left on Buzzville Road/CR 15 from the Eagle Bluff Access Area at the Chautauqua National Wildlife Refuge.

1.1 Stay left on Buzzville Road as it now shares the route with CR 2280 North.

1.9 Take a soft right on CR 2300 North.

3.4 Stay on CR 2300 North.

6.5 Turn left on Cactus Drive/CR 2600 East.

8.5 Turn left on CR 2500 North.

9.3 **Side trip:** Turn right at the sign for a short trip to the Jake Wolf Fish Hatchery. This will add nearly 2 miles to your ride.

10.6 Turn right on Durang Hill Road/CR 2400 East.

11.7 Just after the curve, turn left on Woodley Road/CR 2400 East.

12.8 Turn right on State Park Road just before Larry's Restaurant and Family Bar.

12.9 Turn left on State Park Road as it runs along the shore of Spring Lake.

15.1 Turn right on Spring Lake Road.

17.1 Turn right on Fornoff Road.

19.2 Fornoff Road becomes CR 2750 East.

22.2 Turn right on CR 2300 North.

28.3 Take a soft left on Buzzville Road/CR 2280 North.

29.0 Stay on Buzzville Road as it turns right to join with CR 2250 North.

30.1 Return to the Eagle Bluff Access Area.

Local Information

Havana Area Chamber of Commerce: P.O. Box 116, Havana, IL 62644; (309) 543-3528; www.scenichavana.com.

Peoria Area Convention and Visitors Bureau: 456 Fulton St., Suite 300, Peoria; (800) 747-0302; www.peoria.org.

Local Events/Attractions

Dickson Mounds Museum: On-site archeological museum exploring American Indian culture as it existed in the Illinois River Valley; free admission; 10956 North Dickson Mounds Rd., Lewistown; (309) 547-3721; www.museum.state.il.us/ismsites/dickson.

Jake Wolf Memorial Fish Hatchery: Has exhibits focusing on fish production at the hatchery, antique fishing tackle, and the Illinois River at the turn of the century; daily tours; 25410 North Fish Hatchery Rd., Topeka; (309) 968-7531; http://dnr.state.il.us/education/interprt/jwolf.htm.

Restaurants

Cup and Saucer: Downtown Havana lunch spot with soups and baked goods; 305 West Main St., Havana; (309) 543-0000.

Accommodations

Dale Roberts Lodging: Clean and affordable; 301½ West Main St., Havana; (309) 543-4156.

Spring Lake State Fish and Wildlife Area: Two small, somewhat primitive campgrounds; quiet and out of the way; 7982 South Park Rd., Manito; (309) 968-7135; http://dnr.state.il.us/lands/Landmgt/parks/r1/spl.htm.

Sycamore Motor Lodge: 371 East Dearborn St., Havana; (309) 543.4454.

Bike Shops

Bushwhacker: Combination bike, outdoors, and patio furniture shop has a loyal following in the area; 4700 North University in the Metro Centre, Peoria; (309) 692-4812; http://bushwhacker.com.

Restrooms

Start/finish: Eagle Bluff parking area has vault toilets; no water.

Mile 5.5: The equestrian campground in Sand Ridge State Forest has restrooms and water.

Mile 6.5: The state forest campground has restrooms and water.

Mile 12.9: Restrooms are available at the boat ramp.

Mile 15.3: Spring Lake Day Use Area has restrooms.

Mile 23.7: Pass the state forest campground again.

Mile 24.7: Pass the equestrian campground again.

Maps

USGS: Manito quad, Duck Island quad, Havana quad, Topeka quad.

DeLorme: Illinois Atlas & Gazetteer: Page 50.

29 Siloam Springs-Griggsville Classic

This long ride through west-central Illinois starts with a tour of the rolling—often hilly—landscape between Siloam Springs State Park and the Illinois River. The landscape is transformed upon reaching the Illinois River floodplain, where you'll follow the bottom edge of the river bluff while taking in long views toward the river. Arriving in Griggsville, purple martins and their dwellings take center stage. The final part of the ride takes you on quiet roads through gently rolling farmland.

Start: Siloam Springs State Park, located about 25 miles east of Quincy.
Length: 75.4 miles.
Terrain: An equal amount of rolling and sometimes hilly woodland mixed with flat or gently rolling areas through cropland.

Traffic and hazards: There are just a few brief stretches where you're likely to encounter traffic: SR 107 at mile 14.2, CR 2 west of New Salem at mile 52.5, and the short stretch on SR 104 at mile 67.8. Be sure to bring an ample supply of food and water; it's a long way between some of the pit stops.

Getting there: From northeast Illinois, take I-55 south to US 136 and head west. After crossing the Illinois River, turn left on US 24. After passing through Mount Sterling, turn left on East 2950th Street. Turn right on North 1200th Avenue, then left on East 2873rd Lane. The entrance to the park is on the right. Park at the Main Shelter House area—it's the first large picnic area on the right. Coordinates for starting point: 15S 676370E 4417531N

The Ride

While exploring the varied landscape of this ride, one of the many pleasures you'll encounter are quiet country roads on which you'll likely see more deer than cars. Indeed, with no sizable cities in the area, the roads on this route are quiet enough to allow biking companions to turn pedals side-by-side for most of the journey. Signs of civilization show up at widely spaced intervals, but you'll come upon the two towns—Versailles and Griggsville—at just the right times for fueling up and flopping down on a picnic table or grassy lawn.

A taste of this route's challenging landscape is delivered early on. The ride out of Siloam Springs State Park will get your wheels whizzing on a fairly steep downhill. East of Kellerville, you'll roll over a series of dips and climbs—many are brief, a few are substantial. Along this section of road are outlying sections of Siloam Springs State Park, a smattering of roadside ponds and wetlands, and a ravine containing Cronin Creek.

After the brief (and busy) stretch along SR 107, the roads become narrow, winding, and intimate. Woodland occasionally gives way to pastoral grassland. After enjoying the view from a 30-foot-high bridge over McKee Creek, the road leads you upward for about a mile. While pedaling this leg burner climb, be sure to lift your head now and then to enjoy the big, dramatic wooded ravine to the right. At the top

of the climb, the road widens—as do the views of the surrounding landscape. Cross McKee Creek again on the way into Versailles (pronounced *Ver-sails* in these parts). In Versailles, gather provisions at the small grocery store and take a break at the town park to the right on SR 99.

Just outside of Versailles, expansive views appear during an exhilarating descent of the bluff. After descending nearly 200 feet to the Illinois River bottomlands, the scenery is utterly transformed: For the next 14 miles, the route runs between the bluff on the right and the wide-open bottomland on the left. When the route swings out into the floodplain, you'll be surrounded by unrelenting stalks of corn. Looking east toward the town of Meredosia, the metal latticework of the bridge spanning the Illinois River is visible about 5 miles away.

In the hamlet of Valley City, you'll start to make a gradual climb out of the Illinois River floodplain. In Griggsville, birdhouses are perched on poles in people's yards, and in the town center sits a 40-foot high-rise stacked with multiple birdhouses. The birdhouses are for purple martins, a bluish black member of the swallow family that was headed for the endangered species list not so long ago. Local resident J. L. Wade was largely responsible for the birdhouses and for the bird becoming the town's official hyper-mascot—and, some say, for providing a helping hand in the species' comeback. Wade, owner of a local antenna-manufacturing factory, started making the aluminum birdhouses in the early 1960s and marketed them as a strategy for eliminating mosquito problems. While purple martins do eat mosquitoes, ornithologists generally refute the claim (plastered on a 40-foot wall in downtown Griggsville) that each bird eats 2,000 mosquitoes in a single day. In recent years, after Wade passed away, the birdhouse company was sold to a Chicago manufacturer. While the birdhouses are now made in Chicago, there is still a showroom for them in Griggsville.

Heading out of Griggsville, the rolling terrain brings you through a couple of villages: New Salem (not the same New Salem outside of Springfield, where Lincoln lived) and Baylis. While following the final leg of the route along quiet, gently rolling farm roads, keep an eye peeled for stately old barns and the occasional view from the small hilltops. After crossing SR 104, the hills swell and the woodland grows thicker heading north toward the state park. Getting closer to the park entrance, you'll shoot down into a ravine before crossing McKee Creek for the final time.

Miles and Directions

0.0 From the starting point in Siloam Springs State Park, head back out to the main road.

1.2 Turn right on East 2873rd Lane/Kellerville Road.

3.6 Turn right on North 1200th Avenue. Once you pass Kellerville, this road goes through a succession of name changes: CR 585 North, CR 550 North, CR 575 North, CR 600 North.

10.8 Turn right on CR 450 East.

◀   *This high-rise birdhouse in Griggsville was built for a small bird called the purple martin.*

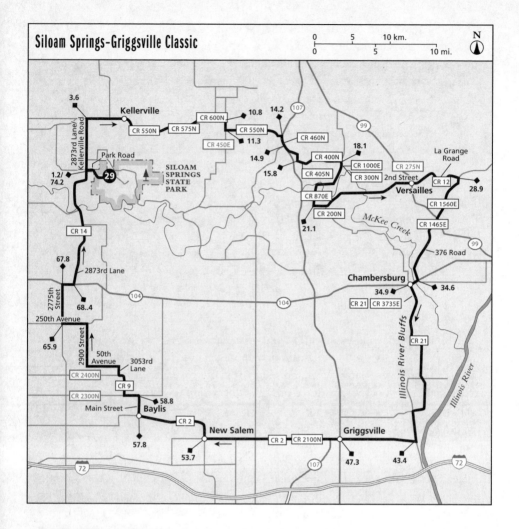

Siloam Springs-Griggsville Classic

11.3 Turn left on CR 550 North.

14.2 Turn right on SR 107. Traffic is steady; stay to the right.

14.9 Turn left on CR 460 North, which becomes CR 795.

15.8 Turn left on CR 405 North. This road soon becomes CR 400 North.

18.1 Turn right on CR 1000 East/CR 300 North.

21.1 Turn left on CR 200 North. As you get closer to Versailles, this road becomes CR 260 North, CR 275 North, and West 2nd Street.

26.3 In Versailles, continue straight ahead on La Grange Road/CR 12.

28.9 Turn right on CR 1560 East. On the way to Chambersburg, this road experiences an intense identity crisis as it becomes CR 1495 East, CR 1465 East, CR 1435 East, and 376 Road.

34.6 Turn right on SR 104 and pass through Chambersburg.

34.9 Turn left on CR 21/CR 3735 East.

43.4 Turn right on CR 2/CR 2100 West.

47.3 Pass through Griggsville.

53.7 Turn right on Pittsfield Road in New Salem. This is a continuation of CR 2, but it is not well marked. Follow this road as it curves to the left into the hamlet of Baylis.

57.8 In Baylis, turn right on Main Street.

58.8 Turn left on CR 2300 North. From here, the route takes a series of steps heading north and west. It may look tricky on a map, but it's easy to navigate on the ground. From CR 2300 North, the road curves right to become CR 9, curves left to become 340th Avenue, curves right to become East 3053rd Lane, curves left to become North 50th Avenue, curves right to become East 2900th Street, and curves left to become North 250th Avenue.

65.9 Turn right on East 2775th Street.

67.8 Turn right on SR 104. Watch for fast-moving traffic.

68.4 Turn left on East 2873rd Lane.

74.2 Turn right into Siloam Springs State Park.

75.4 Return to the parking area where you started.

Local Information

Pike County Chamber of Commerce: 224 West Washington St., Pittsfield; (217) 285-2971; www.pikeil.org.

Quincy Area Convention and Visitors Bureau: 300 Civic Center Plaza, Suite 237, Quincy; (800) 978-4748; www.quincy-cvb.org.

Local Events/Attractions

The Nature Society: This is the purple martin organization founded by J. L. Wade; buy birdhouses and gifts; 109 West Quincy St., Griggsville; www.naturesociety.org.

Restaurants

The Patio Restaurant: Upscale steak and seafood restaurant located in a historic hotel; 133 South 4th St., Quincy; (217) 222-5660; www.patiorestaurant.net.

Purple Martin Inn: Country diner fare; conveniently located at 105 West Quincy St., Griggsville; (217) 833-2600.

Accommodations

Land of Lincoln Motel: 403 East Main St., Mount Sterling; (217) 773-3311.

Siloam Springs State Park: Scenic, out-of-the-way park with 178 campsites; RR 1, Box 204, Clayton; (217) 894-6205; http://dnr.state.il.us/lands/landmgt/parks/r4/siloamsp.htm.

The Victorian Inn: Clean and affordable bed-and-breakfast about 15 miles northwest of Siloam Springs State Park; 217 North Illinois St., Camp Point; (217) 593-6116; www.the victorian-inn.com.

Bike Shops

Madison-Davis Bicycles: 912 South 8th St., Quincy; (217) 222-7262; www.madison-davis bicycles.com.

Restrooms

Start/finish: Restrooms and water are available at the parking area where the ride begins.

Mile 26.3: In Versailles, there are a few stores and a restaurant that may allow use of restrooms.

Mile 47.3: A visitor center is located opposite the birdhouse high-rise in downtown Griggsville.

Maps

USGS: Kellerville quad, Mt. Sterling quad, Versailles quad, Perry East quad, Cooperstown quad, Griggsville quad, New Salem quad, Baylis quad, Fishhook quad.

DeLorme: Illinois Atlas & Gazetteer: Page 66.

30 Springfield Cruise

While touring the environs northwest of Springfield, you'll encounter the rural charm of pastureland and farms, rivers and wetlands, and hills and ravines. And how could any Springfield-area excursion take place without at least one significant Lincolnian encounter? At nearly the halfway point, you'll pass by a small museum that highlights one of Honest Abe's most celebrated achievements as an Illinois politician.

Start: Washington Park, located on the west side of Springfield.
Length: 38.6 miles.

Terrain: Most of the terrain is gently rolling, but a few big hills appear along the way.
Traffic and hazards: Washington Street may get busy as you return to Springfield.

Getting there: Coming from the north on I-55, exit heading south on Sherman Boulevard (Business 55). Stay on this road as it becomes Veterans Drive. Turn left on Bruns Lane. A few miles ahead, turn left on Fayette Avenue. At Feldkamp Avenue, turn right and enter Washington Park. At the next junction in front of the lagoon, turn left. Turn right and then turn left in front of the pavilion. Park in the lot between the pavilion and the lagoon. Coordinates for starting point: 16S 270976E 4407624N

The Ride

With the exception of Washington, D.C., no other city in the nation serves as such an extensive tribute to a national hero. The mark of Lincoln exists throughout the city of Springfield. Plaques commemorate the sites of many of his activities, his name graces multiple businesses and streets, and his tomb and his home are maintained by the state as public shrines. Tour groups move from the Lincoln Presidential Museum to Lincoln's former law office to the Lincoln family pew on display in a local church.

This abundance of Lincolnia can get a bit overwhelming, and may inspire you to look for off-the-beaten-path encounters with this historic figure. If you're interested in visiting one of the lesser-known Lincoln attractions in the area, you may enjoy the museum that appears on this ride in the quiet rural town of Athens (pronounced *AY-thens*). The Long Nine Museum in Athens highlights one of Lincoln's most celebrated accomplishments as a state politician—his role in relocating the Illinois state capital.

Not long after striking out on this ride, it becomes clear that Springfield is a fairly compact city. It also becomes clear that those who name the local infrastructure tend to stick to the tried-and-true. After only 3 miles of riding through residential neighborhoods on Lincoln Avenue and Camp Lincoln Road, you'll arrive at the open, rolling, rural landscape alongside Abraham Lincoln Capital Airport. Traveling on SR 29, you'll zoom down toward the wooded banks of the Sangamon River. Another ravine appears on CR 1, where you'll drop down to cross Cantrall Creek.

A few large hills appear along the Springfield Cruise in the vicinity of the Sangamon River.

Continuing north, a sign in front of an old brick farmhouse on Digiovanna Road describes an event in 1926 when the famous aviator Charles Lindberg spent a night in the house after he landed his mail plane in a nearby field due to engine troubles. Repairing the plane the next day, Lindberg was off to Chicago. After making the first solo transatlantic flight the following year, Lindberg continued the same mail route, and local farmers say he never failed to dip a wing as he flew over the farm.

In the quiet village of Athens, you'll pass the Long Nine Museum located in a former post office at the corner of Jefferson Street and Main Street. The museum commemorates a banquet held upstairs in the building to honor Lincoln and the other men who successfully brought the state capital to Sangamon County. In the 1830s, when large waves of settlers began arriving in central Illinois, talk grew about relocating the state's capital from Vandalia, northeast of Saint Louis, to Springfield and thereby closer to the growing population. Led by Lincoln, a voting bloc of nine state legislators lobbied hard for moving the capital. The bloc was known as the Long Nine because the average height among them was 6 feet. Two years after successfully moving the capital, the boundary of Sangamon County was redrawn, leaving Athens in Menard County. The good feelings of the Athens townspeople fizzled. Despite letters written by Athens residents asking Lincoln and other lawmakers to reconsider, the decision stood.

The museum commemorating this turn of events and Lincoln's role in it contains a post office and general store on the first floor and, upstairs, dioramas depicting the history of the building and Lincoln's early connections to the area. The room upstairs features a large oil painting by the late artist Lloyd Ostendorf showing Lincoln in formal dress toasting his colleagues at the banquet. On the same street corner as the museum is a survey marker placed by Lincoln in 1834 when he was the deputy surveyor for the county. One block west of the museum, you'll find a small, no-frills grassy park perfect for taking a break.

Leaving Athens, the route proceeds south through a checkerboard of level cornfields. The woodland increases as you briskly descend a steep, winding hill into the Sangamon River floodplain. After crossing the river, the road shadows the river for half a mile, passing a series of roadside turnoffs that allow better views of the 60-foot-wide waterway. From the densely tangled banks of the river, a stretch of steep, winding road guides you back up the bluff. After the ascent, you'll follow the top of a bluff above the river and then drop down again to cross an iron trestle bridge over Richland Creek.

In the hamlet of Salisbury, consider having a slice of homemade apple pie in the pleasantly rustic atmosphere of the Morningstar Mercantile and Cafe. Next door to the cafe is the Colin Folk Art Gallery, which showcases the paintings and one-of-a-kind furniture of George Colin. Colin's paintings feature a range of local and not-so-local subject matter, such as roosters, cotton pickers, Abraham Lincoln, cowboys, dancers, and ice skaters. Colin, who learned to paint and draw from a Norman Rockwell correspondence course in illustration, has an impressive list of customers including Oprah Winfrey, Michael Jordan, former Illinois governor George Ryan, and U.S. senator Richard Durbin.

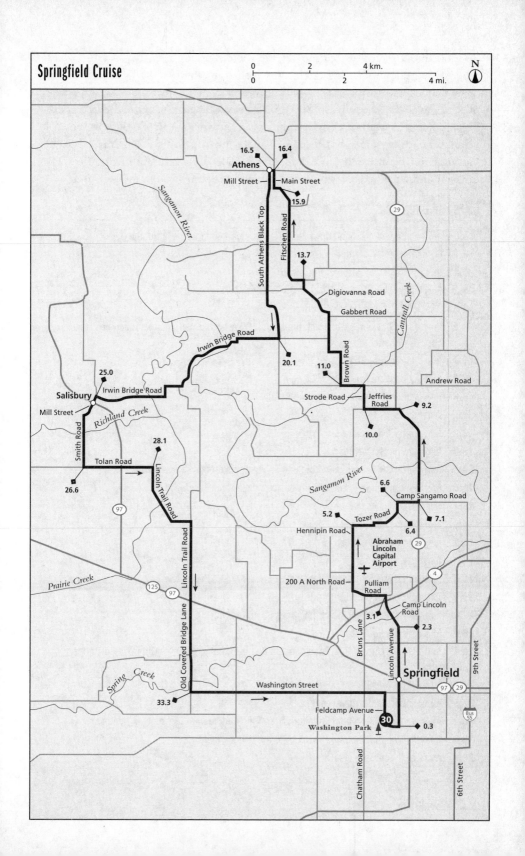

On the return trip to Springfield, the route dips and rises as you cross a continuing progression of creeks: Richland Creek again, followed by Prairie Creek and Spring Creek, from which Springfield gets its name. The open rural landscape fades into memory as you return to Springfield on Washington Street and pass a growing number of newer housing developments. Getting closer to Washington Park, the neighborhoods get older and the streets more urban. Once you've returned to the starting point, be sure to explore the rolling wooded terrain of Washington Park. The east side of the park contains botanical gardens, a lagoon, ravines, and a carillon.

Miles and Directions

0.0 In Washington Park, head down the hill on the park road to the left of the pavilion.

0.1 Go right as the park road splits.

0.2 Turn right again at Williams Boulevard.

0.3 Turn left on Lincoln Avenue.

2.3 Bear left on Camp Lincoln Road.

3.1 Turn left on Pulliam Road, which turns into 200 A North Road and then becomes Hennepin Road after the curve.

5.2 Turn right on Tozer Road.

6.4 Turn left on Ware Road.

6.6 Turn right on West Camp Sangamo Road.

7.1 Turn left on SR 29.

9.2 Turn left on Jeffries Road.

10.0 Turn right on Strode Road.

10.5 Turn left on CR 1 (be mindful of fast-moving traffic on this short stretch).

11.0 Turn right on Brown Road, which becomes Digiovanna Road.

13.7 Turn left on Fitschen Road.

15.9 Turn left on Little Road.

16.1 Turn right on Main Street.

16.4 Turn left on Jefferson Street.

16.5 Turn left on Mill Street, which becomes South Athens Black Top.

20.1 Turn right on Irwin Bridge Road.

25.0 Turn left on Mill Street, which becomes Smith Road.

26.6 Turn left on Tolan Road.

28.1 Turn right on Lincoln Trail Road. Lincoln Trail eventually becomes Old Covered Bridge Lane.

33.3 Turn left on Washington Street.

37.5 Turn right on Feldkamp Avenue.

38.2 After entering Washington Park, turn left on the park road at the edge of the lagoon.

38.5 Bear right on the park road to return to the parking area.

38.6 Arrive at the parking area.

Local Information

Central Illinois Tourism Development Office: 700 East Adams St., Springfield; (217) 525-7980; www.visitcentralillinois.com.

Springfield Convention and Visitors Bureau: 109 North 7th St., Springfield; (217) 789-2360; www.visit-springfieldillinois.com.

Local Events/Attractions

Abraham Lincoln Presidential Museum and Library: This museum dedicated to Illinois' most famous figure features a few high-tech attractions; 212 North 6th St., Springfield; (800) 610-2094; www.alplm.org.

Colin Folk Art Gallery: 6111 Mill St., Pleasant Plains; (217) 626-1204.

Illinois State Museum: Permanent and changing exhibits on Illinois' land, life, people, and art; 502 South Spring St., Springfield; (217) 782-7386; www.museum.state.il.us.

Lincoln's New Salem State Historic Site: 15588 History Lane, Petersburg; (217) 632-4000; www.lincolnsnewsalem.com.

Long Nine Museum: Open most summer afternoons; 200 South Main St., Athens; (217) 636-8755.

New Salem Country Opry: Old-style music venue featuring local and traveling country music performers; located next to Lincoln's New Salem State Historic Site; 14305 SR 97, Petersburg; (217) 632-2630; www.springfield-illinois.com/opry.

Old State Capitol State Historic Site: Restored with period furnishings; 1 Old State Capitol Plaza, Springfield; (217) 785-7960; www.oldstatecapitol.org/osc.htm.

Restaurants

Cafe Brio: Downtown restaurant with good food and a pleasant atmosphere; 524 East Monroe St., Springfield; (217) 544-0574.

Cozy Dog Drive-In: Credits itself for inventing the corn dog; decorated with Route 66 memorabilia; 2935 South 6th St., Springfield; (217) 525-1992; www.cozydogdrivein.com.

Morningstar Mercantile and Cafe: Known for its pies; located just off the route on SR 97, Salisbury; (217) 626-2022; www.morningstarcafe.com.

Accommodations

Carpenter Street Hotel: Affordable lodging north of downtown; 525 North 6th St., Springfield; (217) 789-9100; www.carpenterstreethotel.com.

Henry Mischler House: 803 East Edwards St., Springfield; (217) 525-2660; www.mischlerhouse.com.

Lincoln's New Salem State Historic Site: Contains a campground; see contact info above.

Bike Shops

BikeTek: Located close to the route; 957 Clock Tower Dr., Springfield; (217) 787-2907; www.biketekinc.net.

Restrooms

Start/finish: There's a water fountain next to the parking area in Washington Park. Restrooms are available near the park entrance off of South Grand Avenue.

Mile 16.5: A convenience store in Athens has restrooms. Head north on Main Street, turn right on Hargrave Street, and ride for a few blocks (Hargrave Street is 1 block north of Jefferson Street).

Maps

USGS: Athens quad, Farmingdale quad, Springfield West quad, Salisbury quad.

DeLorme: Illinois Atlas & Gazetteer: Pages 61 and 60.

Southern Illinois

Cyclists looking for hills are in luck in southern Illinois. One of only a few regions in the state not steamrolled by the last glacier, southern Illinois is known for its hills, valleys, and bluffs within the enormous Shawnee National Forest. The back roads of the Shawnee offer some of the most exhilarating riding in the state. Those who enjoy climbing will be thrilled with rides such as the Garden of the Gods Cruise, where level terrain comes in short supply.

In addition to the usual tectonic forces, the landscape in southern Illinois was sculpted by the forces of wind and water. The Big Muddy River carves an especially impressive gorge on the west side of the Shawnee. Rides such as the Ohio River Challenge, the Shawnee–Pomona Ramble, and the Shawnee West Ramble explore river bluffs as well as flat floodplain. Mississippi River bluffs figure prominently on the American Bottoms Cruise south of Saint Louis, and on the Kampsville River Bluff Cruise and the Pere Marquette Challenge north of Saint Louis.

Of course, not all of southern Illinois is composed of soaring bluffs, big hills, and deep valleys. A topographically mellower, but no less beautiful, riding experience can be found on the Hillsboro, Rend Lake, and Olney rambles. These less strenuous rides focus on the pockets of hilly terrain in the northern section of the region.

The fact that southern Illinois has fewer urban areas than the rest of the state is reflected in the intensely rural nature of nearly all the rides in this section. Be prepared to encounter few of the typical roadside facilities, such as convenience stores, parks, and gas stations. Some people may find this bothersome; others find it appealing because they say it adds to the beauty and remote ambience that typifies this part of the state.

31 American Bottoms Cruise

This ride consists of two parts, each very different from the other. The west half tours the straight, wide-open roads that run through a vast Mississippi River floodplain (and super-fertile farming territory) called the American Bottoms. The east half follows a series of twisting, hilly roads through the wooded bluffs about 400 feet above the floodplain.

Start: The old village of Valmeyer at Bosch Community Park. Old Valmeyer is located about 35 miles south of Saint Louis.
Length: 41.4 miles.
Terrain: Half of the ride is flat Mississippi floodplain; the other half is rolling and hilly, with a few long climbs. At mile 6.2, you'll start climbing for 3 or so miles. Most of the climbing is gradual, but some of it is steep.

Traffic and hazards: Be careful while traveling up and down the river bluffs. These roads are curvy and there are blind turns. Patches of loose gravel may appear as well. While cycling through the floodplain, the route is totally exposed to sun and wind.

Getting there: From the Saint Louis area, head south on SR 3. In Waterloo, turn right on SR 156. Pass the new town of Valmeyer on the right and then head down the bluff. As you enter old Valmeyer, Bosch Memorial Park appears on the right. Park along Maple Street or on 4th Street. Start the ride by heading south on 4th Street. Coordinates for starting point: 15S 735196E 4241999N

The Ride

If the village of Valmeyer seems especially quiet, there's good reason for it: The townspeople, by and large, have left the village. In 1993, after getting hit with two severe floods in quick succession, 90 percent of the town's buildings were damaged beyond repair. As a result, the Valmeyer residents decided to pull up stakes and move their town out of the floodplain to a spot 2 miles up the river bluff. Houses, churches, stores, businesses, a school, and a post office were built in the new town with funding from a variety of sources. While most of Valmeyer's 900 residents decided to move 400 feet up the bluff, some did not. Now, about 1,200 residents live in the new Valmeyer, while a dozen or so families decided to remain in the old Valmeyer.

Heading west from old Valmeyer, the bluffs and limestone outcroppings come into view as you get farther into the floodplain. Within the vast gridded cropland of the floodplain, the rare farmhouse looks like the last remaining chess piece on the board. After meandering a few miles through crops and wetlands, you'll head back toward the wooded bluffs and then start climbing.

As you start gradually ascending the bluff on this wiggler of a road, look for Monroe City Creek as it flows beside you within the ravine. Wooded bluffs rise up about 200 feet on each side of the road. While admiring the surroundings, be sure to keep

These ruins of an old limestone church appear on the American Bottoms Cruise.

an eye on the roadway—a few blind curves require your full attention. Just before reaching the hamlet of Monroe City, the road becomes more winding and the climbing intensifies. Over the next 2 miles, the road rises about 300 feet. A handful of turns bring you up on a ridge, densely wooded with hickory and maple.

The stately limestone church in the hamlet of Madonnaville marks the top of the 3-mile leg-burning climb up the bluff. Immaculate Consumption Catholic Church dates to 1855; the former school and rectory, built in a similar style with local stone, were both built in 1861. Pull up next to the cemetery for an expansive view of the nearby hills and woodland.

Another stone church, this one without a roof and partly covered in vines, appears on Old Baum Church Road. A plaque near the entrance explains that this church was built by a German evangelical congregation in 1883 and was used until the 1930s. Continuing ahead, the road winds past an increasing number of residences, including a few sparkling new subdivisions that appear out of place in these rural environs. A short stint on SR 156 drops you off on the delightfully curvy and rolling Deer Hill Road, which runs through a mixed landscape of pastureland, wooded swatches, and scattered houses.

The end of Deer Hill Road at about mile 20 signals the beginning of a zigzagging roller coaster ride in and out of the Fountain Creek floodplain. Just before turning on HH Road, a steep downhill plunges you down beside Fountain Creek. The road climbs out of the floodplain, and then turning onto D Road, you'll make another steep descent to cross Fountain Creek. Another climb follows, and then a few ticks later, after crossing Hanover Road, an extended curving downhill drops you into a ravine created by Long Slash Creek.

As you turn onto Steppig Road and commence the 1-mile-long descent back to the Mississippi floodplain, the roadside is speckled with small ponds fringed with stands of trees. While careening downward, sometimes steeply, watch for views of the level floodplain below. Also, keep watch for Little Carr Creek flowing through the wooded ravine parallel to the road. While following this winding road down the bluff, be mindful of troublesome patches of loose gravel.

Back on the floodplain, suddenly you can see for miles. Now that you have a couple of hours of riding under your tires, it may come as a painful realization that the floodplain provides no relief from wind and sun. The wind, which frequently blows through the floodplain, seems to press harder as you mount the 30-foot-high levee alongside Fountain Creek. The nice views, however, offer a reasonable tradeoff for the wind. Fountain Creek hosts turtles basking in the sun as well as waterbirds such as great blue herons, green herons, killdeer, and plovers. The higher position of the levee also helps with spotting American kestrels, a small falcon that often scouts prey while perched on wires and electrical poles.

Coming down from the Fountain Creek levee, you'll turn toward the bluffs and pedal for about 4 miles back to Valmeyer. On the way into Valmeyer, look for the big gap in the face of the bluff. This is the location of a system of caves that once hosted one of the largest mushroom-growing operations in the nation. The caves are now used as a records storage facility for the military.

Miles and Directions

0.0 Start at Bosch Community Park in old Valmeyer. Head south on 4th Street.

0.2 Turn right on SR 156/Main Street.

1.4 Turn left on B Road.

4.4 Turn left on Baer Road. Continue straight ahead as Baer Road merges with Bluff Road.

6.2 Turn left on KK Road. Be careful on the turns while following this winding road.

9.5 Turn left on Ahne Road.

11.7 Turn left on Old Baum Church Road.

13.9 Turn left on SR 156.

15.1 Turn right on Deer Hill Road.

19.6 Turn left on HH Road.

20.4 Turn right on D Road.

25.1 Turn left on Steppig Road.

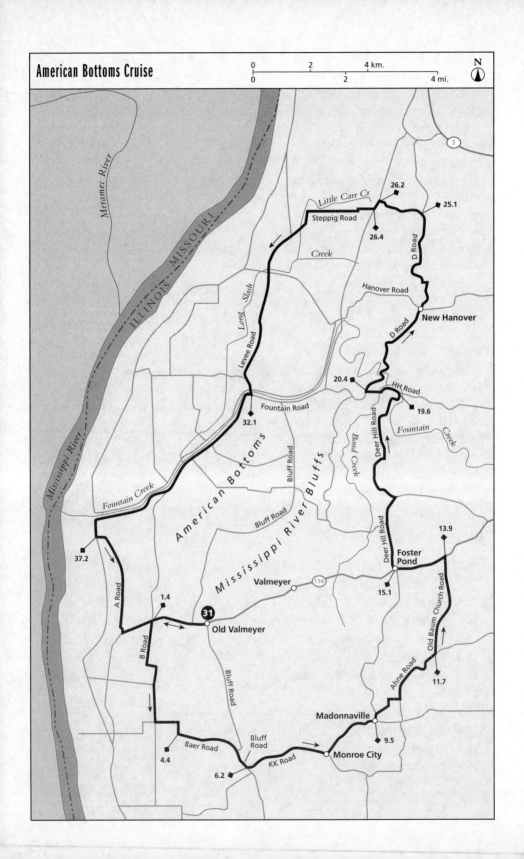

American Bottoms Cruise

0   2   4 km.
0   2   4 mi.

N

Meramec River

ILLINOIS

MISSOURI

Little Carr Cr

26.2

25.1

Steppig Road

26.4

Creek

D Road

Long Slash

Hanover Road

Levee Road

D Road

New Hanover

20.4

HH Road

Fountain Road

19.6

32.1

Fountain   Creek

Mississippi River

Deer Hill Road

Bond Creek

Bluff Road

American Bottoms

Mississippi River Bluffs

Fountain Creek

Bluff Road

37.2

13.9

Foster Pond

A Road

Deer Hill Road

15.1

Valmeyer   156

1.4

31

Old Baum Church Road

B Road

Old Valmeyer

Ahne Road

11.7

Bluff Road

Madonnaville

9.5

Bluff Road

4.4

Baer Road

KK Road

Monroe City

6.2

26.2 Turn left on Bluff Road.

26.4 Turn right on Steppig Road, which soon becomes Levee Road.

32.1 Stay on Levee Road as it turns hard to the right after crossing Fountain Creek.

37.2 Turn left on A Road.

39.6 Turn left on SR 156.

41.4 Turn left on 4th Street in Valmeyer and return to Bosch Community Park.

Local Information

Monroe County Tourism Committee: P.O. Box 1, Waterloo, IL 62298; (618) 939-5300.

Tourism Bureau of Southwestern Illinois: 10950 Lincoln Trail, Fairview Heights; (618) 397-1488; www.thetourismbureau.org.

Local Events/Attractions

Illinois Caverns State Natural Area: Open Thursday through Saturday; spelunking gear required; 4369 G Rd., Waterloo; (618) 458-6699 or (618) 785-2555; http://dnr.state.il.us/lands/landmgt/parks/r4/ilc.htm.

Maeystown: Entire village is on the National Register of Historic Places; features a handful of shops; located several miles south of the route; contact the village for more information; (618) 458-6566; www.maeystown.com.

Restaurants

Dreamland Palace German Restaurant: Bratwurst, knockwurst, and other German specialties; located right on the route; 3043 SR 156, Foster Pond; (618) 939-9922; www.dreamlandpalace.net.

Gallagher's: Steak, seafood, and chicken served in a charming old building with great decor; 114 West Mill St., Waterloo; (618) 939-9933; www.gallagherswaterloo.com.

Accommodations

Corner George Inn Bed and Breakfast: Has seven guest rooms, each with a private bath; corner of Main Street and Mill Street, Maeystown; (618) 458-6660.

Bike Shops

South County Cyclery: 9985 Lin Ferry Dr., Affton, MO; (314) 843-5586; www.angelfire.com/mo/southcountycyclery.

Restrooms and Water

Start/finish: Restrooms and a picnic area are available in Bosch Memorial Park.

Maps

USGS: Columbia quad, Valmeyer quad, Waterloo quad.

DeLorme: Illinois Atlas & Gazetteer: Page 74.

32 Chain of Rocks Ramble

While following paved trails along this stretch of the Mississippi River, you'll encounter a handful of local landmarks, including the Gateway Arch in downtown Saint Louis. On the second half of the ride, the trails take you upstream on a system of levees and through a series of parks. End the ride at one of the great unsung treasures of Illinois and Missouri—the mile-long Chain of Rocks pedestrian bridge.

Start: Across the Mississippi River from Saint Louis at the foot of the Chain of Rocks Bridge.
Length: 24.7 miles.
Terrain: Flat riverbank.

Traffic and hazards: About 5 miles of this route is on streets; the rest follows trails. About 3 miles of trails have a crushed gravel surface that can be slightly rough in places. SR 3 has heavy traffic but a very wide shoulder.

Getting there: From I-270 east of the Mississippi River, head south on SR 3. Immediately turn right on Chain of Rocks Road. Park at the end of Chain of Rocks Road in the lot at the foot of the Chain of Rocks Bridge. Coordinates for starting point: 15S 746443E 4293435N

The Ride

After the Gateway Arch in downtown Saint Louis, the Chain of Rocks Bridge is one of the most captivating human artifacts in the region. At about 1 mile long, the bridge is not only one of the longest steel-truss bridges in the country, it's also been called the longest bike and pedestrian bridge in the world. Measurements aside, the views overlooking the mammoth Mississippi waterway, the nearby wooded island and bluffs, and the distant skyline of Saint Louis are absolutely breathtaking.

A distinctive feature of the bridge is the 22-degree bend in the middle. The bend allowed southbound riverboats to follow the current between the bridge's piers and avoid colliding with two water-intake towers just south of the bridge. These two castlelike water-intake structures were built in 1894 and are still used for gathering the local water supply. The Chain of Rocks Bridge is perhaps best known for serving as the Mississippi River crossing for historic Route 66 from 1936 until the 1960s.

You'll get the full experience of the Chain of Rocks Bridge at the end of the ride. For now, head east from the parking area at the foot of the bridge. The first mile takes you across Chouteau Island and over the Chain of Rocks Canal, an 8.4-mile-long waterway that allows river traffic to bypass a series of treacherous rock ledges in the main channel of the Mississippi River.

After crossing the Chain of Rocks Canal, bike route signs will direct you down to the Confluence Trail as it runs beside the canal. The straight-as-an-arrow canal is treeless and edged by piles of riprap, but the sprawling wetlands on the left and the attending waterbirds help liven the scenery. Eventually, the trail leaves the canal and joins up with SR 3. When the trail ends at 20th Street, you'll embark on a nearly

In Saint Louis, paddleboat tours are offered on the Mississippi River.

3-mile stretch of riding on SR 3. The traffic is fast and thick, but thankfully the paved shoulder is wide, smooth, and somewhat free of roadside detritus. (Local authorities have indicated that a bike path along SR 3 is on the way. Let's hope they follow through with these plans. For now, though, the shoulder works okay.)

The handsome McKinley Bridge was built in 1910 for one of the Illinois interurban train lines that once connected local cities. The bridge offers fine views of downtown Saint Louis, the Gateway Arch, and the nearby wooded shoreline. Coming down off the bridge starts you toward downtown Saint Louis on a 2-mile route that zigzags by numerous heavy industries, including a scrap metal recycler and a salt storage facility. Watch for trucks as the path weaves in and out of the concrete floodwall.

By installing helpful signs, colorful banners, and attractive sculptures along the floodwall, the city of Saint Louis has done an admirable job of making this intensely industrial strip of riverfront more welcoming to cyclists and pedestrians. After the path ends in a trailhead parking area, you'll follow quiet side streets to the foot of the tallest monument in the nation. Visitors can make the 630-foot trip to the top of the steel arch aboard a special tram. Since the Gateway Arch was finished in 1965, eight small planes have flown through its gap.

After ogling this engineering marvel and perhaps grabbing a bite from a vendor or at one of the many eateries in the vicinity, it's time to turn around and start heading north on the Riverfront Trail. After passing the McKinley Bridge, you'll continue to

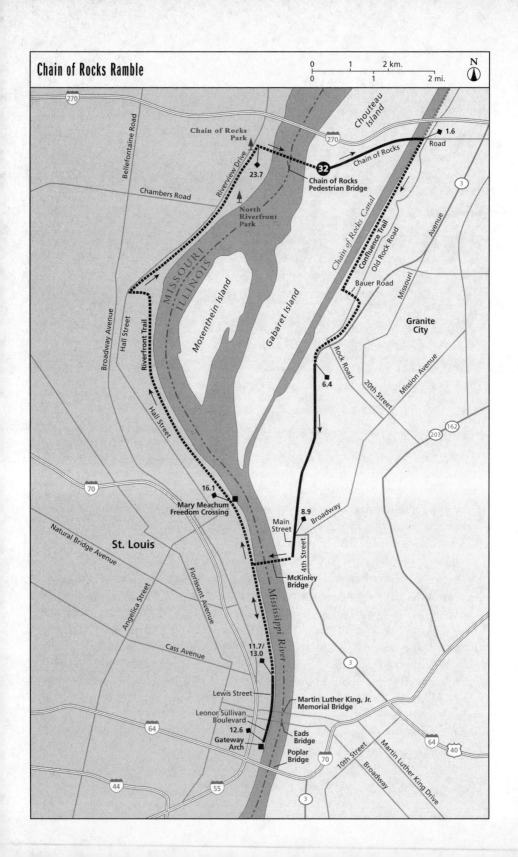

Chain of Rocks Ramble

0   1   2 km.

0   1   2 mi.

N

270

Bellefontaine Road

Chambers Road

Chain of Rocks
Park

Riverview Drive

23.7

North
Riverfront
Park

Chouteau
Island

270

3

1.6

Chain of Rocks
Road

32

Chain of Rocks
Pedestrian Bridge

Chain of Rocks Canal

Confluence Trail

Old Rock Road

Bauer Road

Missouri Avenue

Granite
City

MISSOURI
ILLINOIS

Mosenthein Island

Gabaret Island

Broadway Avenue

Hall Street

Riverfront Trail

Hall Street

Rock Road

6.4

20th Street

Mission Avenue

162

203

70

16.1

Mary Meachum
Freedom Crossing

Natural Bridge Avenue

St. Louis

Angelica Street

Florissant Avenue

Cass Avenue

8.9

Main
Street

4th Street

Broadway

McKinley
Bridge

3

Mississippi River

11.7/
13.0

Lewis Street

Leonor Sullivan
Boulevard

12.6

Gateway
Arch

Martin Luther King, Jr.
Memorial Bridge

Eads
Bridge

Poplar
Bridge

64

10th Street

Broadway

Martin Luther King Drive

64

40

44

55

70

3

weave in and out of the floodwall and then occasionally duck under pipelines that connect the industries with the barges on the river.

Just after passing the Merchants Bridge, the trail passes the Mary Meachum Freedom Crossing, commemorating the efforts of a freed African-American woman who attempted to guide runaway slaves across the Mississippi River at this spot in 1855. Meachum and the slaves were captured before reaching Illinois. Since the runaway slaves were owned by a prominent Saint Louis resident, local papers covered the incident thoroughly, making it one of only a few well-documented events related to the local Underground Railroad.

Continuing north, the trail mounts a 50-foot-high levee that offers glimpses of the river through the trees. In the river, you'll see the dense woodland of Mosenthein Island, named for a family that once lived on this 2.5-mile-long swath of waterbound bottomland.

At mile 20.3, the trail begins accompanying Riverview Drive and passes through a series of open grassy parks on the edge of the river. Just before reaching the Chain of Rocks Bridge, the final park takes you partially up a wooded bluff. Once you've mounted the Chain of Rocks Bridge, you'll likely agree that there is no better place to enjoy this big and wild river. The view south from the bridge of the northern tip of Mosenthein Island hasn't changed a bit since this bridge was built in 1929.

Miles and Directions

0.0 Head east on Chain of Rocks Road from the parking area.

1.6 After crossing the Chain of Rocks Canal, follow the bike route signs to the Confluence Trail. Head south on the Confluence Trail as it follows the shore of the Chain of Rocks Canal.

6.4 At the end of the Confluence Trail, continue straight ahead on SR 3. While there's heavy traffic on SR 3, there's also a very wide shoulder.

8.9 As SR 3 turns left, stay to the right on Main Street and then head toward the McKinley Bridge to the right.

9.1 Before crossing the McKinley Bridge, hop on the pedestrian/bike path on the left.

11.7 When the Riverfront Trail ends at the parking area near the corner of Biddle Street and Lewis Street, turn left on Lewis Street and keep heading south along the river. Lewis Street soon becomes Leonor Sullivan Boulevard.

12.6 At the foot of the Gateway Arch, turn around and retrace your route back to the McKinley Bridge. Instead of crossing back over the bridge, keep heading north on the Missouri side of the river on the Riverfront Trail.

23.7 After crossing Riverview Drive, cross the Chain of Rocks Bridge.

24.7 Return to the parking area at the foot of the bridge.

Local Information

Madison County Transit Trails: c/o Madison County Transit, One Transit Way, Granite City; (618) 874-7433; www.mcttrails.org.

St. Louis Convention and Visitors Commission: 701 Convention Plaza, Suite 300, Saint Louis, MO; (314) 421-1023; www.explorestlouis.com.

St. Louis Department of Parks: 5600 Clayton Rd., Saint Louis, MO; (314) 622-4000; http://stlouis.missouri.org.

Tourism Bureau of Southwestern Illinois: 10950 Lincoln Trail, Fairview Heights; (618) 397-1488; www.thetourismbureau.org.

Local Events/Attractions

Cahokia Mounds State Historic Site and Interpretive Center: Once the largest and most sophisticated prehistoric city north of Mexico; 30 Ramey Dr., Cahokia; (618) 346-5160; www.cahokiamounds.com.

Eugene Field House and the St. Louis Toy Museum: Historic home with a large toy collection; located a few blocks west of the route; 634 South Broadway, Saint Louis, MO; (314) 421-4689; www.eugenefieldhouse.org.

Restaurants

Blues City Deli: Classic deli sandwiches; located south of downtown; 2438 McNair Ave., Saint Louis, MO; (314) 773-8225; www.bluescitydeli.com.

Franco Restaurant: French-influenced cuisine; very affordable lunch menu; 1535 South 8th St., Saint Louis, MO; (314) 436-2500; www.eatatfranco.com.

Accommodations

Beall Mansion: This 1903 mansion contains a museum; on the National Register of Historic Places; 407 East 12th St., Alton; (866) 843-2325; www.beallmansion.com.

Bike Shops

Breese Bicycles: Specializes in service; 3809 Pontoon Rd., Pontoon Beach; (618) 797-0434.

Restrooms

Start/finish: Portable restrooms are available at the beginning of the trail.

Mile 9.1: Water is available at the roadside park at the foot of the McKinley Bridge.

Maps

USGS: Columbia Bottom quad, Granite City quad.

DeLorme: Illinois Atlas & Gazetteer: Page 75.

33 Garden of the Gods Cruise

A magnificent series of ridges and hollows (or "hollers," as Southerners call them) will give your legs a first-rate workout. This ride takes you through dense woodland, along wild and winding roads, and over some of the biggest hills in Illinois. The huge hills let up on the northeastern section of the route. Toward the end of the ride, consider flopping your tired body into a scenic little lake nestled in the bottom of a beautiful holler.

Start: Garden of the Gods Recreation Area, located about 15 miles southeast of Harrisburg.
Length: 37.3 miles.
Terrain: Some of the biggest hills in Illinois, deep ravines, and densely wooded national forest. Some sections of the ride are gently rolling.

Traffic and hazards: Throughout the ride, the big hills and curvy roads require that riders use extra care. This is especially true on the short segments of SR 1 and SR 34, where riders will encounter more traffic. Tackling this route during the dog days of a southern Illinois summer can be grueling. Bring extra water.

Getting there: From Harrisburg, head south on SR 145. Turn left on SR 34, then left on Karbers Ridge Road (CR 4). Turn left again on Garden of the Gods Road. The entrance is on the left. Coordinates for starting point: 16S 377810E 4162654N

The Ride

It's for good reason that Garden of the Gods serves as one of the main tourist draws in southern Illinois. At the edge of the parking area, visitors can stand atop strangely shaped rock formations and take in 30-mile views of distant rolling hills. Some of the rock formations look like enormous dollops of wet sand dropped from above; others resemble forests of giant mushrooms. Garden of the Gods also claims a top-notch system of hiking trails that allows you to explore rocky canyons, sandstone cliffs, and remote wooded bluffs.

This scenic backdrop provides a perfect launching spot for this ride. A couple of miles after leaving Garden of the Gods, Karbers Ridge Road offers a taste of the roller coaster ride to come: You're granted a few far-off views as you crest a hill, dip way down, rise again, and then descend steeply toward SR 34.

From Herod, the route climbs nearly 200 feet before guiding you on a glorious gradual downhill through a lush forest of maple and oak. The road follows Gape Hollow—carved out by Eagle Creek, a little rocky-bottom stream that runs alongside the road. This perfect biking road is so dense with greenery, so quiet and winding, that it seems more like a woodland hiking trail than a road.

Near the junction of Eagle Mine Road and High Knob Road, the strangely beautiful grassy hills seem extraordinarily out of place. Indeed, the bare hills are the result

The Garden of the Gods Cruise takes you through one of the hilliest areas in Illinois.

of a former a strip-mining operation in the area. As you round the side of a hill south of Eagle Mine Road, expansive views open up to the east and south.

More climbs and more hilltop views await you along High Knob Road. This road, sprinkled with pine plantations, traverses a ridge between Rice Hollow to the west and Captain Vineyard Hollow to the east. The terrain mellows for the next several miles: As you pedal through the flat farmland on Leamington Road, more of the formerly strip-mined hills appear to the north and attractive wooded bluffs rise up on the south. Switching to Thacker Hollow Road, you're guided along a narrow and winding country road that mounts a series of small but steep hills.

Take your pick of two places to stop and explore after turning onto Pounds Hollow Road. The first spot is Pounds Hollow Recreation Area, a public camping area and swimming hole. The campground sits on a steep bluff above a small lake set deep in a wooded holler. On hot, muggy summer days, the lake's swimming beach brings in people from miles around. Even if swimming is not on the agenda, consider taking the 1.5-mile loop along the densely wooded park road down to Pounds Lake.

Rim Rock Recreation Area, about 1 mile beyond Pounds Hollow, offers a spot to rest and pick up the primo hiking trails in the area. There's a short paved trail that runs along the top of what's called the Rim Rock Escarpment. You can also hike down into Pounds Hollow and follow the Beaver Trail back to Pounds Lake. Rim Rock contains the crumbling remains of a wall that local Native Americans once used for defense.

Garden of the Gods Cruise

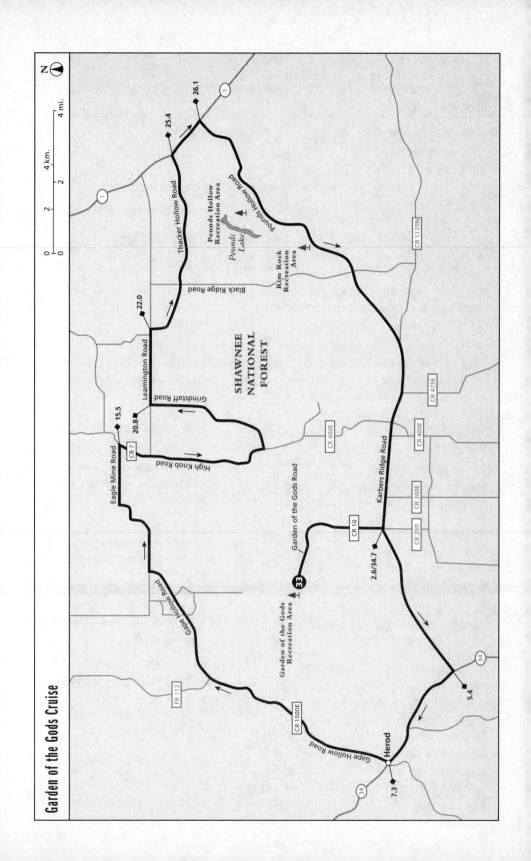

From Rim Rock, several miles of winding wooded roadway lead you back to CR 10 and the entrance to Garden of the Gods.

Miles and Directions

0.0 Start from the parking area at Garden of the Gods Recreation Area.

1.2 Turn right on CR 10.

2.6 Turn left on Karbers Ridge Road.

5.4 Turn right on SR 34. Ride carefully: The shoulder nearly disappears on this road.

7.3 Turn right on Gape Hollow Road (CR 1500 East) in Herod. No road sign for Gape Hollow Road, but it's the only right turn in Herod.

13.3 After crossing CR 15/CR 17, Gape Hollow Road becomes Eagle Mine Road.

15.5 Turn right on High Knob Road (look closely—the road sign may be hidden behind branches).

18.4 Turn left on Grindstaff Road.

20.8 Turn right on Leamington Road.

22.0 Turn right on Thacker Hollow Road.

25.4 Turn right on SR 1. Stay to the right; traffic picks up and moves fast on this road.

26.1 Turn right on Pounds Hollow Road, which eventually turns into Karbers Ridge Road.

27.9 **Side trip:** The 1.5-mile loop down to Pounds Lake is highly recommended—especially if it's swimming weather.

34.7 Turn right on CR 10.

37.3 Return to the Garden of the Gods parking area.

Local Information

Shawnee National Forest: Hidden Springs Ranger Station, 602 North 1st St., Vienna; (618) 658-2111; www.fs.fed.us/r9/forests/shawnee.

Southern Illinois Tourism Development Office: 3000 West DeYoung St., Marion; (888) 998-9397 or (618) 998-1024; http://illinois adventure.com.

Local Events/Attractions

Cave-in-Rock State Park: Best known for its deep sandstone cave that once hosted a tavern and served as a hideout for bandits and river pirates; 1 New State Park Rd., Box 338, Cave-in-Rock; (618) 289-4325; http://dnr.state.il.us/lands/landmgt/parks/r5/caverock.htm.

Garden of the Gods Recreation Area: One of the main attractions in southern Illinois, with stunning rock formations and great views; see Shawnee National Forest contact info above.

Pounds Hollow Recreation Area: Offers camping and swimming; see Shawnee National Forest contact info above.

Restaurants

The Bar BQ Barn: A local favorite specializing in BBQ sandwiches; 632 North Main St., Harrisburg; (618) 252-6190.

Kaylor's Restaurant: Great views of the Ohio River from a bluff in Cave-in-Rock State Park; (618) 289-4545; see Cave-in-Rock information above; http://caveinrockkaylors.com.

Accommodations

Cave-in-Rock State Park: Campground, with showers available; see contact info above.

Garden of the Gods Recreation Area: Campground contains twelve primitive sites, no showers; excellent hiking trails spin off from the campground; see Shawnee National Forest contact info above.

Rim Rock's Dogwood Cabins: Located near the Rim Rock Recreation Area, RR 2, Box 124, Elizabethtown; www.rimrocksdogwoodcabins.com.
River Rose Inn Bed and Breakfast and Cottages: Greek Revival mansion on the Ohio River; 1 Main St., Elizabethtown; (618) 287-8811; www.riveroseinn.com.

Bike Shops

The Bike Surgeon: 404 South Illinois Ave., Carbondale; (618) 457-4521; www.thebikesurgeon.com.

Restrooms

Start/finish: Garden of the Gods has vault toilets and water.
Mile 5.4: Harbisons Country Market at the corner of Karbers Ridge Road and SR 34 has restrooms.
Mile 27.9: Pounds Hollow Recreation Area has a campground with water and restrooms.
Mile 28.7: Rim Rock Recreation Area offers restrooms.

Maps

USGS: Karbers Ridge quad, Herod quad, Equality quad.
DeLorme: Illinois Atlas & Gazetteer: Page 91.

34 Hillsboro Ramble

Much of this ride follows the route of the Hillsboro–Roubaix Spring Classic, a favorite bike race in central Illinois. Cyclists love riding in this area because of the quiet roads and the constantly shifting terrain. As the roads change from flat to rolling to hilly, you'll mount a few hilltops with open views of the surrounding countryside.

Start: South shore of Lake Lou Yaeger, located just outside of Litchfield.
Length: 33.9 miles.

Terrain: The route offers a mix of flat and rolling terrain, with a handful of hill climbs.
Traffic and hazards: Be mindful of occasional cars on the curving roads.

Getting there: From I-55 south of Springfield, head east on SR 16. Pass through Litchfield, then turn left on Lake Lou Yaeger Trail. Keep straight ahead as you pass the park entrance on the left. Park in the dirt lot on the right opposite the lake. Coordinates for starting point: 16S 275459E 4340417N

The Ride

Many Midwestern bike racers have the Hillsboro–Roubaix Spring Classic in mind when they start riding their indoor trainers in December. The early-April race features a 22-mile loop that rumbles through brick streets in Hillsboro and then dips and bobs through the rolling terrain between Litchfield and Hillsboro. There are short but challenging climbs and twisting descents. The event is the largest single-day road race in the Midwest, with nearly 400 riders competing in seven skill levels; top finishers in each class are awarded trophies and cash prizes. The race takes place the same weekend as its namesake, the Paris–Roubaix, held in northern France since 1896. Known for its rough terrain and cobblestone roads, the Paris–Roubaix is one of the most famous bike races in Europe.

While you won't trace the entire route of the Hillsboro-Roubaix race, you'll cover most it on this ride. In order to remain on quiet roads and stretch out the mileage a bit, some notable changes were made. First, the route was extended about 10 miles south to offer riders an added taste of the lovely rolling landscape in the area. Also, in order to avoid some of the more heavily trafficked roads, you'll be starting on the south shore of Lake Lou Yaeger instead of in the town of Hillsboro.

After departing from the shore of Lake Lou Yaeger, the first few miles of the ride zigzag through flat cornfields and pastureland. On Washboard Trail (despite its name, it's actually smooth) the landscape changes: A steep downhill with a curve at the bottom starts the adrenaline moving. Rise again and you're granted views of the surrounding terrain before dropping again to cross Brush Creek. Catch a glimpse of Shoal Creek (the water source for Lake Lou Yaeger) while on Old Litchfield Road. After pedaling through the Shoal Creek floodplain, you'll climb a wiggly road onto a bluff laden with maple and oak trees.

Turns come frequently as you navigate a series of quiet—and often narrow—roads. Concrete silos and wood barns spring up from the pastures and cropland. After the second crossing of Shoal Creek on a bridge about 50 feet above the water, the landscape rolls, flattens, and then rolls again. This pattern continues as you follow the curves of Fox Hunt Trail.

As Waveland Road shoots straight north, watch for American kestrels perched on the roadside electric wires. Occasionally, you may see them hovering perfectly while scouting prey. (The American kestrel is a small falcon with blue-gray wings and a speckled breast.) On the Red Bridge Trail, the road descends steeply before crossing a set of railroad tracks. While on the bridge over the Middle Fork of Shoal Creek, a fetching scene appears in front of you: wooded hills rising from the grassy edges of the bottomland.

Emerging from the floodplain, the landscape transforms again. The gently rolling terrain of Miller Road allows views of the surrounding agricultural checkerboard. On Interurban Circle, the road curves through a wooded stretch before descending to Brush Creek. After completing a short stretch on SR 16, it's 3 miles back to the starting point at Lake Lou Yaeger.

Miles and Directions

0.0 Head east on Lake Lou Yaeger Trail. After the second curve to the right, Lake Lou Yaeger Trail becomes Rainmaker Trail and then soon becomes 13th Avenue.

1.9 Turn right on Parsons Road (CR 650 East).

2.9 Turn right on SR 16.

3.0 Turn left on Washboard Trail.

5.6 Turn right on Old Litchfield Road.

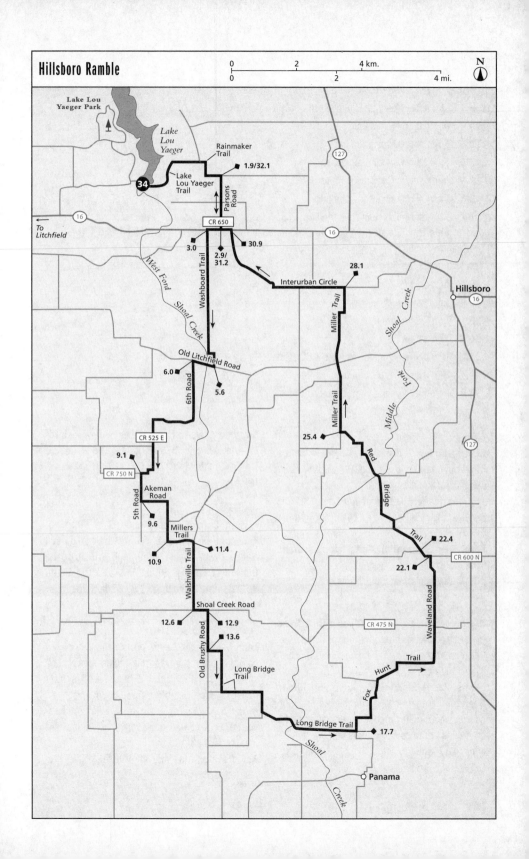

Hillsboro Ramble

0   2   4 km.

0   2   4 mi.

N

Lake Lou
Yaeger Park

Lake
Lou
Yaeger

Rainmaker
Trail

1.9/32.1

Lake
Lou Yaeger
Trail

34

Parsons Road

16

To
Litchfield

CR 650

3.0

2.9/
31.2

30.9

28.1

Interurban Circle

Hillsboro

16

West Ford

Shoal Creek

Washboard Trail

Miller Trail

Shoal Creek

Old Litchfield Road

6.0

5.6

6th Road

Miller Trail

Fork Middle

127

25.4

CR 525 E

9.1

CR 750 N

Akeman
Road

Red

5th Road

9.6

Bridge

Millers
Trail

11.4

Trail

22.4

10.9

Walshville Trail

CR 600 N

22.1

Shoal Creek Road

Waveland Road

12.6

12.9

13.6

Old Brushy Road

CR 475 N

Long Bridge
Trail

Hunt

Trail

Fox

Long Bridge Trail

17.7

Shoal

Panama

Creek

6.0	Turn left on 6th Road. Stay on this road as it curves several times and becomes CR 525 East.
9.1	Turn left on 5th Road.
9.6	Turn left on Akeman Road, which becomes Durban Road as it turns right.
10.9	Turn left on Millers Trail.
11.4	Turn right on Walshville Trail.
12.6	Turn left on Shoal Creek Road.
12.9	Turn right on Old Brushy Road.
13.6	Turn left on Long Bridge Trail.
17.7	Turn left on Fox Hunt Trail; the name changes to Waveland Road as it runs straight north. **Side trip:** Turn right on Fox Hunt Trail to reach the village of Panama, which has a convenience store.
22.1	Turn left on 6th Avenue.
22.4	Turn right on Red Bridge Trail.
25.4	Turn right on Miller Trail.
28.1	Turn left on Interurban Circle.
30.9	Turn left on SR 16.
31.2	Turn right on Parsons Road/CR 650 East.
32.1	Turn left on 13th Avenue.
33.9	Return to parking lot at Lake Lou Yaeger.

Local Information

Central Illinois Tourism Development Office: 700 East Adams, Springfield; (217) 525-7980; www.visitcentralillinois.com.

City of Litchfield Office of Tourism: 120 East Ryder St., Litchfield; (217) 324-5253; www.cityoflitchfieldil.com.

Springfield Convention and Visitors Bureau: 109 North 7th St., Springfield; (217) 789-2360; www.visit-springfieldillinois.com.

Local Events/Attractions

Hillsboro–Roubaix Spring Classic Bike Race: Held in early April; attracts around 400 serious racers; http://web.me.com/iccc_stl/Hillsboro/Welcome.html.

Mother Jones Monument and Union Miners Cemetery: Monument honors the famous labor activist who fought for coal miners' rights; cemetery also contains the miners who were killed in the 1898 mining riots; Lake St., Mount Olive; (217) 999-4261.

Sky View Drive-In Theatre: Last surviving drive-in along historic Route 66; 150 Old Route 66 North, Litchfield; (217) 324-2533; www.litchfieldskyview.com.

Restaurants

Ariston Cafe: Originally opened in 1924 but relocated when Route 66 was rerouted; still owned by the same family and is said to be the oldest cafe on Route 66; 413 Old Route 66 North, Litchfield; (217) 324-2023; www.ariston-cafe.com.

Accommodations

Lake Lou Yaeger Campground: Nicely wooded camping area; the park has picnic areas, playgrounds, a marina, and a beach with shower houses; follow signs for campground just west of the beginning of the ride on Lake Lou Yaeger Trail; (217) 324-4771; www.cityoflitchfieldil.com/news/28-1.html.

Red Rooster Inn: Very affordable 1902 hotel located on the town square in Hillsboro; includes a restaurant; 123 East Seward St., Hillsboro; (217) 532-6332; www.redroosterinn.net.

Bike Shops

Wheelfast Bicycle Co.: 20 Cottonwood Lane, Chatham; (217) 483-7807; http://wheelfast .com.

Restrooms

No restrooms along this route. You will find restrooms and water near the starting point at Lake Lou Yaeger Park and in Panama, which is a short side trip at mile 17.7.

Maps

USGS: Butler quad, Sorento North quad.
DeLorme: Illinois Atlas & Gazetteer: Page 69.

35 Kampsville River Bluff Cruise

Without a doubt, these quiet, winding roads through the river bluffs above the Illinois River offer some of the most scenic riding in the state. Much of the mileage consists of long climbs and long descents through wooded hollows that are at times gradual, at times steep. The bottoms of the hollows typically open up into a yawning floodplain bordered by bluffs. Numerous creeks appear along the way, as do big dramatic bluffs soaring up from the edge of the road.

Start: In Kampsville at a community park at the corner of Marquette Street and 2nd Street. Kampsville is located about 60 miles southwest of Springfield.
Length: 34.5 miles.
Terrain: By Illinois standards, there are some major climbs on this route. The two times the route goes up the bluff, the climbs go on for 2 to 3 miles. The rest of the ride is flat or rolling.

Traffic and hazards: A handful of turns have no road signs; fortunately, none of the turns are confusing. You'll encounter several short stretches of gravel surface on Pleasant Dale Hollow Road. Expect a few farm dogs to give chase along the route.

Getting there: From I-72 to the north, head south on SR 100. Stay on SR 100 all the way to Kampsville. Turn left on Marquette Street and park at the small community park near the corner of Marquette Street and 2nd Street. From Saint Louis to the south, head north on SR 367 from I-270. In Alton, turn left on SR 100 and follow it to Kampsville. Coordinates for starting point: 15S 706219E 4352463N

The Ride

Calhoun County occupies a 40-mile-long strip of rugged terrain hemmed in by two big rivers: the Mississippi River on the west side and the Illinois River on the east. The rivers come together at the southern tip of the county, creating a virtual peninsula of land. Access to the peninsula is limited to the county's 17-mile-wide northern border, four ferry routes, and a lone bridge from East Hardin to Hardin, Illinois.

The isolated location of the Kampsville River Bluff Cruise makes the roads especially quiet.

The county is good for biking not just because the isolated geography makes for mostly traffic-free riding, but also the riding is top notch because of the stunning terrain. As one of the few areas in Illinois to escape the steamrolling effects of the last glacier, Calhoun County contains many square miles of high wooded bluffs punctuated by hollows carved out by streams flowing down toward the mighty rivers.

There are also some interesting attractions in the area. Kampsville, where this ride starts, hosts the Center for American Archeology, which attracts visitors from across the nation. The center is an education and research organization focusing on the archeology of the Native Americans and European settlers in the region. The visitor center, which occupies a historic storefront building in Kampsville's downtown area, displays exhibits and artifacts that document the prehistory of the lower Illinois River Valley. Another local attraction is the McCully Heritage Project, which you'll encounter less than 2 miles into the ride. The McCully Heritage Project is a 940-acre nonprofit preserve with ponds, wetlands, rugged bluffs, scenic overlooks, and plenty of hiking trails.

After saddling up in Kampsville and heading south along the foot of the river bluff, you'll turn east and enter one of the many local hollows. Pass the farmhouse and picnic pavilion at the entrance to the McCully Heritage Project, then continue ahead as the road meanders upward alongside Crawford Creek. The hollow narrows considerably as you ascend 250 feet during the final 2 miles up the bluff. At the top of the bluff, everything changes. Wide fields sprinkled with small farms cover a gently

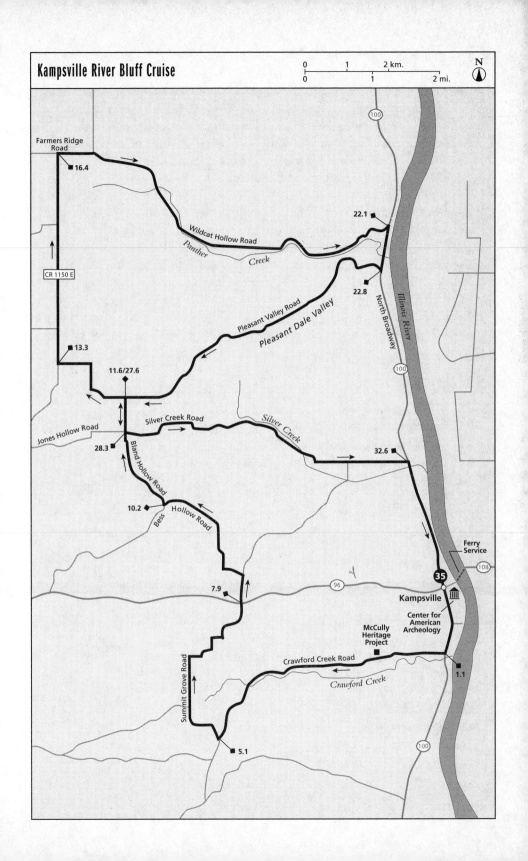

Kampsville River Bluff Cruise

0   1   2 km.

0   1   2 mi.

N

Farmers Ridge Road

■ 16.4

■ 22.1

CR 1150 E

Wildcat Hollow Road

Panther   Creek

■ 22.8

Pleasant Valley Road

Pleasant Dale Valley

North Broadway

Illinois River

■ 13.3

◆ 11.6/27.6

Jones Hollow Road

Silver Creek Road

Silver Creek

■ 32.6

28.3 ■

Bland Hollow Road

10.2 ■

Bess   Hollow Road

Ferry Service

7.9 ■

96

35

Kampsville

Summit Grove Road

McCully Heritage Project

Center for American Archeology

108

Crawford Creek Road

Crawford Creek

■ 1.1

■ 5.1

100

rolling landscape. On Bess Hollow Road, a gradual downhill leads you through a wooded ravine containing Fox Creek. Hillcrest Cemetery, at the corner of Pleasant Valley Road and CR 1150 East, offers shady spots to take a break and admire the surrounding fields and prairie. Rest up because the next 3 miles present a continuous roller coaster ride through a series of short but steep ravines, one after the other.

The joyride continues as you jet down the bluff on Wildcat Hollow Road. After an initial steep plunge underneath a canopy of oak trees, settle in for a long, gradual descent along Panther Creek. Now and then bluffs soar upward—almost vertically—from the side of the road. Soon, the hollow widens into a flat floodplain. With the bluffs spread farther apart, their wooded undulations are revealed. Occasionally, you'll catch glimpses of the rocky-bottomed creek twisting alongside the road.

While crossing Panther Creek on the short stretch of SR 100, look left to see where the creek joins the quarter-mile-wide Illinois River. It's then back to higher ground on Pleasant Valley Road and another peaceful, winding roadway up the wooded bluff. Look for patches of exposed rock where the road hugs the side of these broad hills. The final descent traces Silver Creek along another wooded and winding roadway. The short ride back to Kampsville along SR 100 takes you under a craggy limestone bluff high above the road.

Miles and Directions

0.0   Head left (south) on 2nd Street, then turn right on Oak Street.

0.1   Turn left on North Broadway/SR 100.

1.1   Turn right on Crawford Creek Road.

5.1   Turn right on Summit Grove Road (no road sign at this junction).

7.9   As you cross SR 96, jog to the right slightly and then continue straight ahead on Bess Hollow Road.

10.2   Turn right on Bland Hollow Road (no road sign at this junction).

11.6   Turn left on Pleasant Valley Road (Some signs identify this road as Pleasant Dale Valley Road).

13.3   Turn right on CR 1150 East.

16.4   Turn right on Wildcat Hollow Road (no road sign at this junction).

22.1   Turn right on SR 100.

22.8   Turn right on Pleasant Valley Road.

27.6   Turn left on Bland Hollow Road.

28.3   Turn left on Silver Creek Road (no sign for this road, but there is a sign for Jones Hollow Road going to the right).

32.6   Turn right on SR 100.

34.4   Turn left on Marquette Street.

34.5   Return to the parking area.

Local Information

Calhoun County Tourism (Alton Regional Convention and Visitors Bureau): 200 Piasa St., Alton; (618) 465-6676; www.visitcalhoun .com.

Local Events/Attractions

Center for American Archeology: Contains a museum and gift shop; Marquette St. and Broadway, Kampsville; (618) 653-4316; www .caa-archeology.org.

McCully Heritage Project: Private nonprofit preserve that offers 15 miles of hiking trails; on Crawford Creek Road about 1 mile west of SR 100; (618) 653-4687; www.mccully heritage.org.

Restaurants

Illinois Riverdock Restaurant: Known for its smoked meats and homemade pies; 310 South Park St., Hardin; (618) 576-2362.

Kampsville Inn Restaurant: Located next to the starting point; watch the ferryboat while dining; 2nd St. and Joliet St., Kampsville; (618) 653-4413.

Accommodations

Pere Marquette Lodge and Conference Center: Rooms, cabins, and a campground at one of the most scenic state parks in Illinois; 13653 Lodge Blvd., Grafton; (618) 786-2331; www .pmlodge.net.

Ruebel Hotel and Saloon: Offers twenty-two rooms in a historic hotel above a restaurant; cottages and lodge rooms also available; 217 East Main St., Grafton; (618) 786-2315; www .ruebelhotel.com.

McCully Heritage Project: Three walk-in campsites; see contact info above.

Bike Shops

Wild Trak Bikes: Just off SR 100 in downtown Alton; 202 State St., Alton; (618) 462-2574.

Restrooms

Start/finish: Public restrooms are available at the Kampsville Village Campground located south of Oak Street and east of Broadway/SR 100.

Mile 1.8: Restrooms and water are available at the McCully Heritage Project near the barn on the right.

Maps

USGS: Pearl West quad, Pleasant Dale Valley quad.

DeLorme: Illinois Atlas & Gazetteer: Page 66.

36 Nickelplate-Quercus Grove Ramble

The first section of this route on the Nickelplate Trail tours the lush landscape alongside Judy Creek. In Edwardsville, the trail runs through the historic district of Leclaire before sending you into farmland outside of town. Following the Quercus Grove Trail on the return trip, you'll shoot back toward Edwardsville on a route that resembles a quiet country road.

Start: Glen Carbon, located in Madison County across the Mississippi River from Saint Louis.
Length: 25.4 miles.
Traffic and hazards: Only 5.1 miles of this ride follow streets; the rest of the ride follows trails. Among the trails, there's roughly an equal amount of surface that is asphalt and crushed gravel. The surface of the Nickelplate Trail is asphalt west of Edwardsville and is crushed gravel to the east; the surface of the Quercus Grove Trail is nearly all crushed gravel.

Getting there: Park at Citizens Park on Main Street in Glen Carbon. From I-270, head south on SR 157. Turn left on Main Street and use the trailhead parking area on the right. From the parking area, follow the sign toward Edwardsville on the Nickelplate Trail. Coordinates for starting point: 16S 240546E 4292822N

The Ride

Madison County, located across the Mississippi River from Saint Louis, claims the largest concentration of rail trails in southern Illinois. This ride offers a great introduction to this top-notch system of trails while following most of the Nickelplate Trail and the all of the Quercus Grove Trail.

After starting the route in the suburban Saint Louis town of Glen Carbon, you'll encounter several inviting parks while following Judy Creek. The first is Miner Park, which contains the Glen Carbon Library. Next to the library is a recently constructed covered bridge spanning Judy Creek. After passing under I-270, a spur trail on the right leads up a steep bluff on a series of switchbacks to the Green Space North Conservation Area, where you'll find a small collection of biking and hiking trails set within woodland and savanna. Judy Creek plays hide-and-seek with you on the way toward Edwardsville Township Park, the third park along this stretch of the Nickelplate Trail.

North of the five-way trail junction at mile 4, the Nickelplate Trail cuts through the historic factory town of Leclaire (now part of Edwardsville). The town was founded by a man named N. O. Nelson, an industrialist who provided a striking contrast to his fellow captains of industry at the turn of the century. Nelson sought to create a

The old water tower marks the historic community of Leclaire
on the Nickelplate Trail.

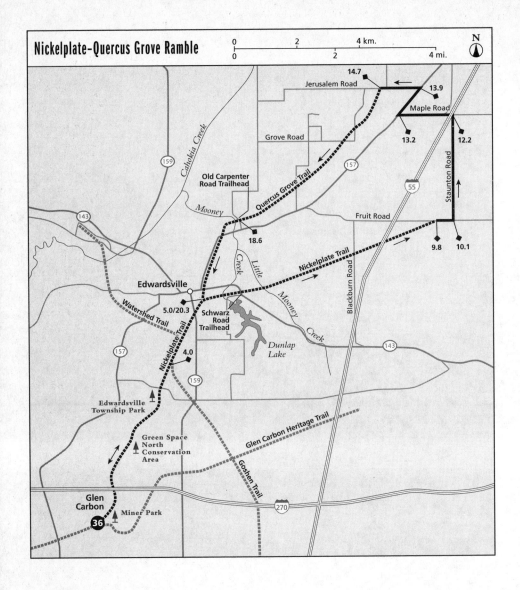

Nickelplate-Quercus Grove Ramble

0   2   4 km.
0   2   4 mi.

N

14.7
Jerusalem Road
13.9
Maple Road
13.2   12.2
Grove Road
159
Cahokia Creek
157
Old Carpenter
Road Trailhead
Mooney
55
Staunton Road
Fruit Road
143
18.6
Little Creek
Nickelplate Trail
9.8   10.1
Edwardsville
Watershed Trail
5.0/20.3
Nickelplate Trail
Schwarz
Road
Trailhead
Mooney Creek
Blackburn Road
143
Dunlap
Lake
157
4.0
159
Edwardsville
Township Park
Green Space
North
Conservation
Area
Glen Carbon Heritage Trail
Goshen Trail
270
Glen
Carbon
36   Miner Park

company where workers were treated in an exemplary fashion, with profit sharing and excellent working conditions. The town provided good schools for children and entertainment for adults. Modest but attractive houses were built for workers along curving, tree-lined streets. Local streets still bear the names of Nelson's intellectual heroes from the United States and Europe, such as John Ruskin, Thomas Jefferson, and Henry Wadsworth Longfellow.

Heading toward the rural landscape outside of Edwardsville, you'll pass the junction with the Quercus Grove Trail, followed by a brick manufacturer with huge stacks of red and brown bricks sitting beside the trail. (Coal mining and brick making both enjoyed a long history in Edwardsville.) Just after the brickyard, the trail mounts a

75-foot-high earthen train embankment above Mooney Creek. As the agricultural land takes over, a thin strip of trees borders each side of the trail. Finishing the Nickelplate Trail, you'll zigzag for 5 miles along quiet rural roads.

Heading back toward Edwardsville on the Quercus Grove Trail, a leafy buffer often grows between the trail and the cropland stretching into the distance. Small ravines appear alongside the trail now and then, as do big vine-covered oak trees set within patches of lush greenery. In Edwardsville, the trail cuts through a bustling mix of residential neighborhoods, businesses, and industrial areas. At the trail crossing of Chapman Road, consider a visit to Springers Creek Winery, which has a back door opening right onto the trail. After locking up in the bike rack, the back patio offers a perfect spot to sip a glass of local wine. From the winery, it's 5.4 miles of pedaling back to the starting point.

Miles and Directions

0.0 Head north on the Nickelplate Trail.

4.0 When you arrive at the five-way junction, simply follow the signs for the Nickelplate Trail painted on the asphalt trail surface.

5.0 Keep right on the Nickelplate Trail at the junction with the Quercus Grove Trail.

9.8 The Nickelplate Trail ends. Turn right on Fruit Road to begin the on-street section of the route.

10.1 Turn left on Staunton Road.

12.2 Turn left on Maple Road.

13.2 Turn right on the path that runs alongside SR 157.

13.9 Turn left on Jerusalem Road.

14.7 Pick up the Quercus Grove Trail on the left.

20.3 Follow the Nickelplate Trail back to the trailhead.

25.4 Return to the trailhead parking area.

Local Information

Edwardsville/Glen Carbon Chamber of Commerce: 200 University Park Dr., Suite 260, Edwardsville; (618) 656-7600; www.edglen chamber.com.

Madison County Transit Trails: c/o Madison County Transit, One Transit Way, Granite City; (618) 874-7433; www.mcttrails.org.

Tourism Bureau of Southwestern Illinois: 10950 Lincoln Trail, Fairview Heights; (618) 397-1488; www.thetourismbureau.org.

Local Events/Attractions

Cahokia Mounds State Historic Site and Interpretive Center: Once the largest and most sophisticated prehistoric city north of Mexico;

30 Ramey Dr., Cahokia; (618) 346-5160; www .cahokiamounds.com.

Springers Creek Winery: 817 Hillsboro Ave., Edwardsville; (618) 307-5110; www.springers creekwinery.com.

Restaurants

Erato on Main: Eclectic contemporary cuisine with emphasis on seafood; somewhat pricey; 126 North Main St., Edwardsville; (618) 307-3203; www.eratoonmain.com.

Mr. Currys Gourmet Indian Restaurant: Affordable lunch buffet, plenty of vegetarian options; 7403 Marine Rd. (SR 143), Edwardsville; (415) 577-2274; www.mrcurrys.com/restaurants.htm.

Nori Sushi and Japanese Grill: Casual atmosphere with extensive sushi menu; 1025 Century Dr., Edwardsville; (618) 659-9400; www .norisushi.net.

Accommodations

Bilbrey Farms: Bed-and-breakfast and an exotic animal farm featuring a zebra, emus, peacocks, and a miniature horse, among others; 8724 Pin Oak Rd., Edwardsville; (618) 692-1950; www .bilbreyfarms.com.
Country Hearth Inn and Suites: 1013 Plummer Dr., Edwardsville; (618) 656-7829; www .countryhearthedwardsville.com.
Horseshoe Lake State Park: Has forty-eight campsites located on an island; (618) 931-0270; http://dnr.state.il.us/lands/landmgt/parks/r4/horsesp.htm.

Bike Shops

The Cyclery and Fitness Center: 2472 Troy Rd., Edwardsville, 62025; (618) 692-0070; http:// thecyclerys.com.

Restrooms

Start/finish: Restrooms and water are available at Miners Park near the trailhead.
Mile 3.0: Water and restrooms are available at Edwardsville Township Park.
Mile 22.4: Again pass Edwardsville Township Park.

Maps

USGS: Edwardsville quad, Marine quad.
DeLorme: Illinois Atlas & Gazetteer: Page 76.

37 Ohio River Challenge

The lion's share of this route follows the Ohio River Scenic Byway, a series of roads that traces the waterway for nearly 1,000 miles from Pennsylvania to Cairo, Illinois. The northern section of this loop contains hills laced with quiet roads that wind through woods and pastureland. While paralleling the Ohio River to the west, you'll pass two creeks that widen into small lakes. A succession of rolling hills takes you down to the Ohio River floodplain on Unionville Road and back to Brookport.

Start: Downtown Brookport at the corner of 2nd Street and Ohio Street.
Length: 43.9 miles.
Terrain: A rolling, sometimes hilly landscape dominates the northern and eastern sections

of this ride. The rest of the route is mostly flat or very gently rolling farmland.
Traffic and hazards: Most of these roads are quiet. A bit more traffic appears in the vicinity of Brookport.

Getting there: From I-24 to the west, exit on US 45 and head east. In Brookport, turn right on 2nd Street and park near the intersection of Ohio Street. Coordinates for starting point: 16S 355118E 4109595N

The Ride

The small town of Brookport, where this ride begins, sits between a couple of historic sites worthy of your attention. The first spot, located upstream from Brookport

Enjoy a long, steep descent on the bluff that slopes toward the Ohio River.

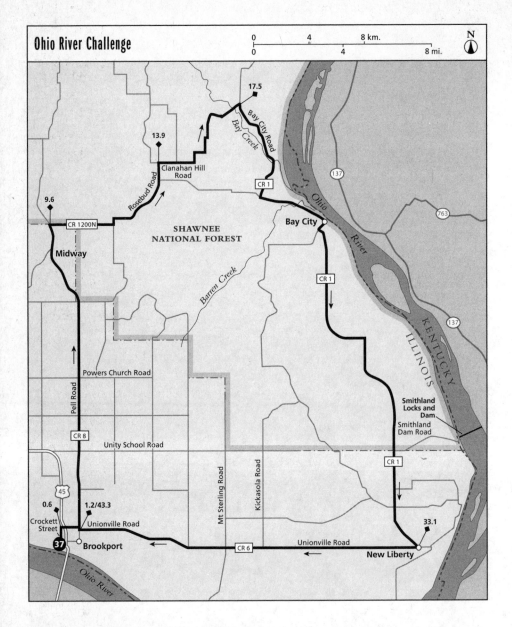

0   4   8 km.

0   4   8 mi.

N

17.5

13.9

Bay City Road

Bay Creek

Clanahan Hill
Road

Rosebud Road

CR 1

137

Ohio River

9.6

CR 1200N

Bay City

763

Midway

SHAWNEE
NATIONAL FOREST

Barren Creek

CR 1

Powers Church Road

Pell Road

Smithland
Locks and
Dam

Smithland
Dam Road

KENTUCKY

ILLINOIS

137

CR 8

Unity School Road

CR 1

0.6

1.2/43.3

Mt Sterling Road

Kickasola Road

45

Crockett
Street

Unionville Road

33.1

37

Brookport

CR 6

Unionville Road

New Liberty

Ohio River

along the Ohio River, is a series of earthen mounds built by the first Native Americans to practice large-scale agriculture in the area. Constructed nearly 1,000 years ago, nineteen mounds remain, the highest about 30 feet tall. Archeologists say that the Native American leaders lived on or ruled from the flat-topped mounds; they also built thatch-roofed homes, ceremonial buildings, and temples on them. During the past century, researchers have uncovered a variety of artifacts in the area, as well as the remains of a series of buildings and protective walls that were built near the mounds.

Downstream from Brookport, the second historic spot, Fort Massac, occupies the shore of the Ohio River on the outskirts of Metropolis. A full-size replica of a timber fort from 1802 serves as the centerpiece of the park (Illinois' first state park). Between 1757 and the Civil War, France, England, and United States each housed troops here. The park's visitor center features a collection artifacts from Fort Massac, including bowls, cutlery, and other items that offer a sense of everyday life at the fort.

As you start the ride and head northward from Brookport, you're guided through a rolling pastoral landscape containing a mix of hills, woods, and open space. After about 7 miles of riding on a gently rolling straightaway, the road starts to wind and the hills grow in size as you get closer to Shawnee National Forest. In the hamlet of Midway, you'll pass St. Stephens Lutheran Church and an adjoining cemetery. Rosebud Road takes you past a couple of ponds before the forest suddenly becomes extremely dense and lush.

The wind will press hard against your face as the road plunges downward on the final section of Clanahan Hill Road. Enjoy the distant views as you descend 250 feet and then cross Bay Creek at the bottom of the bluff. The road traces a levee along the edge of Bay Creek, which grows wide and sluggish as it nears the Ohio River in this area. Tall wooded bluffs rise above the opposite shore of the creek; down in the water, look for waterbirds serving as the sentinels of the shoreline. Cross Bay Creek again, and the Ohio River appears in the distance. On the way to the hamlet of Bay City, you'll see another body of water that looks like a large pond but is actually another creek—Barren Creek.

Bay City is no more than an antiques store and a few houses in the shadow of the wooded bluffs to the south along the Ohio River. The 1997 film *U.S. Marshals* features an airplane crash that occurs in the Ohio River at Bay City, and the antiques store appears in the film as a rundown general store. From Bay City, the road climbs more than 200 feet up the bluff. A few miles ahead, you'll pass the turnoff for Smithland Lock and Dam, which possesses the world's largest twin navigational lock, at about three-quarters of a mile long (access to the lock and dam is restricted). Once you get on CR 6, the route back to Brookport is mostly straight and mostly flat.

Miles and Directions

0.0 Head west on 2nd Street.

0.1 Turn right on Crockett Street.

0.6 Turn right on Unionville Road.

1.2 Turn left on Pell Road/CR 8.

9.6 Turn right on CR 1200 North. After a couple of turns, this road becomes Rosebud Road.

13.9 Turn right on Clanahan Hill Road.

17.5 Turn right on CR 1/Bay City Road.

33.1 Turn right on CR 6/Unionville Road.

43.3 Turn left on Crockett Street.

43.8 Turn left on 2nd Street.

43.9 Return to the starting point at the corner of Ohio Street and 2nd Street.

Local Information

Metropolis Tourism: 607 Market St., Metropolis; (877) 424-5025; www.metropolistourism.com.

Southernmost Illinois Tourism Bureau: P.O. Box 378, Anna, IL 62906; (618) 833-9928 or (800) 248-4373; www.southernmostillinois.com.

Local Events/Attractions

Harrah's Casino: Over 1,000 slot machines await your coins on this "riverboat" casino (it doesn't really leave the shore); new hotel; 100 East Front St., Metropolis; (800) 929-5905; www.harrahsmetropolis.com.

Kincaid Mounds State Historic Site: Local Native Americans constructed a series of mounds at this site nearly 1,000 years ago; located between Brookport and CR 1 on Unionville Road, head south for about 5 miles on New Cut Road; (877) 248-4373; www.kincaidmounds.com.

Super Museum: Museum dedicated to Metropolis's most famous resident; located downtown next to the bronze statue of Superman; 611 Market St., Metropolis; (618) 524-5518; www.supermuseum.com.

Restaurants

Bill's BBQ: Serving up ribs for more than forty years; located 2 blocks west of Fort Massac State Park; 1105 East 7th St., Metropolis; (618) 524-2503.

Farley's Cafeteria: Old-fashioned cafeteria, open since 1954; 613 Market St., Metropolis; (618) 524-7226.

Accommodations

Bay City General Store and Lodging: Walk-out porch overlooking the Ohio River; affordable; located right on the bike route, above an antiques store; CR 1, Bay City; (618) 683-4305; www.baycitystoreandlodgingohioriver.com.

Dixon Springs State Park: Campsites with electric hookups and excellent walk-in sites; showers offered at the pool; located about 15 miles north of Metropolis; RR 2, Box 78, SR 146, Golconda; (618) 949-3394.

Old Bethlehem School Cottage Bed and Breakfast: One-room schoolhouse that's been converted into a three-bedroom cottage; 6162 Old Marion Rd., Metropolis; (618) 524-4922 or (618) 645-0319; www.bethlehemschool.com.

Bike Shops

Bikeworld: Located across the Ohio River from Brookport; 809 Joe Clifton Dr., Paducah, KY; (270) 442-0751.

Restrooms

None on the route, but there are a couple of diners in the vicinity of downtown Brookport that may allow you to use their restrooms and fill up water bottles.

Maps

USGS: Brownfield quad, Smithland quad, Little Cypress quad, Paducah quad.

DeLorme: Illinois Atlas & Gazetteer: Page 94.

38 Olney Ramble

While pedaling through Olney, keep watch for this town's famous white squirrels, depicted on street signs, police uniforms, and in front yards as lawn ornaments. In the park where the ride kicks off, you may even see live examples of the squirrels the town adores so much. South of Olney, take a break from scouting for squirrels and explore the quiet farm roads that are frequently interrupted by patches of woodland and sandy-bottomed creeks. North of town, the wooded shores of East Fork Lake will escort you back toward downtown Olney.

Start: Olney City Park in Olney, located about 35 miles southeast of Effingham.
Length: 18.2 miles.
Terrain: Gently rolling agricultural land and some wooded areas.

Traffic and hazards: Ride with care after crossing US 50 on CR 1400 East (St. Marie Road), as traffic increases and the road has no shoulder.

Getting there: From I-70/57 in Effingham, head south on SR 33. In Newton, turn right on SR 130. Olney City Park is on the left as you enter Olney. From I-57 to the west, head east on US 50. In Olney, turn left on SR 130. Olney City Park is on the right. Park along White Squirrel Drive. Coordinates for starting point: 16S 405117E 4287762N

The Ride

People in Olney feel affection for their century-old colony of albino gray squirrels. Patches on the uniforms of the Olney Police and Fire Departments are adorned with images of white squirrels. Signs throughout the town feature them, and there's even a weird song about the squirrels (available on the town's Web site) that goes, "I want to tell you about a place I know where the squirrels are whiter than the whitest snow, and they can cross any road because the streets are paved with joy."

Regarding the origins of the colony, two different creation stories vie for dominance—both describe local residents who trapped albino squirrels and then set them free when state laws were established that forbade the keeping of squirrels. Proud and protective of their furry white treasures, the town's government enacted laws in recent years protecting the squirrels (cats and dogs may not be outside without leashes). The town enacted the laws in response to a precipitous drop in the white squirrel population during the past fifty years. In 1941 Olney boasted 800 of the rodents; annual counts now come up with around 120. One of the best places to catch a glimpse of these critters is Olney City Park, where this ride begins.

On the way out of town along Elliot Street, you'll encounter a string of impressive houses—in the styles of Queen Anne, late Victorian, and Colonial Revival—between Chestnut Street and South Avenue. The houses on this stretch of street, constructed around the turn of the century, are included on the National Register of Historic Places.

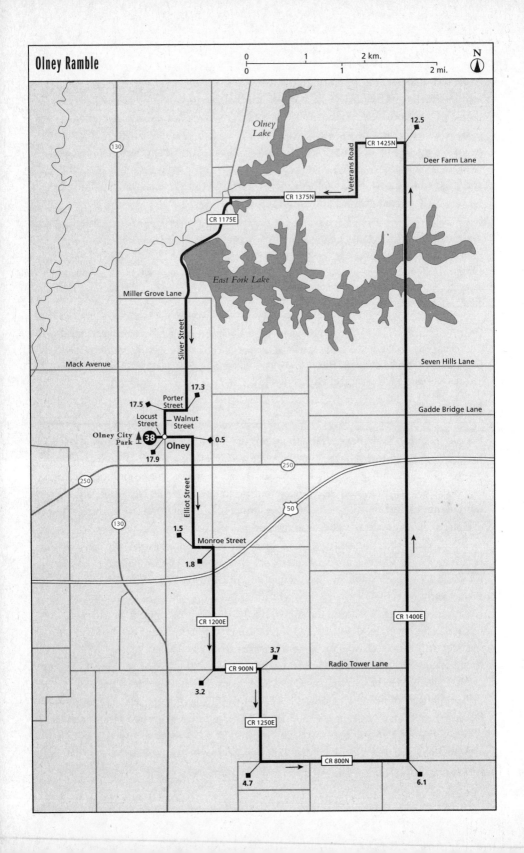

Olney Ramble

0   1   2 km.

0   1   2 mi.

N

Olney Lake

12.5

CR 1425N

Veterans Road

Deer Farm Lane

CR 1375N

CR 1175E

East Fork Lake

Miller Grove Lane

Silver Street

Seven Hills Lane

Mack Avenue

Gadde Bridge Lane

17.3

Porter Street

17.5

Locust Street

Walnut Street

Olney City Park

38

Olney

0.5

17.9

250

250

Elliot Street

50

CR 1400E

1.5

Monroe Street

1.8

130

CR 1200E

Radio Tower Lane

3.7

CR 900N

3.2

CR 1250E

CR 800N

4.7

6.1

Also on the way out of town, you'll pass a historic marker at the corner of East Street and US 50 honoring Robert Ridgway, a naturalist, scientist, artist, and author of an eight-volume work on the birds of Central and North America. With no more than a high school education, Ridgway was one of the most prominent ornithologists of his day and served as the curator of birds for the Smithsonian Institution. Ridgway bought property near Olney in 1906 for his family's summer cottage. North of Olney, you'll have an opportunity to visit this site, now a park called Bird Haven.

South of the Ridgway marker, corn country takes over, but first the road cuts through a tunnel-like grove of big pine and oak trees. On CR 900 North, you'll make the first of several crossings of Big Creek. Here, the creek's wooded banks momentarily interrupt the rolling pastureland. Continuing through the gently undulating farmland, the route crosses the main stem of Big Creek and passes the wooden supports of a former train overpass before climbing a short, steep hill. Heading north, the road takes a sharp drop into a wooded wetland before crossing Big Creek again. Trilliums grow on the banks of the sandy-bottomed stream.

Continuing north, the route makes a gradual climb through agricultural fields toward US 50. Beyond US 50, views open up as you crest a hill and then descend toward East Fork Lake. You'll likely see some people fishing on the lake as you cross two of its many arms and then mount the lake's dam and spillway. The 934-acre lake, created in 1970, was the third in a series of local lakes built to serve as Olney's water supply. As you traverse the dam, the lake and its picturesque wooded shores are on the left; on the right, the landscape drops dramatically 100 feet or so toward wetlands.

As you head back into Olney, consider turning left on CR 1275 North and riding for 0.3 mile to visit Bird Haven Park, the location of Robert Ridgway's summer home and a site where he performed ornithological research.

Miles and Directions

0.0 Start in Olney City Park and head east on White Squirrel Drive. Continue straight ahead on Locust Street as you leave the park.

0.5 Turn right on Morgan Avenue.

0.6 Turn left on Laurel Avenue.

0.7 Turn right on Elliot Street.

1.5 Turn left on Monroe Street.

1.8 Turn right on East Street (turns into CR 1200 East).

3.2 Turn left on CR 900 North.

3.7 Turn right on CR 1250 East.

4.7 Turn left on CR 800 North.

6.1 Turn left on CR 1400 East. After crossing US 50, ride with care—traffic picks up and the road offers no shoulders.

12.5 Turn left on CR 1425 North. As this road makes a couple of turns, it becomes Veterans Road and then CR 1375 North.

14.8 Turn left on CR 1175 East. This road becomes Silver Street as you approach Olney.

16.1 **Side trip:** Turn left on CR 1275 North to visit Bird Haven. It's 0.3 mile off CR 1175 East.

17.3 Turn right on Porter Street.

17.5 Turn left on Walnut Street.

17.9 Turn right on Locust Street.

18.2 Return to Olney City Park.

Local Information

City of Olney: 300 South Whittle Ave., Olney; (618) 395-7302; www.ci.olney.il.us.

Olney and the Greater Richland County Chamber of Commerce: 210 East Chestnut St., Olney; (618) 392-2241; www.olneychamber.com.

Southeastern Illinois Convention and Visitors Bureau: 1707 East Main St., Suite 5, Olney; (877) 273-4554 or (618) 392-0925; www .southeastillinois.com.

Local Events/Attractions

Bird Haven and the Robert Ridgway Memorial Arboretum: Located north of Olney on CR 1200 East; (618) 395-7302.

Carnegie Building Museum: Displays focus on Native American artifacts, early farm equipment, a one-room school, and the local oil industry; 401 East Main St., Olney; (618) 395-7430.

Olney Bicycle Classic: The Olney Chamber of Commerce organizes a series of bike rides and races for riders of all levels in early September in Olney City Park; see Olney Chamber contact information above.

Richland Heritage House Museum: Guided tours are offered of this century-old home with period furnishings; 122 West Elm St., Olney; (618) 392-2318.

Restaurants

Daylight Donuts: A local morning hangout; 320 West Main St., Olney; (618) 395-1333.

Ophelia's Cup: Coffee drinks, breakfasts, sandwiches, and desserts in a friendly atmosphere on the downtown strip; 205 South Whittle Ave., Olney; (618) 392-6287.

White Brothers BBQ: Specializing in pulled pork, ribs, and chicken; operates in the same building as Daylight Donuts; 320 West Main St., Olney; (618) 392-2727.

Accommodations

Motels: Several affordable motels are located near the intersection of SR 130 and West Main-Street in Olney.

Red Hills State Park: Large campground offers many sites on the park's small lake; pleasant hiking trail in the north section of the park; located 15 miles west of Olney on US 150; (618) 936-2469; http://dnr.state.il.us/lands/landmgt/parks/r5/redhls.htm.

Restrooms

Start/finish: Olney City Park has restrooms.

Maps

USGS: Dundas quad, Olney quad.

DeLorme: Illinois Atlas & Gazetteer: Page 80.

39 Pere Marquette Challenge

The first and final parts of this ride follow the wonderfully scenic Vadalabene Great River Road Trail as it hugs the shore of the Mississippi River between the town of Alton and Pere Marquette State Park. When you reach the state park, you'll climb a bluff that resembles more of a vertical wall than a big hill. After the park, winding rural roads guide you through a rolling—and often hilly—landscape of quiet rural bliss.

Start: Piasa Park, located northwest of Alton on SR 100.

Length: 58.2 miles.

Terrain: The terrain is extremely varied on this route: You'll encounter flat riverbank while following the Mississippi River and huge river bluffs at Pere Marquette State Park. The rest of the route offers sizable hills and ravines as well as rolling woodland.

Traffic and hazards: The Vadalabene Trail's only notable drawback is its close proximity to SR 100, which tends to be especially busy with traffic on summer weekends. To avoid heavy traffic, consider a midweek trip or go early in the day on a weekend. The northernmost sections of the route follow a series of narrow winding roads. Be mindful of traffic on the turns. At mile 32.6, you'll encounter about 1 mile of gravel road surface.

Getting there: From the Saint Louis area, take US 67 north across the Mississippi River. Turn left on SR 100 in Alton. The parking area is on the right at the foot of the bluff decorated with a large painting of the Piasa bird. From I-55, head west on SR 140. Stay on SR 140 through Alton until reaching Broadway Street. Turn right on Broadway Street and then turn right on SR 143. Keep straight ahead on US 67. Turn left again on SR 100. Coordinates for starting point: 15S 742986E 4308901N

The Ride

This ride starts at the foot of a bluff adorned with a painting of the Piasa bird, a dragonlike creature with antlers, wings, and a long tail. According to local folklore, the Illini people who once lived in the area were plagued by a ferocious flying creature with a strong taste for human flesh that lived in the cliffs above the river. After the bird was finally killed by archers wielding poison arrows, Native Americans painted an image of the Piasa bird on a rock wall to commemorate the event. The original pictograph of the Piasa bird is long gone; the current image was painted in 1998.

As you begin the ride, it soon becomes clear why the Vadalabene Great River Road Trail is considered one of the most scenic multiuse trails in the state. The Mississippi River runs 1 mile wide on the left, and wooded, sometimes rocky bluffs soar up on the right. Within the first few miles, a series of small roadside parks offer places to stop and soak up the scenery.

On the opposite shore of the Mississippi River in the small town of Portage des Sioux, Missouri, look for a 25-foot fiberglass sculpture dedicated to Our Lady of the Rivers. The sculpture, which sits on a 20-foot pedestal, was erected after the town was spared from a major flood in 1951. Today the monument is the site of an annual

From the top of the high bluff at Pere Marquette State Park, you can see many miles of farmland and wooded floodplain.

blessing of the boats. While looking out over the river, you'll see a handful of islands and occasional barges chugging through the massive waterway. A few more ticks bring you to a roadside water park with a waterslide that runs down the bluff into a big pool.

The village of Grafton is lined with shops, bars, and eateries, many catering to the tourist set. In Grafton, the trail drops down by the river and runs behind the main business strip through an open, grassy floodplain sprinkled with a few houses. North of Grafton, after passing an old stone building that houses the Illinois Youth Center, the trail runs underneath a small stone cross that marks the point where Jacques Marquette became the first European to enter what is now Illinois.

Before reaching Pere Marquette State Park, the trail ascends the bluff just a bit and winds along its sides. You'll zigzag through rugged terrain, dense with stands of maple and sassafras trees. From a trail bridge about 100 feet up on the bluff, you can see the Illinois River, nearby wetlands, and the Grafton Car Ferry below. As you come down off the bluff, the Pere Marquette riding stables signal your entrance into one of the best state parks in Illinois.

Pere Marquette Challenge

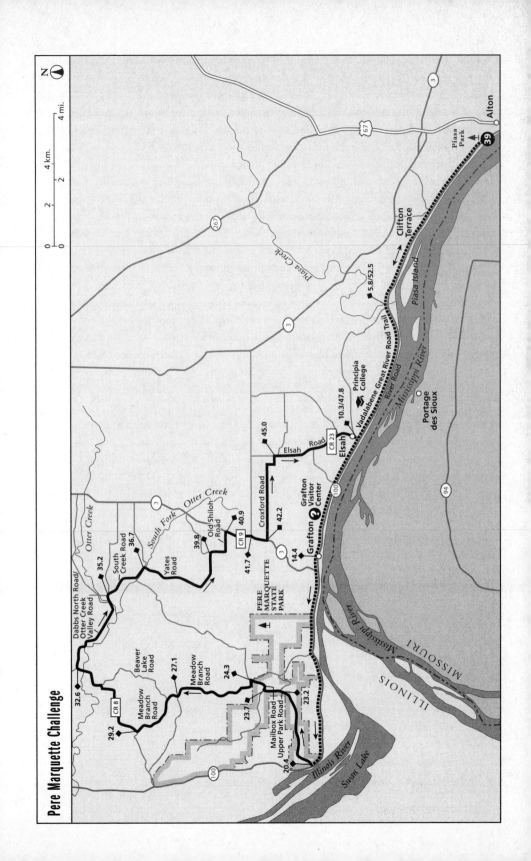

At Pere Marquette State Park, be sure to drop in at the Great Lodge, which contains a magnificent open room with comfortable chairs. The lodge sits at the foot of what is likely the steepest climb in Illinois: The initial mile of this road rises about 350 feet. After this arduous ascent, you're rewarded with stunning views of the Illinois River and its backwater, Swan Lake. On a clear day, the Gateway Arch is visible in downtown Saint Louis. A series of scenic overlooks each offer slightly different views of the endless floodplain down below.

With the big bluffs behind you, the road mounts a ridge thick with walnut, maple, hickory, and sassafras trees. Ravines tumble down on each side as the road takes a twisting route through a persistently rolling landscape. Occasional views open up along the ridge that you follow for several miles. Not long after landing on CR 8, a screaming downhill takes you on a winding route to Otter Creek. Look for patches of exposed rock on the hillsides as you meander through the Otter Creek floodplain for the next 4 miles. After climbing out of the Otter Creek floodplain, the landscape dips, rises, and continues to roll. Minor hills come and go. Near CR 9, the topography starts leveling out, and the landscape grows increasingly residential and agricultural.

Heading down the bluff back to the shore of the Mississippi, you'll pass through the storybook village of Elsah. The village, situated at the mouth of a little valley, contains dozens of well-kept homes from the 1850s, many of them constructed of native limestone. The entire village is on the National Register of Historic Places. Askew Creek trickles through the center of the village, and irises, tulips, and roses grow along walkways in front of stone cottages. Elsah is also where you'll see signs for Principia College, a Christian Science school founded up on the bluffs in the 1930s.

On the return trip to Alton along the Vadalabene Trail, you'll be using the wide shoulder on the opposite side of the road for much of the route. This puts you closer to the river and farther away from the bluffs, allowing better views of the exposed rock and craggy cliffs.

Miles and Directions

0.0 Head northwest on the Vadalabene Great River Road Trail.

20.4 At the end of the trail, turn right on the Pere Marquette park road as it heads up the bluff between the park lodge and the visitor center.

23.2 Turn left on Upper Park Road.

23.7 Turn right on Mailbox Road.

24.3 Turn left on Branch Road. There are no road signs at this four-way junction.

27.1 Turn right on Meadow Branch Road.

29.2 Turn right on CR 8.

32.6 Turn right on Dabbs North Road/Otter Creek Valley Road. This is where you'll encounter about 1 mile of gravel road surface.

35.2 Turn right on South Creek Road.

36.7 Turn right on Yates Road.

39.8 Turn right on Old Shiloh Hollow Road/CR 1000 East.

40.9 Turn right on CR 9.

41.7 Turn right on SR 3.

42.2 Turn left on Croxford Road.

45.0 Turn right on Elsah Road/CR 23.

47.8 Turn left on the Vadalabene Great River Road Trail.

58.2 Return to Piasa Park.

Local Information

Alton Regional Convention and Visitors Bureau: 200 Piasa St., Alton; (618) 465-6676; www.visitalton.com.

Tourism Bureau of Southwestern Illinois: 10950 Lincoln Trail, Fairview Heights; (618) 397-1488; www.thetourismbureau.org.

Local Events/Attractions

Alton Museum of History and Art: One of the rooms pays tribute to Alton resident Robert Wadlow, the world's tallest man; 2809 College Ave., Alton; (618) 462-2763; www.altonmuseum.com.

National Great Rivers Museum: Delves into many aspects of Mississippi River culture; includes video exhibits, a gift shop, and a model historic riverboat; located at Melvin Price Locks and Dam 26, SR 143 in East Alton; (618) 462-6979.

Restaurants

Fin Inn Aquarium Restaurant: Contains four 2,000-gallon aquariums; menu leans toward finned creatures; 1000 West Main St., Grafton; (618) 786-2030; www.fininn.com.

Pere Marquette Lodge and Conference Center: Breakfast, lunch, and dinner available in the great lodge; 13653 Lodge Blvd., Grafton; (618) 786-2331; www.pmlodge.net.

Piasa Winery: Offers sandwiches in addition to local wines; 211 West Main St., Grafton; (618) 786-8439; www.piasawinery.com.

Tony's: Known for steak and Italian food; 312 Piasa St., Alton; (618) 462-8384; www.tonysrestaurant.com.

Accommodations

Beall Mansion: This 1903 mansion contains a museum; the house is on the National Register of Historic Places; 407 East 12th St., Alton; (866) 843-2325; www.beallmansion.com.

Pere Marquette Lodge and Conference Center: Rooms, cabins, and campground at one of the most scenic state parks in Illinois; see contact info above.

Ruebel Hotel and Saloon: Offers twenty-two rooms in a historic hotel above a restaurant; cottages and lodge rooms also available; 217 East Main St., Grafton; (618) 786-2315; www.ruebelhotel.com.

Bike Shops

Wild Trak Bikes: Located just off SR 100 in downtown Alton; 202 State St., Alton; (618) 462-2574.

Restrooms

Start/finish: Water and restrooms are available at the trailhead.

Mile 5.6: The gas station at Piasa Creek has beverages and restrooms.

Mile 13.2: The visitor center east of Grafton has restrooms and water.

Mile 20.5: The visitor center and the lodge at Pere Marquette contain restrooms and water.

Mile 52.5: Pass the gas station again at Piasa Creek.

Maps

USGS: Alton quad, Brussels quad, Grafton quad, Elsah quad, Otterville quad.

DeLorme: Illinois Atlas & Gazetteer: Pages 75 and 67.

40 Rend Lake Ramble

Get to know Rend Lake and its environs on this ride that cuts through nearly all of the lake's numerous recreation areas. About one-third of the ride follows paved bike trails near the shore of the lake; the remainder follows mostly quiet rural roads.

Start: The Rend Lake Visitor Center, located about 20 miles south of Mount Vernon.
Length: 34.9 miles.

Terrain: The landscape is flat and gently rolling.
Traffic and hazards: SR 154 is somewhat busy; SR 37 has steady traffic.

Getting there: Coming from the north on I-57, exit on SR 154 heading east. Turn right on SR 37, right on Illinois Street, and then right again on Mine 24 Road. As you approach Rend Lake, the visitor center is on the right. Coordinates for starting point: 16S 328446E 4211660N

The Ride

Rend Lake is a new addition to the landscape of southern Illinois. Built in the early 1970s by damming up the Big Muddy River and Casey Creek, state and federal agencies created the 19,000-acre reservoir that serves as a water supply for a two-county area. The lake, which is shaped like a broad Y, was built to also serve as a recreation spot. Indeed, anglers from southern and central Illinois come in large numbers for the largemouth bass, crappies, bluegills, channel catfish, and white bass. But, as the travel brochures point out, Rend Lake is much more than an oversize fishin' hole: The 13-mile-long lake draws pleasure boaters and beachgoers, and the wooded shores lure throngs of campers, hikers, hunters, and wildlife watchers. Visitors also come for golf, lodging, and the shooting facility at the Rend Lake Recreation Complex on the east side of the lake.

Starting from the lake's visitor center on the south shore, the Big Muddy River spillway is the first thing you'll encounter after crossing Rend Lake Dam Road. Crossing the pedestrian bridge over the Big Muddy takes you to rich wetlands fed by the river's backwater. While tracing the route of a canal, watch for legions of turtles and frogs, as well as large pike and catfish sunning themselves near the shore. After a peaceful 1.2-mile-long ramble between the 70-foot-high Rend Lake Dam on the right and dense stands of oak, hickory, maple, and cypress on the left, you'll cross Rend Lake Dam Road again.

The next several miles take you through a series of picnicking areas and campgrounds along the west shore of Rend Lake. Two places to watch for are the Rend Lake Marina and the sandy beach at Sandusky Creek South Recreation Area. The rolling terrain near the South Sandusky Campground is blanketed with cypress and silver maples. Continuing ahead toward the North Sandusky Campground, the trail crosses Sandusky Creek and travels along Rend City Road.

A train passes by on a quiet rural road near Rend Lake.

In the North Sandusky Campground, bike route signs lead you along the quiet park road to the entrance of the campground. Along Rend City Road, you'll pass St. Mary's of the Woods, a pleasant outdoor location where Catholic mass is held for campers visiting Rend Lake campgrounds. You'll become acquainted with the immense size of Rend Lake as you cross its 2-mile-wide west arm on SR 154.

The ride into Wayne Fitzgerrell State Park could be an out-and-back trip on the park road, or, if you don't mind riding on a crushed gravel trail, you can use the park trail for a portion of the trip (both options have similar mileage). The trail winds next to the Rend Lake Resort and through several miles of bottomland woods sprinkled with small ponds and open grassy areas. While riding through the park, don't be surprised if wild turkeys cross in front of you.

Leaving the park and returning to SR 154, you'll cross another arm of Rend Lake. After turning off SR 154, you might consider stopping at the Southern Illinois Artisans Shop, which contains a wide selection of arts and crafts created by Illinois artists. The shop also hosts a small gift shop and a gallery that features exhibitions of Illinois-related artwork.

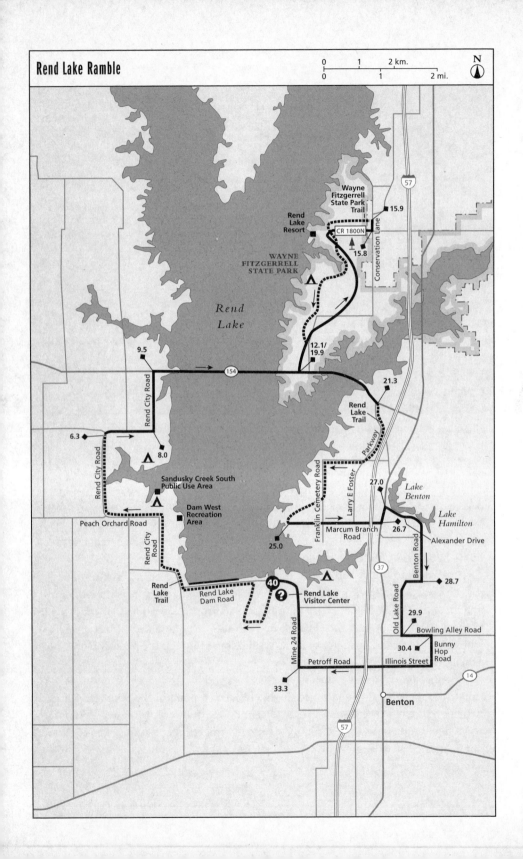

Rend Lake Ramble

0   1   2 km.

0   1   2 mi.

N

Rend Lake

WAYNE FITZGERRELL STATE PARK

Wayne Fitzgerrell State Park Trail

15.9

Rend Lake Resort

CR 1800N

15.8

Conservation Lane

57

9.5

154

12.1/19.9

21.3

Rend City Road

Rend Lake Trail

6.3

8.0

Sandusky Creek South Public Use Area

Peach Orchard Road

Rend City Road

Dam West Recreation Area

Franklin Cemetery Road

Larry E Foster

Parkway

27.0

Lake Benton

Lake Hamilton

Marcum Branch Road

26.7

Alexander Drive

25.0

Benton Road

Rend City Road

Rend Lake Trail

Old Lake Road

28.7

40

?

Rend Lake Dam Road

Rend Lake Visitor Center

29.9

Bowling Alley Road

37

30.4

Bunny Hop Road

Mine 24 Road

Illinois Street

Petroff Road

14

33.3

Benton

57

As you ride beneath the water tower painted like an enormous teed-up golf ball, you'll squeeze between I-57 and the Rend Lake Golf Course and its restaurant and lodgings. When the path starts meandering through the gently rolling woodland and open fields, you'll catch glimpses of Rend Lake through the trees.

The final section of this ride takes you east of Rend Lake to the pleasant wooded shores of Lake Benton and Lake Hamilton. From Lake Hamilton, you'll tour quiet, mostly flat farm roads sprinkled with houses. As you draw closer to the Rend Lake Visitor Center, where the ride started, patches of woodland start to appear and the landscape acquires a gentle roll.

Miles and Directions

0.0   From the Rend Lake Visitor Center, cross Rend Lake Dam Road and head south on the trail.

6.3   As you enter the North Sandusky Campground, the trail ends; follow the signs along the quiet park road.

8.0   Turn left on Rend City Road.

9.5   Turn right on SR 154. Traffic moves steadily on this road, but there is an adequate shoulder for riding. (Plans are under way to install a bike trail along this section of roadway.)

12.1   Turn left into Wayne Fitzgerrell State Park. Continue on the main park road toward Rend Lake College. At the Rend Lake Resort, keep to the right.

15.8   Before reaching Rend Lake College, turn left on Conservation Lane.

15.9   Pick up the trail on the left.

18.8   Where the trail starts a small loop, head back out to the park road. Take the first right, and then take the first left.

19.1   Turn right on the main park road.

19.9   Turn left on SR 154.

21.3   Turn right on Larry E. Foster Parkway. One block ahead, hop on the trail that accompanies the road on the left.

25.0   In the Marcum Branch North Public Use Area, leave the trail and turn left on Marcum Branch Road.

26.7   Turn left on SR 37 (watch for traffic on this road).

27.0   Turn right on Alexander Drive. Your feet may get wet as you ride through several inches of water on the ford bridge. Alexander Drive turns into North Benton Road as it curves to the south.

28.7   Turn right on Old Lake Road.

29.9   Turn left on Bowling Alley Road.

30.4   Turn right on Bunny Hop Road. As Bunny Hop Road curves right, it becomes Illinois Street. Farther ahead, Illinois Street becomes Petroff Road.

33.3   Turn right on Mine 24 Road.

34.9   Return to the Rend Lake Visitor Center.

Local Information

Southern Illinois Tourism Development Office: 3000 West DeYoung St., Marion; (888) 998-9397 or (618) 998-1024; http://illinois adventure.com.

U.S. Army Corps of Engineers, Rend Lake Project Office: 12220 Rend City Rd., Benton; (618) 724-2493; www.rendlake.com.

Local Events/Attractions

Sesser Historic Opera House: Erected in 1914 on the west side of Rend Lake, the opera house hosts community theater and musical programs; contains a cafe; 108 West Franklin Ave., Sesser; (618) 625-5116; www.sesser.org.

Southern Illinois Artisans Shop and Visitors Center: A store for local artists to display and sell their work; contains a small museum with changing exhibitions focusing on a range of Illinois arts; 14967 Gun Creek Trail, Whittington; (618) 629-2220; www.museum.state.il.us/ism sites/so-il.

Restaurants

Jack Russell Fish Company: Fish and seafood; 106 East Main St., Benton; (618) 439-3474; www.jackrussellfishco.com.

Mike's Drive-In: Serving homemade root beer and barbecue sandwiches since 1953; 1007 West Main St., West Frankfort; (618) 932-2564.

Windows Restaurant: Located at the Rend Lake Resort in Wayne Fitzgerrell State Park; outdoor seating; 11712 East Windy Lane, Whittington; (800) 633-3341; http://rendlakeresort.com/dining.php.

Accommodations

Days Inn: In Benton, south of Rend Lake; 711 West Main St., Benton; (618) 439-3183.

Gretchen's Country Home Bed and Breakfast: On a small lake; inexpensive; 14186 Cherry St., Sesser; (618) 625-6067.

Hard Days Night Bed and Breakfast: George Harrison stayed here while visiting his sister; 113 McCann St., Benton; (618) 438-2328; www.harddaysnitebnb.com.

Rend Lake Resort: Lakeside lodging in Wayne Fitzgerrell State Park; some rooms with Jacuzzis; 11712 East Windy Lane, Whittington; (800) 633-3341.

Wayne Fitzgerrell State Park: Huge RV camping area, plus tent sites in the park's north section; 11094 Ranger Rd., Whittington; (618) 629-2320; http://dnr.state.il.us/lands/landmgt/parks/r5/region5.htm.

Bike Shops

The Bike Surgeon: 404 South Illinois Ave., Carbondale; (618) 457-4521; www.thebike surgeon.com.

Restrooms

Start/finish: Rend Lake Visitor Center has restrooms and water.

Mile 4.5: Sandusky Creek South Public Use Area has water and restrooms.

Mile 20.0: Wayne Fitzgerrell State Park has restrooms and water.

Maps

USGS: Rend Lake Dam quad.

DeLorme: Illinois Atlas & Gazetteer: Page 84.

41 Shawnee Hills Wine Trail Ramble

Wineries with porches overlooking the vineyards, expansive views of the surrounding countryside, a choice of bed-and-breakfasts, and one of the best state parks in Illinois—what could be better? How about throwing in a bike ride along a series of quiet, scenic roads?

Start: Picnic shelter 4 at Giant City State Park, located next to the park's visitor center at the corner of Church Road and Giant City Park Road.
Length: 28.7 miles.
Terrain: Rolling woodland and farm fields are often interrupted by large hills with far-off views.

Traffic and hazards: Consuming great amounts of wine before bicycling narrow, winding, hilly roads is a treacherous enterprise. Use care when combining the vino with the velo. Also, watch for narrow bridges with boards (yes, wooden boards) on the surface. Be sure to cross these bridges on the raised boards lined up for car wheels.

Getting there: From Carbondale, head south on SR 51. Follow signs to Giant City State Park by turning left on Makanda Road (CR 29). In Makanda, keep straight ahead on Baptist Hill Road and enter the park. Follow the signs to the visitor center. Park at picnic area 4, located just north of the visitor center. Coordinates for starting point: 16S 306815E 4163891N

The Ride

Wineries in Illinois have rapidly multiplied in recent years. Since the mid-1990s the number of wineries went from about a dozen to more than seventy, and now Illinois is among the top twelve wine-producing states in the nation. Many of Illinois' new wineries have sprouted up within the Shawnee Hills. Kirby Pringle, a wine columnist for the *News-Gazette* in Champaign-Urbana, recommends trying Shawnee Hills wines made with the following grapes: Chardonel, Vignoles, Vidal Blanc, Chambourcin, and Norton (also known as Cynthiana). The wines range in price, but nearly all the vineyards offer bottles starting at around $12.

Cyclists with a taste for wine (including those schlepping wine bottles back with them) may be glad to know that the second half of this ride is where you'll encounter four wineries. The second half also hosts the quietest and most scenic roads—as well as the most hill climbing.

The ride starts with a trip from Giant City State Park to the town of Cobden, which is nestled among the big Shawnee Hills. On the way into Cobden, enjoy long views of the surrounding countryside—particularly as you descend the steep hill into town. A community park sits along the railroad tracks in the center of this hilly town. Like so many other small towns in Illinois, Cobden was named after one of the bigwigs of the Illinois Central Railroad.

After crossing SR 51 east of Cobden, you're greeted with more expansive views of the surrounding landscape sprinkled with farms and swaths of woodland. After

Shawnee Hills Wine Trail Ramble

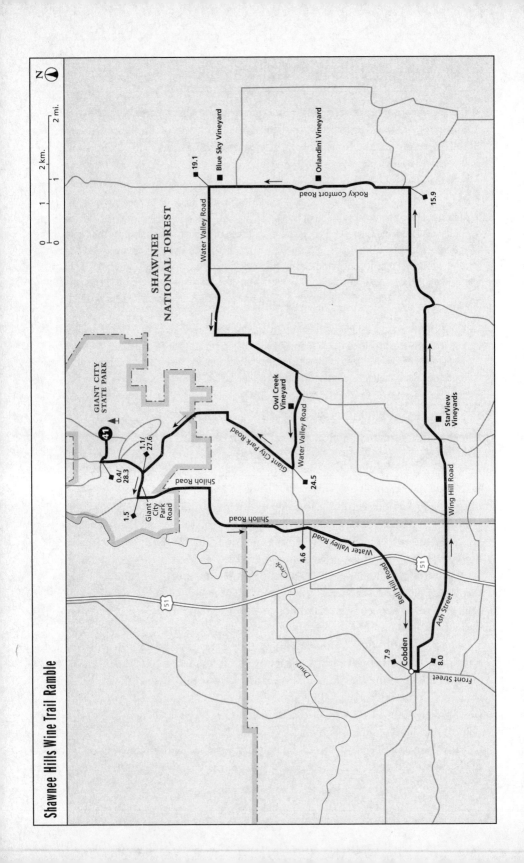

N

0 1 2 km.

0 1 2 mi.

SHAWNEE
NATIONAL FOREST

Blue Sky Vineyard ■ 19.1

Orlandini Vineyard ■

Rocky Comfort Road

15.9

Water Valley Road

GIANT CITY
STATE PARK

41

0.4/
28.3

1.1/
27.6

1.5

Giant
City
Park
Road

Giant City Park Road

Owl Creek
Vineyard ■

Water Valley Road

24.5

Shiloh Road

StarView
Vineyards ■

Shiloh Road

Creek

4.6

Water Valley Road

Wing Hill Road

Drury

51

Bell Hill Road

51

Ash Street

7.9

Cobden

8.0

Front Street

passing StarView Vineyard on the right, Wing Hill Road accompanies Bradshaw Creek for a short stretch. Knock out a steep climb, then turn onto Rocky Comfort Road, where you'll follow a gradual downhill. In between the several substantial climbs on Rocky Comfort Road, you'll encounter two more wineries—Orlandini and Blue Sky. Before turning on Water Valley Road, you can't miss Blue Sky Vineyard's Tuscan-style building on the right.

Water Valley Road is quiet, narrow, and never flat, with plenty of hilltop views. Use care as you cross a wooden bridge and what's called a "ford-bridge," where you'll pedal through a small stream as it runs over the road. This lovely stretch of road hosts Owl Creek Vineyard, which offers an array of red, white, and dessert wines.

As you head north back to the state park, you'll climb a ridge and enter a large orchard. On top of the ridge, watch for the sprawling view of the Shawnee Hills on the left. In particular, look for a big white cross that sits on a hill about 8 miles west. The 100-foot steel and marble cross was erected in 1963 on Bald Knob Mountain. The final miles back to the state park offer up more spine-tingling views as you make a long descent down from the ridge.

Miles and Directions

0.0 Head west on Church Road from picnic shelter 4.

0.4 Turn left on Giant City Park Road.

1.1 Stay right on Giant City Park Road.

1.5 Turn left on Shiloh Road (CR 1).

4.6 Turn right on Water Valley Road; it soon becomes Bell Hill Road, and near Cobden, Bell Hill Road becomes Poplar Street.

7.9 Turn left on Front Street.

8.0 Turn left on Ash Street, which soon becomes Wing Hill Road.

15.9 Turn left on Rocky Comfort Road.

19.1 Turn left on Water Valley Road.

24.5 Turn right on Giant City Park Road.

27.6 Turn right at the three-way junction for Giant City Park Road.

28.3 Turn right on Church Road.

28.7 Return to picnic shelter 4.

Local Information

Shawnee Hills Wine Trail Association: Another half-dozen vineyards are located west of this ride along SR 127; c/o Pomona Winery; 2865 Hickory Ridge Rd., Pomona; (618) 967-4006; http://shawneewinetrail.com.

Southern Illinois Tourism Development Office: 3000 West DeYoung St., Marion; (888) 998-9397 or (618) 998-1024; http://illinois adventure.com.

Local Events/Attractions

Blue Sky Vineyard: The largest of the vineyards on this route offers sandwiches, snacks, and a big outdoor terrace, in addition to lodging; open year-round; 3150 South Rocky Comfort Rd., Makanda; (618) 995-9463; www.bluesky vineyard.com.

Giant City Stables: Guided trail rides on some of the park's many equestrian trails; 722 Giant City Rd., Makanda; (618) 529-4110; www .giantcitystables.com.

Orlandini Vineyard: Has a new tasting room and hosts several events near harvest time; open April through November; 410 Thorn Lane, Makanda; (618) 995-2307; www.orlandinivineyard.com.

Owl Creek Vineyard: Open March through December; 2655 Water Valley Rd., Cobden; (618) 893-2557; www.owlcreekvineyard.com.

StarView Vineyards: Features a gift shop, an expansive deck with a view of the vineyard, koi ponds; open year-round; 5100 Wing Hill Rd., Cobden; (618) 893-9463; www.starview vineyards.com.

Shawnee Hills Wine Trail Festival: Typically held on Labor Day weekend; music, food, and, of course, wine are offered; see Shawnee Hill Wine Trail Association contact info above.

Restaurants

Dar Salaam: Highly regarded Middle Eastern restaurant; 218 North Illinois Ave. (US 51), Carbondale; (618) 351-9191.

Giant City Lodge: Dining room, cocktail bar, and gift shop; steak and seafood served; open for lunch and dinner; 460 Giant City Lodge Rd., Makanda; (618) 457-4921; www.dnr.state.il .us/lodges/gc.htm.

Accommodations

Blue Sky Vineyard: Offers lodging on the bike route; see contact information above.

Giant City Lodge: Offers thirty-four cabins in several different sizes; reasonable prices; see contact information above.

Giant City State Park Campground: Quiet, wooded campground with electric hookups and walk-in sites near hiking trails and lake access; (618) 457-4836; http://dnr.state.il.us/lands/ landmgt/parks/r5/gc.htm.

Shawnee Hills Bed and Breakfast: Three rooms with antique furnishings; occupies a beautiful stretch of road on the route; 290 Water Valley Road Rd., Cobden; (618) 893-2211; www .shawneehillbb.com.

Water Valley Inn Bed and Breakfast: Sits on 100 acres on the route; enjoy the wraparound porch; 3435 Water Valley Rd., Cobden; (618) 534-2244; www.1watervalleyinn.com.

Bike Shops

The Bike Surgeon: 404 South Illinois Ave., Carbondale; (618) 457-4521; www.thebike surgeon.com.

Restrooms

Start/finish: Restrooms are available at picnic shelter 4.

Mile 7.9: Pass a gas station/convenience store in Cobden.

Mile 12.3: Restrooms at StarView Vineyards.

Mile 18.8: Restrooms at Blue Sky Vineyard.

Mile 23.5: Restrooms at Owl Creek Vineyard.

Maps

USGS: Lick Creek quad, Makanda quad.

DeLorme: Illinois Atlas & Gazetteer: Page 89.

42 Shawnee-Pomona Ramble

Get ready for a 22-mile-long roller coaster ride as you negotiate a series of steep climbs and descents that will have you either trying to catch your breath or searching for the brake levers. Along with four deep ravines—including some that plunge nearly 300 feet—you'll encounter two wineries, a handful of tree-lined creeks, winding roads, thick fairy-tale forests, and a well-appointed barbecue joint.

Start: The Little Grand Canyon parking area, located about 12 miles west of Carbondale.
Length: 22.1 miles.
Terrain: Except for the final few miles of rolling terrain, you're constantly going up and down wooded bluffs. Some of these bluffs are steep.

Traffic and hazards: The half-mile section on SR 127 will likely be busy, but there is a small shoulder for riding.

Getting there: From downtown Carbondale, take SR 13 west. On the way out of Carbondale, turn left on South Oakland Avenue. Turn right on West Chautauqua Street, then turn left on SR 127. At Etherton Road, turn right and follow the signs for the Little Grand Canyon. Coordinates for starting point: 16S 288747E 4172858N

The Ride

While exploring the Shawnee Hills, you'll sometimes find so many interesting places to visit that it's difficult to decide among your options. In the vicinity of this ride are a cluster of great spots that deserve a visit, such as the Pomona Natural Bridge, Bald Knob Mountain Cross, Cliff View Park and the Northwest Passage Root Beer Saloon in Alto Pass, and several orchard markets along SR 127. But one of the greatest thrills in southern Illinois happens to be where this ride begins.

Often called the best short hike in southern Illinois, the Little Grand Canyon Trail takes you down through a dramatic sandstone canyon that leads to the floodplain of the Big Muddy River. Thanks to the handiwork of the Civilian Conservation Corps, a series of steps have been carved in the solid rock canyon, making the passage much easier. The return trip back up the ridge takes you through another canyon and then passes a sublime point overlooking many miles of river valley. The entire hiking loop is 2.7 miles long.

Similar to the hike in the Little Grand Canyon, this bicycle ride is short and rugged. Starting from the parking area, you'll pedal for a little more than a mile before embarking on a 300-foot descent to the Cave Creek floodplain. The long and winding trip into the ravine offers up a landscape that is lush with vines and trees. Cross the creek, and back up the bluff you go, again through dense woodland: Ravines tumble downward on one side of the road, and bluffs rise up on the other. Halfway through the climb, consider stopping to get your chain greased at the Pomona Winery, which specializes in

There's barely a moment of straight and flat roadway on the Shawnee–Pomona Ramble.

wines made from locally grown fruits such as apples, strawberries, and peaches.

Arriving back on top of the bluff, open grassy areas alternate with deep woods. Swing onto Jerusalem Hill Road, and you'll pass a hilltop church surrounded by an old cemetery. From the cemetery, take in long views of far-off wooded hills as you begin another high-velocity downhill stretch. Near the hamlet of Pomona, the gorgeous riding continues along the main stem of Cave Creek. Bluffs rise on both sides of the road, some topped with exposed rock.

After crossing SR 127, old dilapidated barns and a sprinkling of houses appear on the roadside. A steep downhill brings you to a bridge over Cedar Creek; an equally steep uphill segment leads you back up the bluff under a canopy of maple and hickory limbs. As the terrain levels off, you'll pass a fruit farm, another hilltop cemetery, Kite Hill Winery, and more grand views of the surrounding landscape.

The final leg of this roller coaster ride gets under way as you zoom down toward SR 127 and Sugar Creek. The last big climb takes you up to a ridgetop road that bobs and weaves through a series of horse and cow pastures before returning you to the parking area where you started.

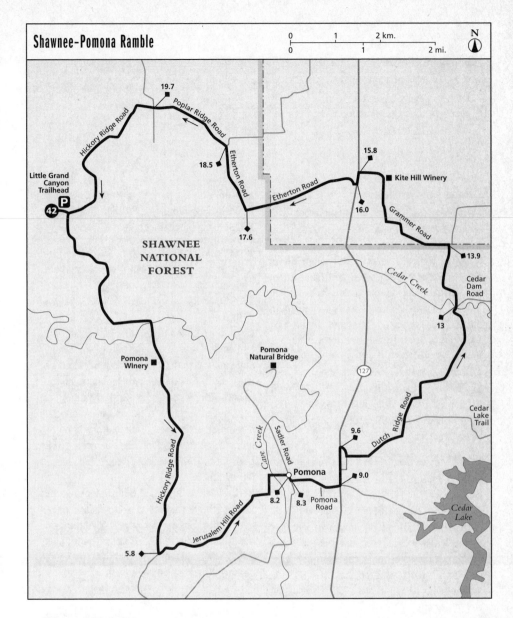

0   1   2 km.
0   1   2 mi.

N

19.7

Poplar Ridge Road

Hickory Ridge Road

18.5

Etherton Road

15.8

Kite Hill Winery

Etherton Road

16.0

17.6

Grammer Road

Little Grand
Canyon
Trailhead

42

P

13.9

SHAWNEE
NATIONAL
FOREST

Cedar Creek

Cedar
Dam
Road

13

Pomona
Wlnery

Pomona
Natural Bridge

127

Cedar
Lake
Trail

Cave Creek

Sadler Road

Hickory Ridge Road

9.6

Dutch Ridge Road

Pomona

9.0

8.2   8.3   Pomona
Road

Cedar
Lake

Jerusalem Hill Road

5.8

Miles and Directions

0.0 From the Little Grand Canyon parking area, turn right on Hickory Ridge Road.

5.8 Turn left on Jerusalem Hill Road.

8.2 Turn right on Sadler Road.

8.3 Turn left on Pomona Road.

9.0 Turn left on SR 127.

9.6 Turn right on Dutch Ridge Road.

13.0 Stay left on Dutch Ridge Road.

13.9 Turn left on Grammer Road.

15.8 Turn left on SR 127.

16.0 Turn right on Etherton Road.

17.6 Stay right on Etherton Road.

18.5 Turn left on Poplar Ridge Road.

19.7 Turn left on Hickory Ridge Road.

22.1 Return to the starting point.

Local Information

Murphysboro Chamber of Commerce: 203 South 13th St., Murphysboro; (618) 684-6421; www.murphysboro.com.

Shawnee National Forest, Mississippi Bluffs Ranger Station: The Little Grand Canyon Trail and 14-mile-long Cedar Lake Trail system, which is accessible along Cove Hollow Road on the east edge of the ride, are both managed by Shawnee National Forest; 521 North Main St., Jonesboro; (618) 833-8576; www.fs.fed.us/r9/forests/shawnee/recreation/trails.

Southern Illinois Tourism Development Office: 3000 West DeYoung St., Marion; (888) 998-9397 or (618) 998-1024; http://illinois adventure.com.

Local Events/Attractions

General John A. Logan Museum: Focuses on local history and contains a gallery featuring local artists; 1613 Edith St., Murphysboro; (618) 684-3455; www.loganmuseum.org.

Kite Hill Winery: Located alongside a small lake, the wine selection focuses on dry reds; open April through November; 83 Kite Hill Rd., Carbondale; (618) 684-5072; www.kitehill vineyards.com.

Pomona Natural Bridge: A 0.3-mile loop trail takes you to the 90-foot-long sandstone arch situated 25 feet above the stream; follow signs in Pomona; see Shawnee National Forest contact information above.

Pomona Winery: Produces a variety of apple wines as well as dessert wines made with various types of locally grown fruit; bottles afford-

ably priced; open April through December; 2865 Hickory Ridge Rd., Pomona; (618) 893-2623; www.pomonawinery.com.

Restaurants

17th Street Bar and Grill: Serves up award-winning barbecued ribs and pork; 32 North 17th St., Murphysboro; (618) 684-3722; www.17thstreetbarbecue.com.

Cummare's Italian Ristorante: Pizza, pasta with homemade sauces, salads, and paninis; lunch and dinner buffet; 1023 Chestnut St., Murphysboro; (618) 687-3700; www.cummares.com.

Mase's Place Bar and Grill: Features an impressive selection of local wines; specializes in barbecue; inviting outdoor porch; on the route; 5162 Hickory Ridge Rd., Pomona; (618) 684-8000; www.masonridgesites.com/Mases Place.htm.

Northwest Passage Root Beer Saloon: Serves root beer on tap as well as gourmet sandwiches and seafood dishes; the place is filled with taxidermy specimens and other kitschy items; Main St., Alto Pass; (618) 893-1634; www.northwest passage2001.net/saloonpg1.html.

Accommodations

Kite Hill Vineyard: Offers a bed-and-breakfast; see contact information above.

Lake Murphysboro State Park: Contains rolling hills covered with groves of oak and hickory; walk-in campsites put you on the shore of the lake; 52 Cinder Hill Dr., Murphysboro; (618) 684-2867; http://dnr.state.il.us/lands/landmgt/parks/r5/murphysb.htm.

Mason Ridge Bed and Breakfast: Located on the route close to the starting point; 47 Powder Ridge Rd., Pomona; (618) 684-8000; www.masonridgesites.com/MasonRidgeBandB.htm.
The Stone House: Former church built in 1846; sits on a bluff overlooking the Mississippi River; 509 West Harrison St., Chester; (618) 604-9106; www.bbonline.com/il/stonehouse.

Bike Shops

The Bike Surgeon: 404 South Illinois Ave., Carbondale; (618) 457-4521; www.thebikesurgeon.com.

Restrooms

Start/finish: Vault toilets are available at the Little Grand Canyon Trail parking area.

Maps

USGS: Cobden quad, Gorham quad, Pomona quad.

DeLorme: Illinois Atlas & Gazetteer: Pages 88 and 89.

43 Shawnee West Ramble

The startling contrast between the Mississippi River bluffs and the flat-as-a-pancake floodplain creates a surprisingly dramatic landscape on this ride. Far-off views crop up frequently as you follow narrow, winding roads over the bluff. In the floodplain, raised levees allow you to catch glimpses of the Mississippi River and admire the river bluffs in the distance.

Start: Piney Creek Ravine State Natural Area, located 25 miles west of Carbondale.
Length: 28.5 miles.
Terrain: South of SR 3, flat Mississippi floodplain rules; north of SR 3, it's high bluffs and deep ravines with hardly a stretch of flat roadway.

Traffic and hazards: Watch for traffic during the short stretch on SR 3. Also, on the northern edge of the loop, be mindful of truck traffic generated by a local gravel-mining operation.

Getting there: From I-64 to the north, take SR 4 south all the way to Campbell Hill. In Campbell Hill, turn right on Rock Crusher Road. Turn right on Piney Creek Road. The parking area is less than a mile ahead on the right (it's slightly hidden). From Carbondale, take SR 149 west to SR 3. Turn right on SR 3, then turn right on Hog Hill Road. Hog Hill Road becomes Rock Crusher Road. Turn left on Piney Creek Road. Coordinates for starting point: 16S 268760E 4195242N

The Ride

Before or after this ride, be sure to spend a couple of hours exploring the Piney Creek Ravine State Natural Area. The preserve, which is the ride's starting point, contains the largest collection of prehistoric petroglyphs in Illinois. A 2.5-mile hike will take you down into a sandstone canyon adorned with some 200 different designs made between 1,500 and 500 years ago. Researchers say that Native Americans created the

On the Shawnee West Ramble, bluffs rise above the agricultural land in the Mississippi River floodplain.

rock art by either pecking or grinding the rock or painting it with pigments. This outdoor gallery features animal figures of deer, birds, and snakes, as well as human figures, human hands, crosses, and a canoe.

Rolling terrain with open grassy pastureland and patches of cropland dominates the first several miles of this biking route. Kinkaid Stone Road leads you downward to Kinkaid Creek (beware of the big trucks; this is also where you'll pass a large gravel-mining operation). From the creek, the road climbs. Back on high ground, you'll feast upon expansive views of the surrounding wooded hills.

On Logan Hollow Road, your diligent pedaling is rewarded with 1.5 miles of downhill euphoria. Get ready—this descent to the Mississippi River floodplain features a few sections steep enough to melt your brake pads. Primarily, though, the downward progression is gradual enough so that you have time to admire the tree-lined rocky stream that runs alongside the road. Like most Mississippi River floodplains in Illinois, this swath of fertile land is dominated by corn and soy plants. Levees and irrigation ditches crisscross the terrain, and a sprinkling of wetlands flood the low spots.

For several reasons, rides that combine big river bluffs and flat river floodplain offer a special appeal. Unless you're training for the Alpe d'Huez stage of the Tour de France, the floodplain offers a welcome break from pedaling through rugged terrain. Once you get into the flat floodplain the dramatic beauty of the soaring bluffs can be

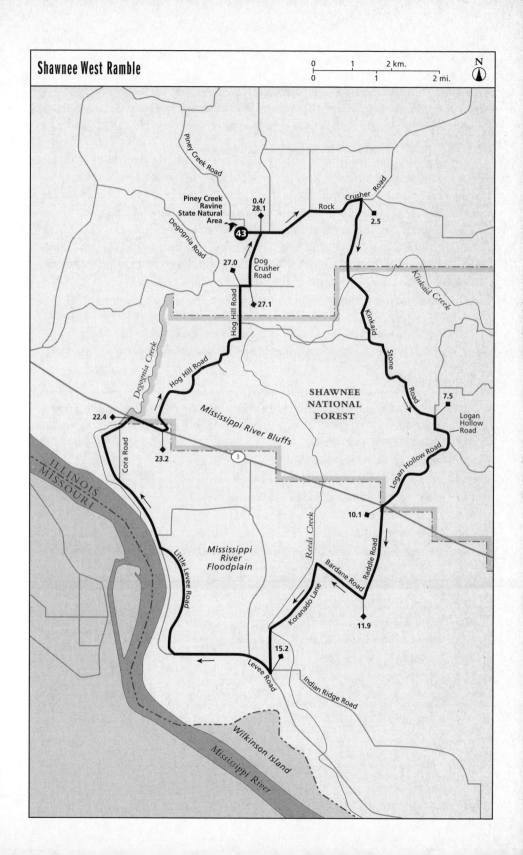

Shawnee West Ramble

0   1   2 km.
0   1   2 mi.

N

Piney Creek Road

Piney Creek
Ravine
State Natural
Area

43

0.4/
28.1

Degognia Road

Rock

Crusher Road

2.5

27.0

Dog
Crusher
Road

27.1

Kinkaid Creek

Hog Hill Road

Degognia Creek

Kinkaid

Stone Road

7.5

Logan
Hollow
Road

SHAWNEE
NATIONAL
FOREST

22.4

Cora Road

Mississippi River Bluffs

23.2

3

Logan Hollow Road

ILLINOIS
MISSOURI

10.1

Little Levee Road

Mississippi
River
Floodplain

Reeds Creek

Raddle Road

Bardane Road

11.9

Koranado Lane

15.2

Levee Road

Indian Ridge Road

Wilkinson Island

Mississippi River

fully realized—like a mountain range that rises up from the prairie. Many people find the stark contrast between soaring bluffs and the achingly flat floodplain downright dramatic. That contrast becomes more acute on this route as you follow the train track embankment on Bardane Road and when you mount the levee on Levee Road. These sections take you slightly above the floodplain and allow views of 10 miles or so across its flat, open expanse.

Levee Road runs about 50 feet above a wetland sprinkled with sand willows on the left. This wetland was taken over by the U.S. Fish and Wildlife Service after a protective levee failed during the flood of 1993, making farming on the land no longer viable. The 2,800-acre site is now a mix of wet meadows and floodplain forest.

Continuing ahead on the levee, openings in the trees reveal glimpses of the Mississippi River and possibly some its mind-bogglingly long river barges. The levee soon passes an enormous coal transport facility, where giant mounds of coal nearly repeat the shape of the high bluffs in the background.

As you leave the floodplain and embark on the gut-busting climb up Hog Hill Road, look for the small rocky cliff within the grove of trees on the left close to SR 3. This thickly wooded road takes you through open grassy areas and past a hilltop cemetery on the way back to Piney Creek Ravine State Natural Area.

Miles and Directions

0.0 Start at the Piney Creek Nature Preserve and head to the left on Piney Creek Road (a brief section of this road is gravel).

0.4 Turn left on Rock Crusher Road.

2.5 Turn right on Kinkaid Stone Road.

7.5 Turn right on Logan Hollow Road.

10.1 At SR 3, continue straight ahead on Raddle Road.

11.9 Turn right on Bardane Road.

13.0 Turn left on Koranado Lane.

15.2 Turn right on Indian Ridge Road and then right again on Levee Road. For a stretch, you'll follow Little Levee Road and then return to Levee Road.

22.4 Turn right on SR 3.

23.2 Turn left on Hog Hill Road.

27.0 Turn right on Degognia Road.

27.1 Turn left on Rock Crusher Road.

28.1 Turn left on Piney Creek Road.

28.5 Return to the parking area.

Local Information

City of Chester: 1330 Swanwick St., Chester; (618) 826-5114; www.chesterill.com.

Southern Illinois Tourism Development Office: 3000 West DeYoung St., Marion; (888) 998-9397 or (618) 998-1024; http://illinois adventure.com.

Local Events/Attractions

Fort Kaskaskia State Historic Site: Occupying a wooded bluff 200 feet above a big bend in the Mississippi River, the park commemorates an old fort; Pierre Menard Home State Historic Site is at the bottom of the bluff; traditional music festival held the third weekend in September; park contains a small campground; located north of Chester on SR 3; (618) 859-3741; www.illinoishistory.gov/hs/fort_kaskaskia.htm.

General John A. Logan Museum: Focuses on local history and contains a gallery featuring local artists; 1613 Edith St.; Murphysboro; (618) 684-3455; www.loganmuseum.org.

Mary's River Covered Bridge: Built in 1854 as part of a toll road between Bremen and Chester; located northeast of Chester on SR 150.

Piney Creek Ravine State Natural Area: For more information about the preserve, contact the Randolph County Conservation Area, 4301 South Lake Dr., Chester; (618) 826-2706; http://dnr.state.il.us/lands/landmgt/parks/r4/pcr.htm.

Restaurants

Cummare's Italian Ristorante: Pizza, pasta with homemade sauces, salads, and paninis; lunch and dinner buffet; 1023 Chestnut St., Murphysboro; (618) 687-3700; www.cummares.com.

Ol' Farmhouse Café and Bakery: Includes a small gift shop and bakery; 639 State St., Chester; (618) 826-1870.

Accommodations

Lake Murphysboro State Park: Contains rolling hills covered with groves of oak and hickory; walk-in campsites put you right on the shore of the lake; 52 Cinder Hill Dr., Murphysboro; (618) 684-2867; http://dnr.state.il.us/lands/landmgt/parks/r5/murphysb.htm.

The Stone House: Former church built in 1846; sits on a bluff overlooking the Mississippi River; 509 West Harrison St., Chester; (618) 604-9106; www.bbonline.com/il/stonehouse.

Bike Shops

The Bike Surgeon: 404 South Illinois Ave., Carbondale; (618) 457-4521; www.thebike surgeon.com.

Restrooms and Water

No public restrooms or water along the route.

Maps

USGS: Raddle quad, Rockwood quad.
DeLorme: Illinois Atlas & Gazetteer: Page 88.

Appendix: Illinois Bicycling Clubs and Advocacy Organizations

Active Transportation Alliance, 9 West Hubbard St., Suite 402, Chicago, IL 60654; (312) 427-3325; www.activetrans.org

Arlington Heights Bicycle Association; (847) 255-3468 or (847) 577-4275; web@ cyclearlington.com; www.cyclearlington.com

Bicycle Club of Lake County, P.O. Box 521, Libertyville, IL 60048; www.bikebclc.com

Bike Psychos, P.O. Box 652, Oak Lawn, IL 60454; (708) 802-1804 or (815) 254-8370; www.bikepsychos.org

Blackhawk Bicycle and Ski Club, P.O. Box 6443, Rockford, IL 61125-1443; (815) 222-8088; www.blackhawkbicycleclub.org

Carbondale Bicycle Club; (618) 687-2546; http://pctt.tripod.com/cbc.htm

Chain Link Cyclists, P.O. Box 839, Freeport, IL 61032; www.chainlinkcyclists.org

Champaign County Bikes, P.O. Box 2373, Champaign, IL 61825-2373; (217) 898-2587; www.champaigncountybikes.org

Chicago Area Tandem Society, 302 East Willow Rd., Barrington, IL 60010; (847) 358-7797; www.chicagotandems.com

Chicago Cycling Club; P.O. Box 1178, Chicago, IL 60690-1175; (773) 509-8093 or (773) 528-7690; www.chicagocyclingclub.org

Decatur Bicycle Club; (217) 865-2163; www.decaturbicycleclub.org

DeKalb County Bicycle Club, P.O. Box 192, DeKalb, IL 60115-0192; (815) 758-1562

Elmhurst Bicycle Club, P.O. Box 902, Elmhurst, IL 60126-0902; (630) 415-2453; www.elmhurstbicycling.org

Evanston Bicycle Club, P.O. Box 1981, Evanston, IL 60204-1981; (847) 604-1225 or (847) 869-1557; www.evanstonbikeclub.org

Folks on Spokes Bicycle Club, P.O. Box 763, Matteson, IL 60443; (708) 730-5179 or (708) 748-7596; www.folksonspokes.com

Fox Valley Bicycle & Ski Club, P.O. Box 1073, Saint Charles, IL 60174-7073; (630) 584-7353 or (630) 443-0280; www.fvbsc.org

Illinois Valley Wheelm'n, 6518 North Sheridan Rd., Suite 2, Peoria, IL 61614-2933; (309) 293-8637; www.ivwheelmn.org

Joliet Bicycle Club, P.O. Box 2758, Joliet, IL 60436; (815) 436-7701; www.joliet bicycleclub.org

Macomb Area Bicycling Club, P.O. Box 248, Macomb, IL 61455-0248; (309) 836-3706; http://cycling.macomb.com

McHenry County Bicycle Club, P.O. Box 917, Crystal Lake, IL 60039-0917; (815) 477-6858 or (847) 587-6234; www.mchenrybicycleclub.org

McLean County Wheelers, P.O. Box 947, Bloomington, IL 61702-0947; (309) 454-7800; www.wheelers.mcleancountywheelers.com

Naperville Bicycle Club, P.O. Box 150, Winfield, IL 60190; (630) 968-6713; www.napervillebikeclub.com

Oak Park Cycle Club, P.O. Box 1488, Oak Park, IL 60304; (708) 383-1244; www.oakparkcycleclub.org

Prairie Cycle Club, P.O. Box 115, Urbana, IL 61803; (217) 359-1995; www.prairiecycleclub.org

Quad Cities Bicycle Club, P.O. Box 3575, Davenport, IA 52808; (309) 762-8252; www.qcbc.org

Rock River Valley Bicycle Club, P.O. Box 37, Oregon, IL 61061; (815) 284-1203 or (815) 284-1203

Schaumburg Bicycle Club, P.O. Box 68353, Schaumburg, IL 60168-0353; (630) 668-5204; www.schaumburgbicycleclub.org

South Chicago Wheelmen; (708) 789-4443; www.southchicagowheelmen.com

Springfield Bicycle Club, P.O. Box 2203, Springfield, IL 62705; (217) 789-4823; www.spfldcycling.org

Velo Club Roubaix, Chicago; (847) 433-8941; www.vcrbiketeam.org

Wheeling Wheelmen, P.O. Box 7304, Wheeling, IL 60089-7304; (847) 520-5010; www.wheelmen.com

Index of Rides by Name

About the Author

Ted Villaire is a year-round cyclist who lives in Chicago and has ridden extensively in the upper Midwest. He is the author of *Camping Illinois* and *Best Rail Trails Illinois* (both FalconGuides) as well as *60 Hikes within 60 Miles: Chicago* and *Easy Hikes Close to Home: Chicago*. His freelance articles have appeared in a variety of magazines and newspapers, including the *Chicago Tribune* and the *Des Moines Register*. He was the editor of a weekly Chicago neighborhood newspaper and now works as a part-time editor and writer for the Active Transportation Alliance in Chicago. Get in touch with him and see more photos of the rides in this book by visiting www.tedvillaire.com.